DESPERATE DECEPTION

British Covert Operations
in the United States, 1939–44

Thomas E. Mahl

BRASSEY'S

Copyright © 1998 Brassey's

First paperback edition 1999

Library of Congress Cataloging-in-Publication Data
Mahl, Thomas E., 1943–
        Desperate deception : British covert operations in the United States, 1939–44 / Thomas E. Mahl.—1st ed.
        p.   cm.
    Includes bibliographical references and index.
    1. World War, 1939–1945—Secret service—Great Britain. 2. World War, 1939–1945—Secret service—United States. I. Title.
D810.S7M254 1998
940.54'8641—dc21   97-19550
                                                                        CIP

    ISBN 1-57488-223-8 (alk.paper)

Designed by Page Graphics, Inc.

Printed in Canada on acid-free paper that meets the American National Standards Institute Z39-48 Standard.

Brassey's
22883 Quicksilver Drive
Dulles, Virginia 20166

10 9   8   7   6   5   4   3   2   1

To Ben and Mary Ternes Mahl,
my grandparents

Contents

•••

Foreword

Brassey's Intelligence and National Security Library is intended to provide citizens, students, scholars, and national security experts with a select set of books that make a unique or significant contribution to understanding the world of intelligence.

The intelligence literature contains much discussion but few studies of covert action—the secret influencing of events in other countries without revealing one's involvement. Much of the focus has been on sensational paramilitary activities, and most of this has been about failures. There has been little detailed study of other aspects of covert action.

Desperate Deception helps fill the gap. It is a very readable account of British covert action in the United States in the years just before and during World War II. Faced with the growing prospect of war with Germany, the British government mounted in 1939 a massive secret political campaign in the United States (including the use of front groups, agents, collaborators, manipulation of polling data, involvement in election campaigns, etc.) to weaken the isolationists, bring the United States into the war, and influence U.S. war policy in England's favor. This campaign helped change not only the course of World War II but also the face of American politics in succeeding decades.

While bits and pieces of the story have been told before and some of the details of the British campaign are lost to history, this is probably the best-researched and best-documented account we are likely to see on this crucial period of Western history. It is also a well-written story

111

that combines both journalistic and academic skills. *Desperate Deception* is a milestone book on covert action and intelligence.

Roy Godson
General Editor
Brassey's Intelligence and National Security Library

•••

Preface

"What you're looking for, what I've looked for, is the file with the whole story in it. That file doesn't exist," retired CIA historian Thomas F. Troy told me when I began my research on this book. "The material you want has been scattered to the winds—a sentence here, a paragraph there. You'll have to hunt them out just as I've had to." This wild scattering is only one of the problems that confront scholars who attempt to explore the covert operations of intelligence agencies as they indistinctly reveal themselves in the public events of diplomatic and domestic history.

As Yale historian Robin Winks has written, "There is, in fact, very little careful, solid research on the...intelligence community...even though intelligence history is an essential component of our times." Intelligence is truly "the missing dimension," not only of diplomatic history, but of the domestic history dealt with in this book. A consequence of this void has been elementary errors that appear in academic histories. One better-informed study notes: "The distinguished editor of a major volume of military diaries published in 1972 failed to realize that the references to 'C' and 'C's information' referred to the head of the Secret Intelligence Service."[1]

British historian Ronald Lewin pointed out in his essay "A Signal-Intelligence War" that strict official secrecy has caused "most of the significant volumes in the United Kingdom series of Official Histories of the Second World War [to be] fundamentally misleading, inadequate and out-of-date." Lewin points to the ruses used to camouflage the Normandy invasion which tied down the German 15th Army.

ix

These deceptions led to the deceptions in the official histories about the invasion. He asserts that most of the official histories and war studies published before the mid-1970s should be rewritten.[2]

What Lewin and others have written about the secrecy surrounding code-breaking and signals intelligence is even more relevant to this book's topic: the covert action and dirty tricks used to move the United States toward war and destroy isolationism as a respectable intellectual position.

Several research problems confront the intelligence research scholar. First, many of the particulars were never put on paper. Among his many tasks, lawyer Ernest Cuneo (code name CRUSADER) was liaison between British Security Coordination and several departments of the U.S. government. Here he is writing to Dick Ellis, who had been second-in-command for British intelligence operations in the Western Hemisphere during World War II: "I saw Berle at State, Eddie Tamm, J. Edgar and more often the Attorney General; on various other matters Dave Niles at the White House and Ed Foley at the Treasury, but so far as I know [there] wasn't a sentence recorded. I reported to Bill Donovan and George Borden [Bowden], and never in writing."[3]

Even those within the intelligence agencies have sometimes lacked a clear understanding of how events proceeded; it sometimes appears that the insider's only advantage over the outsider has been the insider's knowledge that he did not know. In a recently declassified 1968 book review of Ladislas Farago's *The Broken Seal: The Story of "Operation Magic" and the Pearl Harbor Disaster*, CIA reviewer Edwin C. Fishel wrote of Pearl Harbor: "It is becoming increasingly clear that if we want a straight story…—and that is surely a reasonable want—it is going to have to be produced by professionals. This is true not only because of the unlikelihood of getting an adequate 'outside' study but also because a really complete study involves information still classified. Much of it does not even exist on paper."[4]

Much of that information which is on paper and stored in a rational, readily retrievable way remains classified. In Great Britain the Official Secrets Act was first passed in 1911 under fear of Irish and German subversion; it was tightened as recently as the 1980s and acts as a powerful inhibition against research. The British government has an arbitrary right to withhold any document it wishes, the "thirty-year rule" for release notwithstanding. Harford Montgomery Hyde worked for

British intelligence in New York and later wrote about its personnel and operations. After his death in 1989 the British government closed many of his papers at Churchill College, Cambridge, until 2041. Fortunately several scholars, Canadian historian David Stafford and Timothy Naftali of Harvard being two, had scrutinized these papers before the veil fell.

In the United States the Freedom of Information Act would appear on the surface to be a solution to the problem of hidden documents, but in reality it is of limited usefulness. Firstly, there is what author James Bamford has called "quite likely the most secret agreement ever entered into by the English-speaking world," the 1947 UKUSA agreement between the United States and Britain prohibiting the United States from releasing any document that the British will not allow released.[5] In effect the Official Secrets Act operates in the United States for some of the embarrassing information covered by this book.

Secondly, since a researcher must know exactly what he is looking for, he is often asked the impossible: to supply the very information for which he is looking. Thirdly, using the Freedom of Information Act is very time-consuming. Begging too large a workload, government agencies seldom release material in timely enough fashion for a researcher to keep on a reasonable writing schedule. Fourthly, even after half a century the authorities often plead that the release of the requested information threatens national security.

Probably even more damaging than these research problems is the fact that until recently, the study of the intelligence history of World War II has lacked respectability. The conventional charge is that it smacks too much of *conspiracy*—a word with a very unprofessional ring among American historians. How does the historian avoid the charge that he is indulging in conspiracy history when he explores the activities of a thousand people, occupying two floors of Rockefeller Center, in their efforts to involve the United States in a major war? What should we properly call the rigging of a public opinion poll, the planting of a lover, or a fraudulent letter by an intelligence agency in order to gain information or influence policy?

Graduate students are warned against the "furtive fallacy." In fact, the only book similar to this one that was written by a respected historian—Charles Beard—and published by a respected publisher was criticized by the reviewers for this very reason and became an object lesson used to train young historians. Beard's *President Roosevelt and the Coming of the War 1941* was cited for being "deeply flawed by the furtive fallacy in its thesis that Franklin Roosevelt and his cronies secretly manipulated American policy by a series of subtle and sordid tricks to bring their nation into war…. The errors and distortions in [Beard's] interpretation are rather the result of his erroneous assumptions…in the way he believed history happened."[6]

There is, in fact, far more information available than one might expect, though it is often difficult to find because historians have only recently begun to build the base of recognizable names, theories, and verifiable facts that smooths the path for new research. Although the archives of the intelligence agencies may be officially closed, or their files "lost," much information is available to those who will persevere.

Also, although intelligence agencies have strict procedures that theoretically prevent information from reaching outsiders, bureaucracies are populated by human beings. Human beings make mistakes. Clerks misfile documents; weeders lack perfect knowledge, get sick, let their attention wander. One department weeds what another does not. Agents acquire the telltale baggage of life—spouses, children, inquisitive relatives, lovers, ex-spouses. Ex-agents collect details on those with whom they worked as a hobby; they die, and their children give the musty papers away. Diaries are kept and memos made and misplaced. Professional busybodies collect vast troves of information. All of these tangential sources have supplied information for this book.

Last, but perhaps paramount, governments leak, sometimes inadvertently, many times intentionally. A substantial relevant leak took place more than three decades ago. Strangely, these stunning revelations went unexplored by "outside" journalists and historians.

How and why Harford Montgomery Hyde's *The Quiet Canadian* (published as *Room 3603* in the United States) came to be published is not fully clear and remains a subject of controversy. What is indisputable is that the book, particularly the British edition, was much too candid and that many in the intelligence community breathed a sigh of relief when no one followed up. Although the book sold well, no well-circulated American academic journal mentioned it, nor did any respectable journalist or historian pursue its fertile leads.

Unknown to the innocent in the press and academia, there was a tumultuous uproar behind the scenes. Intelligence professionals in both America and Britain were "astounded." A classified CIA review said, "The publication of this study is shocking....Exactly what British intelligence was doing in the United States...was closely held in Washington, and very little had hitherto been printed about it....One may suppose that Mr. Hyde's account...is relatively accurate, but the wisdom of placing it on the public record is extremely questionable."[7]

After reading this, A. M. "Bill" Ross-Smith, a World War II British agent in the United States, wrote me: "I am most interested in CIA review on *QC*....Last paragraph classes *QC* as relatively accurate—I agree with him; it should not have been published...." Earlier Ross-Smith wrote that he was "astounded that he [Hyde] revealed Bellmonte Letter and L.A.T.I. operations at all."[8] Hyde's discussion of the "Bellmonte" and "L.A.T.I." operations revealed the success British intelligence had with phony documents it created. Along with a number of other relevant items these two operations are explained in the Glossary of Individuals and Organizations at the back of this book.

Other major sources of information on the organization and operation of British intelligence during this period are the papers of the head of the OSS, William J. Donovan, at the U.S. Military History Institute, Carlisle Barracks, Carlisle, Pennsylvania, and the Ernest Cuneo Papers at Franklin D. Roosevelt Library, Hyde Park, New York.

I would like to extend my appreciation to Dr. Lawrence S. Kaplan for his patience and timely advice. Dr. Frank L. Byrne, Dr. John Jameson, Dr. James Best, and Dr. Allan C. Dooley also read the manuscript and made useful comments and suggestions. I profited greatly from conversations with Dr. Nicholas J. Cull and from reading his doctoral dissertation, which he graciously supplied me. Dr. Timothy Naftali shared with me his insights into the operations of British intelligence and several pages of valuable notes. Dr. Francis MacDonnell was similarly generous with a prepublication copy of an article. Mary S. Lovell was more than generous with her insights and notes used for the book *Cast No Shadow*. The late A. M. "Bill" Ross-Smith saved me much wasted effort and gave me valuable insights into the operations of British Security Coordination. Thomas F. Troy gave me valuable help in starting my research, as did Walter Trohan and Edmond Taylor.

Dan and Steve Farrow and Richard Henson were helpful in allowing me to see documents from the Francis Henson Papers held by the family. Peter Griffith answered my questions and gave me valuable leads on the activities of his father, Sandy Griffith. Peter's sister Brenda McCooey generously shared not only her memories but a number of photographs from the family album.*

There were a multitude of librarians and archivists without whose help this book could not have been written. Foremost among them was Nanci A. Young, who presides over the Fight for Freedom Papers at Princeton.† Mary K. Knill at the Lyndon Baines Johnson Library was very helpful with my requests for files from the Drew Pearson Papers, as were Ronald M. Bulatoff and Carol A. Leadenham at the Hoover Institution. Others who deserve mention: Rebecca Campbell Cape, at the Lilly Library, Indiana University; Theresa Salazar at the University of Arizona; Matthew Gilmore of the Washington, D.C., Public Library; Harold L. Miller of the State Historical Society of Wisconsin; Thomas Featherstone of the Walter Reuther Library, Wayne State University; George F. Henderson of the Queen's University Archives, Kingston, Canada; John Taylor of the National Archives; Nancy R. Bartlett of the Bently Historical Library, University of Michigan; Carolyn A. Davis of the George Arents Research Library at Syracuse University; Barbara R. Daily of the Baker Library, Harvard University; Bernard R. Crystal of the Butler Library, Columbia University; William R. Massa, Jr., and Judith Ann Schiff of Yale University Library; Nancy E. Metger of the Penrose Library, University of Denver; Cora F. Pederson of the Herbert Hoover Library; Raymond Teichman and Nancy Snedeker of the Franklin D. Roosevelt Library; Dr. Richard J. Sommers at the U.S. Military History Institute, Carlisle Barracks; and the staff of the reference department of the Elyria Public Library.

No list of acknowledgments would be complete without mention of my neighbors John and Sylvia McKenna, who valiantly read early drafts of this book. Their suggestions and the wonderful editing job by Ted Johnson account for whatever clarity is to be found in my prose.

---

*Louise G. Parry shared her memories of Fight for Freedom and the activities of her husband, Albert Parry. United States Congressman Sherrod Brown and his staff helped me gain access to the Dies Committee files.

†Duncan Stuart, CMG, the SOE adviser at the Foreign and Commonwealth, patiently helped me trace cover symbols and operations from the SOE files.

•••

A Calculated Risk

I went up to father's [Winston's] bedroom....

"Sit down, dear boy....I think I see my way through." He resumed his shaving. I was astonished, and said: "Do you mean that we can avoid defeat?"—which seemed credible—"or beat the bastards?"—which seemed incredible.

He...swung around, and said:—"Of course I mean we can beat them."

Me: "Well, I'm all for it, but I don't see how you can do it."

By this time he had dried and sponged his face and turning round to me said with great intensity:—"I shall drag the United States in."

—Randolph Churchill[1]

This is the story of the covert operations mounted by British intelligence to involve the United States in World War II and destroy isolationism. These operations profoundly changed America forever, helping it become the global power we see today—a power whose foreign policy leaders were freed to make, after the war, a multitude of global commitments unhampered by any significant isolationist opposition.

Little information on these operations has hitherto found its way into standard history texts. As recently as the fall 1995 issue of *Diplomatic History*, prominent historian Justice Doenecke could write that "a full-scale study of secret British operations in the United States is much needed...."[2] Without a fuller understanding of British intelligence operations in the United States, there is little chance of understanding the political behavior of the world's greatest power during those crucial years when it emerged to dominate the globe.

That these operations are little known or publicly debated is a mark of their success. Though covert operations often produce spectacular public results, one of their essential qualities is that the origins of events remain secret—that the historical credit or blame falls on the innocent, on citizens acting independently, or even better, on mere chance. The very fact that a covert operation is known to have been run by an intelligence agency marks it as a significant failure. Covert operations thus present conundrums for a republic that are not easily solved.

How can decisions be made about the efficiency of tactics about which even those thought well educated and informed are ignorant? In small part, this history of Britain's effort to drag the United States into World War II is a contribution to the discussion over the usefulness of covert operations—an exchange presently unbalanced by the preponderance of examples of operations blown and bungled.

To understand British intelligence operations in the United States during the war it is necessary to review briefly the situation in which Britain, with her worldwide commitments and inadequate resources, found herself as World War II approached. Britain and France had been able to win World War I only by the intervention of the United States. Two decades later their prospects appeared grim. Germany on the eve of World War II had a population of 80 million with a workforce of 41 million; Great Britain had a population of 46 million with less than half Germany's workforce. Germany's total income at market prices had been £7,260 million in 1938, the last full year of peace, while Britain's had been £5,242 million. More ominously, the Germans had spent five times what Britain had spent on armaments—£1,710 million versus £358 million. While rearmament and public works had given Germany full employment by late 1936, Britain still had 1.3 million unemployed when war came in September 1939.[3]

Britain simply did not have the money for the three-year war her strategic planners envisioned. This had gradually become more and more apparent since 1936, when the British Admiralty had proposed a building program to meet the potential dangers from Germany, Italy, and Japan. The cabinet flatly responded that this lay "beyond the bounds of financial possibility."[4]

The need for dollars, a hard currency, was the problem; earning them was difficult. Hancock and Gowing have written that in 1939 "and for some years past a net deficit on the international balance of payments had announced that the nation, even in advance of the war, was already beginning the process of overseas disinvestment."[5]

Not only were the British failing to generate net trade dollars, they could not borrow dollars from the United States. The Johnson Act of 1934 stopped American citizens from lending dollars to any government in default on its debts to the United States. So the prospects for financial help from the United States appeared just as grim as the prospects for war.

The attitude of the American population was even more worrisome. Most Americans seemed determined to stay out of any European conflict. They had, in large measure, been profoundly disillusioned by both the consequences of World War I and the devious way they had come to participate in it. The public's disillusionment had started very quickly with John Maynard Keynes's erratically brilliant attack on the Versailles Peace Treaty, *The Economic Consequences of the Peace* (1919). Over the next twenty years it had been followed by a whole series of books, many from respected authors and publishers, exposing how deft British propaganda and clever British agents such as Sir William Wiseman had maneuvered the United States into the Great War.

Adding to this in the mid-1930s came the startling revelations of the Senate's Nye Committee linking banks and munitions makers to American entry into the World War. From these disclosures sprang a raft of neutrality laws. The Neutrality Act of 1935 stopped the shipment of arms to all belligerents whenever the president officially declared a state of war. The Neutrality Act of February 1936, though in many ways similar to the 1935 law, forbade loans and credits to the warring parties. In May 1937, Congress made permanent the principal provisions of the above acts and, in addition, forbade travel by Americans on belligerent ships.

Supporting the resolve to stay out of any European conflict were a number of active groups, some motivated by pacifism, others by nationalistic isolationism. Most Americans, however, were not pacifists—they simply wanted to stay out of another European conflict.

As the British once again faced the looming threat of war, in the summer and fall of 1939, there was very little likelihood of defeating Germany without the help of the United States. It is the contention of this book that with the use of its intelligence agents and influential members of the American policy elite who made up various "front groups," the British expected to be able to involve the United States in the war. This was a calculated risk, to be sure—but entirely rational.

There had been encouraging signs of cooperation from President Franklin Roosevelt. One was his "Quarantine Speech," of October 5, 1937, in Chicago, denouncing aggressor nations and calling for collective action to maintain order. John Buchan, Lord Tweedsmuir, the governor-general of Canada, who was intimately associated with the British intelligence services and covert propaganda, wrote that FDR's speech "was the culmination of a long conspiracy between us. (This must be kept secret!)"[6]

But FDR's pronouncement at Chicago, whether "trial balloon" or prod for others to take action, was met by strong public protest. Roosevelt had characteristically backpedaled under the criticism. Less public indications of FDR's pro-British sentiments include the military talks to which he agreed in a December 16, 1937, meeting with the British ambassador, Sir Ronald Lindsay.

In the summer of 1939 large crowds enthusiastically welcomed the new British king, George VI, to the United States for a four-day visit to New York and Washington. On June 11, a Sunday, the president entertained King George and Queen Elizabeth at a grand public relations picnic at Hyde Park, the Roosevelt home on the Hudson River, north of New York City. There for all the American public to see in a profusion of newspaper photographs was flesh-and-blood royalty: not pompous aristocrats, but friendly, informal people who ate the president's hot dogs and drank his beer—just like regular folks.

Besides cultivating goodwill with the great American masses, the visit gave the opportunity for two important conversations between George VI and President Roosevelt exploring the help Britain might expect from the United States in the looming war. Both talks contained hints of the Destroyer Deal consummated more than a year later. According to historian Benjamin Rhodes, the first of these dialogues was on the morning of June 11 at Hyde Park in the presence of Canadian Prime Minister Mackenzie King.

Roosevelt suggested that the United States could help patrol the Atlantic if the British would make Halifax, Nova Scotia, available to the U.S. Navy. Mackenzie King wrote in his diary that the mood of the conversation "was to the effect that every possible assistance short of actual participation in war could be given."[7]

The next afternoon, in a private conversation the president told the king the United States had an interest in acquiring access to British bases in Trinidad and Bermuda. The president indicated that given these bases the United States could patrol the Atlantic for a thousand miles out to sea. Throughout these conversations the president's attitude was warlike. He said that U-boats seen would be sunk and that if the Nazis bombed London, the United States "would come in."[8]

Roosevelt's heart was in the right place, but evidence soon accumulated that these bellicose words had only modest practical significance; the president was not even able to push changes in the neutrality law out of the obstinate and unpredictable Senate Foreign Relations Committee. Prime Minister Neville Chamberlain wrote to the Canadian governor-general that the U.S. Congress was "incorrigible." He continued, "Their behavior over the Neutrality Legislation is enough to make one weep...these pig-headed and self-righteous nobodies."[9]

The president favored the British, but FDR was by nature both cautious in the face of public opinion and a procrastinator. As a result, he would have to be prodded and cajoled into action.

There were other potential British allies on the American scene. These were the people sociologist C. Wright Mills later identified in his book *The Power Elite* (1956). The United States, wrote Mills, was controlled not by the mass of its citizens as described by democratic theory, but by a wealthy Anglo-Saxon Protestant elite from Ivy League schools. In a flurry of caustic reviews, critics, often Cold War liberals, heatedly denied that there was such an elite.[10] That debate now seems over, as Douglas Little noted in a recent review article in *Diplomatic History*: "Far from rejecting the idea of a power elite...[the books under review] celebrate its short lived 'Periclean Age' during the quarter century after 1945."[11] In slight contradiction to Douglas

Little, this book will show that this elite existed and was in a position of pivotal influence at least as early as 1939 and probably much earlier.

The British had not displayed any similar doubts about the existence of an American "power elite," certainly not during World War I. There is substantial testimony that the views of Lord Robert Cecil, expressed to his cabinet colleagues in 1917, remained the view of the British ruling class for much of the next three decades. Cecil wrote that "though the American people are very largely foreign, both in origin and in modes of thought, their rulers are almost exclusively Anglo-Saxons, and share our political ideals."[12]

Most of the members of this establishment were middle- or upper-class Protestants of Northern European, often English, descent. They were college-educated professional men often from Ivy League colleges or prestigious private schools at a time when fewer than two in every hundred Americans held a college degree even from the most lowly normal school.[13]

These people were concentrated in the Northeast, though there were enough of them scattered across the country that with a concerted effort, their voices could be projected to seem to be the will of the country. Politically, they came from either party, the Democrats among them tending to liberalism of the Woodrow Wilson, League of Nations variety, the Republicans to various degrees of conservatism.

Many in this "power elite" were practitioners of the law, particularly international law. There was also a considerable number of academics, and a number of bankers and clerics. These people were oriented toward Europe and a stable international order; they were largely prosperous and respected. If there were to be any changes, they wished them to be predictable and orderly and largely controlled by people they respected and felt comfortable with—the British—or by themselves. The policy makers of this establishment were generally white males, though there were occasionally women, included either because they were in positions of power or for appearances—Mrs. Ogden Reid and Irita Van Doren were in the former category, Mrs. Wendell Willkie and Mrs. Calvin Coolidge in the latter.

This Anglo-Saxon East Coast establishment not only shared England's political ideals but literally loved England and English culture. A surprisingly large number had gone to school in or lived in

England. A number divided their time between homes in Great Britain and the United States. Despite their pro-British bias, these Anglophiles were able to represent themselves as loyal, independent, disinterested Americans at the same time that German-Americans or Italian-Americans were easily belittled as biased "foreigners." This image of objectivity was a gross distortion of the facts; for example, the Anglophiles in the British intelligence front group Fight for Freedom were willing tools of British intelligence.

Ernest Cuneo was attorney to two columnists who worked closely with British intelligence—Walter Winchell and Drew Pearson. He was also liaison between British intelligence, the White House, the FBI, the Treasury, and OSS. In January 1988, in a five-page single-spaced letter to H. Montgomery Hyde, Cuneo wrote: "...as far as the British tricking the U.S. into war, FDR was at war with Hitler long before Chamberlain was forced to declare it. I was eyewitness and indeed, wrote Winchell's stuff on it (volunteer). Of course the British were trying to push the U.S. into war. If that be so, we were indeed a pushover. It reminds me of that Chaucerian line, "He fell upon her and would have raped her—but for her ready acquiescence!"[14]

I have organized my discussion of this book's complex subject as follows.

Chapter 1 describes British Security Coordination (BSC), the British intelligence organization run by Sir William Stephenson—"Intrepid"—and identifies several key personnel. This chapter also describes how and why "Intrepid" had President Roosevelt create the Coordinator of Information—later the OSS—despite the strong objections of the FBI and military intelligence.

Chapter 2 examines the origins and operations of several British intelligence front groups, among them Fight for Freedom, Friends of Democracy, France Forever, and the American Irish Defense Association. This chapter also describes how these fronts worked with the White House to build support for the president's dynamic interventionist policies.

Chapter 3 discusses a number of influential Americans who aided British intelligence efforts. Among those mentioned in the British documents, and in this chapter, are prominent newspaper columnists of the day Walter Lippmann, Drew Pearson, and Walter Winchell; presidential speechwriter Robert Sherwood; and the heads of the *New*

York Post, PM, the *New York Herald Tribune*, the *Baltimore Sun*, and the *New York Times*.

Chapter 4 covers the influence of British intelligence on World War II public opinion polls. This influence ranged from BSC's penetration of Gallup to the rigged polls done by BSC intelligence agent Sanford Griffith that were used to influence Congress.

Chapter 5 documents the activities of British intelligence agent Sanford Griffith as he created front organizations, rigged public opinion polls, organized election opposition to the isolationist Republican congressman Hamilton Fish, and worked on the British intelligence effort to convict German propagandist George Sylvester Viereck in federal court.

Chapter 6 examines the extensive efforts of British intelligence and President Roosevelt to rid the Congress of Hamilton Fish.

Chapter 7 chronicles the switch from isolationism to internationalism by Senator Arthur Vandenberg and relates that change to three female British lobbyists who insinuated themselves with him, including British intelligence's most famous female agent, "Cynthia."

Chapter 8 reexamines an old idea in the light of new evidence. It details how the Republicans, in the most bizarre convention of the twentieth century, forsook their isolationist front-runners—Taft, Dewey, and Vandenberg—in order to nominate a longtime Democrat, Wendell Willkie. It documents the work of British intelligence agents (subagents) in getting Willkie the nomination; Willkie's trip to England at the request of BSC head William Stephenson; Willkie's work for the British intelligence front Fight for Freedom; his closeness to President Franklin Roosevelt; and his part in ridding the Congress of Hamilton Fish.

Through these efforts, British intelligence, as an instrument of British foreign policy, finally prevailed. The prewar isolationists were driven from their places of power and their philosophy lost respectability. Hitlerism was destroyed.

CHAPTER 1

Organization, Methods, and Offspring

British Security Coordination (BSC) was a wide-ranging, full-service, offensive intelligence agency that for its own purposes begot two American agencies in its own image and likeness. One of these agencies, the Coordinator of Information, is the direct lineal predecessor of the OSS and thus today's CIA. The other agency, the "Rockefeller Office," as it became known, had a briefer but no less useful existence.[1]

The man in charge of British intelligence in the United States in 1940 was a prosperous forty-four-year-old Canadian-born businessman, William S. Stephenson, better known today by his New York cable address, INTREPID. He had been a flier in World War I. And though he had been shot down and taken prisoner, he had daringly escaped. One of the things he escaped with was a clever can opener he had come upon as a prisoner. This can opener was unpatented in the Allied countries, and by obtaining a patent and manufacturing it Stephenson made his first fortune.[2]

By the 1930s, Stephenson was a millionaire with major interests in a number of businesses that gave him reason to travel widely in Europe and discreetly gather intelligence on military preparations. For our story, Stephenson's most important holding was Pressed Steel, a major producer of steel auto bodies for such assemblers as Morris, Humber, Hillman, and Austin.

It was through the steel business that he became aware that large amounts of German steel were being diverted to the armaments industry in violation of the Versailles Peace Treaty. This information was passed along to the Secret Intelligence Service (MI-6), and from it to the little-known Industrial Intelligence Center under Winston Churchill's friend Major Desmond Morton. The IIC eventually became part of the Ministry of Economic Warfare during World War II.

This was not the coup it might appear. The intelligence gathered by Stephenson and others was erroneous, and it led to policies that might have proved disastrous had not the United States come into the war. They reported prior to the war that the German economy was being fully mobilized for war, and in September 1939 that the German economy was strained to its limits—producing at a rate that was unsustainable. This analysis was totally wrong. The Germans had a great deal of excess capacity. The height of German production proved to be in 1944 during the intense Allied bombing campaign.

These beliefs about the German economy encouraged the British to feel that with the money and productive capacity of the United States behind them a war with Germany was winnable even if the United States was not a combatant.[3]

The interwar cover for the Secret Intelligence Service, SIS or MI-6, had been Passport Control offices throughout the world. William Stephenson was appointed to this position in New York in the spring of 1940. His predecessor had been Commander Sir James Francis Paget, RN,[4] a competent man but without Stephenson's business or political connections, or his ruthless audacity. (According to author Anthony Cave-Brown, Stephenson had once volunteered to shoot Hitler with a high-powered rifle.)[5]

Subsequently, Stephenson had been chosen by "C," Stewart Menzies, the head of MI-6, to go to the United States as his personal representative to "establish relations on the highest possible level between the British SIS and the U.S. Federal Bureau of Investigation." The mandate given to Stephenson was to "assure sufficient aid for Britain, to counter the enemy's subversive plans throughout the Western Hemisphere …and eventually to bring the United States into the War."[6]

Stephenson first arrived in the United States on April 2, 1940, ostensibly on an official mission for the Ministry of Supply. It was on this trip, even before Churchill's May 10, 1940, ascension to prime minister, that the meeting took place which set the early close working relationship between the Federal Bureau of Investigation and British intelligence.[7]

This meeting between Stephenson and J. Edgar Hoover had been smoothed by a mutual friend, the boxer Gene Tunney:[8] "I had known Sir William for several years. He wanted to make...contact with J. Edgar Hoover...[but] he did not want to make an official approach through well-placed English or American friends; he wanted to do so quietly and with no fanfare."[9]

After a short time in the United States, Stephenson took over the thirty-eighth floor of the International Building in Rockefeller Center, which the Rockefellers, anxious to help, let for a penny rent. This was a convenient address. Several British agencies promoting intervention were also housed here. The British Press Service was located on the forty-fourth floor. The British intelligence front group Fight for Freedom located its operations on the twenty-second floor in the same building, also rent-free.[10]

By January 1941, Stephenson no longer worked under the traditional SIS cover name Passport Control but under the new umbrella name British Security Coordination, which covered all the varied secret organizations Intrepid represented in the United States.[11]

First and foremost, Intrepid represented Britain's Secret Intelligence Service (called SIS or MI-6, or Broadway after its address), which was responsible for intelligence outside Britain and the Commonwealth—responsibilities much like those of today's CIA. The London head of SIS had the designation "C," or CSS, Chief of the Secret Service. This is the "M" of Ian Fleming novels. The first head of the SIS after its reformation in 1909 had been Captain Sir Mansfield Cumming. He died in 1923 and was succeeded by Admiral Hugh "Quex" Sinclair. Stewart Graham Menzies (pronounced Minn-giss), Sinclair's right-hand man, became acting "C" on Sinclair's death in early November 1939 and then in late November "C." SIS was nominally under the Foreign Office (FO). Menzies's day-to-day contact with that office was through the permanent head of the FO, Sir Alexander Cadogan.[12]

Stephenson also represented Britain's internal Security Service, MI-5, which is responsible to the home secretary and cares for the internal security of Britain and its empire—responsibilities very similar to those of the FBI. One of MI-5's great assets was its central registry of names that classified the loyalty of thousands who had come to the attention of the service. On June 10, 1940, Vernon Kell, who had headed this organization since 1909, was dismissed. In November, Sir

David Petre took over as the director general. He was the former head of the Delhi Intelligence Bureau of India and thus a man with long experience at fighting subversives.[13]

MI-6 and MI-5 are well known; volumes have been written on them. But Stephenson also represented lesser-known organizations—some of them little known even today. One of these was the Political Intelligence Department (PID). This was ostensibly a section of the Foreign Office. Here we see the shifting kaleidoscope of intertwined, interacting departments and covers that so bedevil the researcher. The PID, housed at Woburn Abbey, the site of a major black propaganda factory, was a real, nonsecret office between 1939 and 1943. The problem arises because from August 1941 until 1943 the name PID was also the cover for the secret Political Warfare Executive (PWE), and when in 1943 the publicly known PID was disbanded, the Political Warfare Executive continued to use the name Political Intelligence Department.

These cover-name practices confused not only later historians but even the smartest of those who lived in this twilight world. One of these, Sir John Wheeler-Bennett, has confessed both his own confusion and his own somewhat idiosyncratic choice of employer labels: "Bruce [Lockhart] was to become the Director-General of what was, for some extraordinary reason which I never mastered, sometimes called P.W.E and sometimes P.I.D. (Political Intelligence Department) and was also to be appointed a Deputy Under-Secretary in the Foreign Office....[Later] I joined what I still prefer to call the Political Intelligence Department of the Foreign Office."[14]

Another of Stephenson's charges was Special Operations Executive (SOE), itself an amalgamation of secret departments prepared in anticipation of World War II. On April 1, 1938, shortly after the Germans took over Austria, SIS had begot "Section D" for "sabotage and subversion." This dirty-tricks department, certainly a great April Fools' creation, grew rapidly under the command of the dynamic and creative Major Lawrence Grand. By July 1940 it had 140 officers, a larger corps than SIS itself.

Though they were spared the details, recruits to Section D were left little doubt about the potential scope of their jobs. One recruit, Bickham Sweet Escott, has left us a record of his interview: "For security reasons, I can't tell you what sort of job it would be. All I can say is that if you join us, you mustn't be afraid of forgery, and you mustn't be afraid of murder."[15]

A surprising number of the recruits of Section D later achieved fame, even notoriety, in the field of intelligence. Kim Philby and Guy Burgess, later discovered to be Soviet agents, worked for Section D. Sir William Stephenson and his biographer, Montgomery Hyde, were there too.

In July 1940, Churchill consolidated Section D with MI R, a War Office guerrilla warfare research group, and Sir Campbell Stewart's covert propaganda unit, called Department EH after its location, Electra House. Churchill gave the new organization, Special Operations Executive (SOE), the mandate to "set Europe ablaze." SOE had three sections: SO.1 for propaganda, SO.2 for dirty tricks, and SO.3 for planning. A year later, SO.1 was separated from SOE, renamed the Political Warfare Executive, and put under the control of Rex Leeper and Robert Bruce Lockhart.

In the British system, countries had code names. As 48 LAND was the MI-6 code name for the United States, the Special Operations Executive code name for the United States was GROSVENOR. This may well be the origin of the prefix to SOE agent numbers in the United States—they had a "G" prefix and a three- or four-digit suffix. Thus journalist Walter Lucas, who worked for black-propaganda specialist Sidney "Bill" Morrell of SO.1 and planted articles in such publications as the *Christian Science Monitor*, was G.124. There was at least one exception to this system: While William "Wild Bill" Donovan's MI-6 code number was standard enough, 48917, his SOE symbol seems to have been "Q," "referring to both him and his office."[16]

Stephenson's importance and position can be seen in the instructions given to agent Valentine Williams, G.131, an experienced playwright and radio broadcaster, who was sent to the United States in July 1941 by SOE operational head (CD) Frank Nelson. Williams had been in Section D of MI-6 since 1939 while claiming to be a member of the Foreign Office. "One reason I am concerned," wrote Nelson in a marginal note, "to get someone out to USA is to regularize our association with 48000. He is 'C' 's man and is 'running' our show out there without remuneration etc. There is much that is unsatisfactory in this, viz, that we cannot just say to him—we are sending this man or that man!... He would be hard to replace—if he says 'Find your own man and run your own show.' "[17]

Stephenson also represented the British Office of Naval Intelligence (ONI), whose chief was Admiral Sir John Godfrey. Godfrey's personal assistant was the stockbroker Ian Fleming of later James Bond fame. Fleming, it seems, was occasionally lent to Stephenson for special projects.

Of all the organizations under Stephenson's BSC umbrella the Security Executive remains one of the least known. Beyond the sketchy fact that Duff Cooper was for a time in charge of it in England and that it supposedly had worldwide security responsibilities in British possessions, the Security Executive is one of the black holes of intelligence history.

Lastly, Intrepid was the New York representative of the undercover section, the Special Branch, of Scotland Yard. Special Branch had been founded in the late nineteenth century to counter Irish terrorists, but by 1940 it worked with MI-5 against all potential subversives—Communist, Irish, Fascist, or Indian.

As representative of these organizations in the Western Hemisphere, William Stephenson conducted covert diplomacy; provided raw positive intelligence to London; ran intelligence operations, including recruitment of agents and surveillance; conducted a whole range of special operations, from political warfare against isolationists to perhaps even murder; mounted covert propaganda operations; ran a hemisphere port security operation; built and operated Camp X, a clandestine training establishment in Canada; built and operated a clandestine international communications network; conducted a hemispheric ship-observer scheme; and played a major role in Britain's air and sea control of the movement of people, mail, and commodities between the Americas and Europe.[18]

An example of the capabilities of the BSC operation was in the forgeries that it was able to effect. The skilled labor to produce this high-quality work was by the latter part of 1941 housed in a BSC forgery factory in downtown Toronto, Canada. It was called Station M, perhaps after its chief, Eric Maschwitz (cover symbol G.106). In more normal times Maschwitz worked as employee of the BBC; he wrote the lyrics of such popular songs as "The Nightingale Sang in Berkeley Square" and "These Foolish Things." Station M, which opened in the summer of 1941, was under cover of the Canadian Broadcasting Corporation.

Evidence needed to frame Britain's enemies or move the United States closer to war could be and was indeed manufactured. This was a truly frontal assault on the rules of evidence. In addition to "an industrial chemist, and two ruffians who could reproduce faultlessly the imprint of any typewriter on earth," Maschwitz later wrote, "I controlled a chemical laboratory in one place, a photographic studio in another."[19]

In *The Quiet Canadian*, based on a secret after-action report on BSC activities (the "BSC Account"), Montgomery Hyde spends twelve pages chronicling the spurious documents spewed out by Station M and the devastating effects of these genuine-looking pieces of paper.

A newly released document stamped MOST SECRET wonderfully illustrates Eric Maschwitz's willingness to do whatever necessary to move the United States toward war. One problem facing British intelligence in the United States was a shortage of good photographs of German atrocities. On November 26, 1941, in a memorandum titled "Atrocity Photographs," Maschwitz proposed a solution: "If asked to do so, my Section could quite easily provide a regular supply of atrocity pictures, manufactured by us in Canada." Most problems seemed small and quite solvable: "the buying and hiring of costumes, the manufacture of small pieces of scenery and of dummies...a first-class make-up man... all of which could be carried out under some sort of cover.

"...For the sake of accuracy," Maschwitz continued, "we should be provided...with as complete a library as possible of photographs of German personnel, equipment, vehicles...also actual specimens of German...equipment...."

Only one problem loomed in G.106's fertile brain, and it had nothing to do with the propriety of duping the American public. If the project was to be done they had better get busy. "The most obvious setting for atrocity pictures at the moment is Russia, so that we should get to work while there is still snow in Canada."[20]

Clearly the major purpose of BSC was to conduct aggressive offensive operations against those it saw as the enemies of Britain. These included not only Hitler's agents in the United States, but those who simply wished to remain uninvolved in the European war.

The ruthless activism of British Security Coordination was one of Britain's few advantages in the war against Hitler. Ernest Cuneo summed up the BSC offensive in a memo:

"Given the time, the situation, and the mood, it is not surprising however, that BSC also went beyond the legal, the ethical, and the proper. Throughout the neutral Americas, and especially in the U.S., it ran espionage agents, tampered with the mails, tapped telephone, smuggled propaganda into the country, disrupted public gatherings, covertly subsidized newspapers, radios, and organizations, perpetrated forgeries—even palming one off on the President of the United States—violated the aliens registration act, shanghaied sailors numerous times, and possibly murdered one or more persons in this country."[21]

No one should be surprised that the British used their intelligence system to help involve the United States in World War II. The British use of intelligence operatives on Americans has been, after all, sort of a tradition, dating back at least as far as the American Revolution.

British intelligence had certainly infiltrated Benjamin Franklin's American embassy in France. Franklin's chief assistant, Dr. Edward Bancroft, was a British intelligence agent who passed all the information he could gather on to England.[22]

In the period 1778–83 the problem was how to get out of a war with the Americans, but in 1916–17 it was how to get the United States into a war. Intrepid's World War I counterpart had been Sir William Wiseman (1885–1962). His family background, sense of taste, good manners, and discretion highly recommended him to Edward M. House, President Woodrow Wilson's closest adviser. "Colonel" House liked to associate with the famous and titled, and Wiseman could trace his lineage back to the time of Henry VIII and his baronetage to 1628.

As Wilson had favored the British in World War I, Franklin Roosevelt was quite willing to work with British intelligence in World War II. One of the unnoticed consequences of Roosevelt's cooperation was that British intelligence promoted the creation of two American intelligence organizations. Most well known of these organizations was the Coordinator of Information, which became the Office of Strategic Services.

The other intelligence organization was so well camouflaged that it was not until 1976 that the first hint appeared that the "Rockefeller Office," or more properly the Office of the Coordinator of Commercial and Cultural Relations Between the American Republics, later the Coordinator of Inter-American Affairs, had been an intelligence operation. The book *A Man Called Intrepid* by William Stevenson (no relation to Intrepid) was, for all its flaws, the first to reveal that the

Rockefeller Office was an intelligence operation—one that brought the soothing balm of Rockefeller dollars to Intrepid's ambitious but money-short Latin American operations.[23]

Although Franklin Roosevelt created the Rockefeller Office by executive order on August 16, 1940, the ostensibly initial move had been made by Nelson Rockefeller on June 14, 1940, when he submitted a memo to FDR's close adviser Harry Hopkins. FDR accepted the plan on the condition that the youthful Republican Rockefeller accept a more mature Democrat, Will Clayton, as one of his assistants.[24]

The German threat in Europe brought together a complex coincidence of ambitions and interests in Latin America—those of the Rockefellers with the family's Creole Oil Company, those of the administration with the Monroe Doctrine and the more recent Good Neighbor Policy, and those of the British with their need to stop German economic and political advances.

Paul Kramer, another of Nelson Rockefeller's assistants, writes that "the goals of the two partners were different. The one, Britain, sought to use BSC New York as a device for destroying Nazis and pro-Germans wherever they might be (and also to bring the US in the war on the side of Great Britain); the other, the U.S., sought to use BSC's assets—an intelligence network and mail intercept system and experience in fighting Nazis by means of operational intelligence—to further its own policy of western hemisphere unity and defense."[25]

The operations set in motion were part of one of the most important but least studied aspects of covert operations in a modern industrial world: economic warfare. By the end of August 1940 the Rockefeller Office was working on a "voluntary program" by which American businesses would eliminate all their Latin American representatives who were Germans or German agents.

Information from BSC went to its New York FBI liaison, Percy Foxworth, who also had offices in Rockefeller Center. The information was transmitted to the Rockefeller Office located in the old State, War, and Navy Building, Washington, D.C. The documents, labeled "personal and confidential," started, "We understand from a confidential source believed to be reliable," or "Information has been received from a reliable confidential source."[26] At the Rockefeller Office this material would be put together in a system implemented by John S. Dickey, later president of Rockefeller's alma mater, Dartmouth

College. Rockefeller and his assistants, Dickey, Will Clayton, Joseph C. Rovensky of the Chase Bank, Berent Friele of A&P, and Percy L. Douglas of the Otis Elevator Company, with others, put the British blacklist into effect. Thus the Rockefeller Office supplied the manpower, the connections, and the money to reinforce the hard-nosed British blockade and blacklist activities.

Seventeen hundred companies were contacted as part of this program. United States exporters eliminated more than a thousand "undesirable" agency accounts in Latin America during the first six months of 1941. These activities also had a salutary effect on the ruling classes of Latin America, writes Kramer: "Persons close to the rulers were plunged into financial oblivion as a result and this had the effect, in a broader sense, of persuading those in power to turn to the U.S. for aid and protection and relief."[27]

Kramer is sure that this program had Roosevelt's blessing, since FDR ordered J. Edgar Hoover personally to comply with Rockefeller's request that an FBI agent be sent to talk to selected businessmen about cooperating with the blacklisting. On July 19, 1941, almost five months before Pearl Harbor, FDR gave the British blacklist the power of American law when the Federal Register included a long list of the proscribed businessmen. British Security Coordination's information thereafter flowed to the State Department's new division of World Trade Intelligence, headed by John S. Dickey. Dickey continued on the Rockefeller payroll, however.[28]

The Rockefeller Office and British intelligence cooperated in two other areas. They worked together in subverting Boston's outwardly independent 50,000-watt shortwave station WRUL by "secret subsidies through intermediaries."[29] Also, both manipulated the Latin American press by buying advertising space. This complemented the existing BSC program of manipulating the Latin American press by controlling its access to newsprint.[30]

The influence of British Security Coordination in America to involve the United States in World War II and to prepare the United States to participate in war is impressive, even startling. In the Cuneo Papers at the Franklin Roosevelt Library is an article written by Cuneo that, while its main purpose was to defend Cuneo's friend Dick Ellis from charges of being a Soviet mole, captures a telling fact known to few people: British intelligence created William Donovan's COI/OSS.

"If the charge against Ellis is true," wrote Cuneo, "...it would mean that the OSS, and to some extent its successor, the CIA, in effect was a branch of the Soviet KGB."[31]

Cuneo is not the only insider to say bluntly that credit must fall to William Stephenson's organization for the "conception and establishment of the COI."[32] Stephenson cabled this to London in mid-June 1941: "Donovan accuses me of having 'intrigued and driven' him into appointment. You can imagine how relieved I am after three months of battle and jockeying for position in Washington that our man is in a position of such importance to our efforts."[33]

Not only were the British the primary force in the conception and creation of the COI, which later became the OSS and whose pieces were finally reconstructed into the CIA, but a British officer, Dick Ellis, then ran the organization. This was done in deepest secrecy, because as Winston Churchill's personal intelligence assistant, Major Desmond Morton, wrote, "It is of course essential that this fact not be known in view of the furious uproar it would cause if known to the Isolationists."[34]

The isolationists never caught on, but Assistant Secretary of State Adolf Berle did, though he was misled by Ellis's cover name, as he passed this explosive information on to Sumner Welles: "For your confidential information, the really active head of the intelligence section in Donovan's group is Mr. Elliott, who is assistant to Mr. Stevenson [sic]. In other words, Stevenson's assistant in The British intelligence is running Donovan's intelligence service."[35]

The British were not deterred from mounting major operations by the fear of discovery and exposure. Those operations deemed important were given sufficient time and planning so that all of the members of the intelligence orchestra played their parts. Some of the protective coloration came from the British penchant for involving the right social and political strata. To push for Donovan's organization, Intrepid had enlisted people close to President Roosevelt—Gilbert Winant, ambassador to Great Britain; presidential speechwriter Robert Sherwood; and Vincent Astor, FDR's kinsman and intelligence operative—to push for Donovan's appointment.[36]

For support back in Great Britain, Stephenson enlisted the help of two men in Churchill's immediate entourage, "C"'s good friend General H. L. Ismay and Sir Desmond Morton.

Years later when dictating a history of the founding of the Coordinator of Information, William Stephenson related how Donovan began sending the White House (he called it by its code name, "the Summit") papers stressing the need for the United States to establish undercover services equivalent to the various British services—Secret Intelligence Service, Political Warfare Executive, Ministry of Economic Warfare, and external Counterespionage. "Of course my staff," said Sir William, "produced the material for these papers and they were usually sent up in practically the original form."[37]

On May 9, 1941, the wealthy, well-connected Vincent Astor, FDR's friend and New York area coordinator of intelligence, sent the president a clipping from the *New York Herald Tribune* that was probably a plant to build the consensus of voices calling for the plan British intelligence wanted. The *Herald Tribune*, as we will see later, was BSC's favorite outlet for planted articles. Moreover, the putative author, George Fielding Eliot, was a devoted British sympathizer, one of the most influential people in the BSC front Fight for Freedom, and a favorite vehicle for planted articles.

Citing the threat from fifth columnists and enemy agents, Eliot pointed with alarm at the lack of a coordinator for FBI, ONI, and G-2 intelligence. The United States needed, wrote Eliot, "a special intelligence service to act as co-ordinator, responsible directly to the President, acting with his own authority, and provided with personnel to conduct investigations of its own when necessary."[38] And there were other members of the intelligence orchestra. One was William Donovan's friend Secretary of the Navy Frank Knox. Another was BSC collaborator Robert Sherwood. Sherwood certainly had the opportunity to plead Intrepid's case. Sherwood spent twelve days as an overnight guest at the White House between April 23, 1941, and May 27, 1941.

Sherwood was positioning himself to be head of what was to become the Foreign Information Service of the Coordinator of Information. On June 16, 1941, Sherwood sent to Donovan a list of people he thought he could trust, "for the work we discussed…yesterday evening at your home." The letter also contains a clear reference to another of those helping Stephenson: "Yesterday evening at your house was a wonderfully interesting one. I saw the Ambassador again today, He's a honey" (letter from Sherwood to Donovan, 16 June 1941, *Exhibits*

Illustrating the History of OSS, vol. 3; quoted in Troy, "Coordinator of Information," 103).

Sherwood's favorite journalists, it should not be surprising, were also favorites of BSC—Edmond Taylor, Douglas Miller, E. A. Mowrer, H. R. Knickerbocker, and Raymond Gram Swing.[39] Fortunately, one of these, Edmond Taylor, has been quite forthright about his activities with American and British intelligence during this period. In his memoir, *Awakening from History*, Taylor wrote: "The propaganda wing, called the Foreign Information Service, was to be headed by Robert E. Sherwood, the noted playwright and one of President Roosevelt's most talented speech writers. I knew Sherwood slightly, from some of the overlapping interventionist committees with which we were both connected, and admired him greatly."[40]

Tom Troy, in his study done for the Central Intelligence Agency's *Studies in Intelligence* series, credits Ambassador Winant as the man who "brought things to a head." He had no fewer than five scheduled meetings with FDR between June 3 and June 15, 1941.[41]

So Intrepid had the American organization he wished to have, with the man of his choice at the helm and with his own man, Dick Ellis, actually running things. "It was conceived by Stephenson," wrote Intrepid's longtime friend and confidant Ernest Cuneo, "as an American solution to British problems in the Western Hemisphere." Given its parentage and the presence of Dick Ellis, it should come as no surprise that Donovan's office was created in the image and likeness of British Security Coordination. Writes Cuneo: "…before Pearl Harbor, Donovan was building a strategic service, a propaganda unit, a special operations service, an economics division, a morale unit, an SIS, and a Commando unit. COI [Coordinator of Information] was by design multi-faceted, multifunctional. Like BSC it was an integrated structure, and a response to BSC's need."[42]

Not only the wide-ranging organization but the aggressive, offensive spirit, the spirit of BSC at war, became embedded in the COI and moved to OSS when the name was changed in mid-1942. BSC passed on an attitude as much as it passed on specific technical skills. It passed on a way of looking at problems and an openness to possible solutions—no matter their legality or morality.[43]

This sometimes shocked others. After reading an OSS psychological warfare manual, the head of army intelligence, the usually tough

General George Strong, "denounced" it as "devoid of every moral consideration."[44] He could, with equal vehemence, have been speaking of any number of BSC documents, including large stretches of Montgomery Hyde's *The Quiet Canadian*.

At the end of the war, President Roosevelt had an army colonel cataloging the "illegalities and improprieties attributable to OSS, and a Congressional investigation was threatened," according to Ernest Cuneo.[45] It is this wartime modus operandi that the CIA was to take into the Cold War.

••••

CHAPTER 2

The Fronts

One thing is evident. Members of the American elite, including President Franklin D. Roosevelt, were not tricked into the war; they were not victims. They were as eager as the British to fight Hitler.[1]

The Americans were eager to dance but did not know the steps; the British knew the steps but needed a rich partner. These elite interventionists invariably worked with and for and through a number of organizations that were fronts for British intelligence.

One of the startling documents that has come to light is a July 1941 report from Special Operations Executive officer Sydney "Bill" Morrell (G.101). In this memorandum, Morrell emphasizes the secret British financial support provided to the interventionist organizations. He stresses that these fronts had been "formed and acquired" by SO.1, the secret propaganda arm of SOE. He listed them:

> (i) *The Non-Sectarian Anti-Nazi League.* Used for the vehement exposure of enemy agents and isolationists. Prints a wide variety of pamphlets, copies of which have been sent to you. Has recently begun to attack Lindbergh and the many other conscious or unconscious native Fascists....

> (ii) *The League for Human Rights.* A subsidiary organization of the American Federation of Labour which in its turn controls 4,000,000 trade unionists....

> (iii) *Friends of Democracy.* An example of the work of this organization is attached. It is a complete attack upon Henry Ford for his anti-Nazi [sic] leanings.

(iv) *Fight for Freedom Committee*. Both this and (iii) above are militant interventionist organizations whose aim is to provide Roosevelt with evidence that the U.S. public is eager for action.

(v) *American Labour Committee to Aid British Labour*. Another branch organization of the American Federation of Labour. It is organized along the lines that British labour is in the front line defending American labour. The latest activity of this organization has been to inaugurate a week during which all American trade unionists are asked to donate towards a fund in aid of British labour....

(vi) *Committee for Inter-American Co-operation*. Used this for sponsoring SO.1 work in Central and South America. It is now being used intensively for penetration in all Latin American countries, both as cover for agents and for sponsoring pamphlets.

(vii) *America Last*. A purely provocative experiment started in San Francisco in an attempt to sting America into a fighting moold (sic).[2]

The secret "BSC Account" reiterates that Fight for Freedom was a BSC front and adds that BSC had close ties with the Italian-American Mazzini Society, headed by the academic and journalist Max Ascoli. Also claimed was a close working relationship with Salloum Mokarzel, editor of *Al Shoda*, the Arabic daily paper of New York City, and president of the Lebanese League for Progress.[3]

British intelligence agents had created and were running several other front groups by the fall of 1941. One of these was France Forever, which ran the United States part of the British effort to finance and promote an obscure French officer, Charles de Gaulle, as the true voice of the real France.

Another organization merits mention because its leadership interlocked with so many of the front groups above, and it was serviced by British agents who also served so many of the other BSC fronts. This was the CDAAA—the Committee to Defend America by Aiding the Allies—better known as the White Committee after its nominal chairman, Kansas newspaperman William Allen White.

By July 1941, when SOE's Bill Morrell wrote his report, the British propaganda themes that had powered the CDAAA—"Give us the tools and we will finish the job," and its concomitant "We don't need your men"—had run their course. Taken off propaganda support, the White Committee withered, to be superseded by the more militant Fight for Freedom, which better spoke more aggressive themes.

These fronts had interlocking directorates, which worked closely together doing the things the British needed done but did not wish to be seen doing: disseminating propaganda, promoting an American peacetime military draft, pushing through the Destroyer Deal, destroying or turning around the isolationists, making sure that the Republican Party nominated an interventionist in 1940.

In his memorandum describing his stewardship of SO.1, Morrell contended that these fronts were all unaware "of British influence, since this is maintained through a permanent official in each organization, who in turn, is in touch with a cut-out, and never with us direct." Earlier, at the beginning of his report, Bill Morrell laid out his duties: "The activities of SO.1 in New York are three-fold: (1) Subversive propaganda in the United States for the exposure and destruction of enemy propaganda...; countering isolationist and appeasement propaganda.... (2)...directing ostensibly American propaganda towards the three Axis powers and enemy-occupied territories. (3) Subversive propaganda in South American countries as in (1) above."[4]

Morrell's memorandum with its simple declaration that the front groups he listed had been formed or acquired by British intelligence is, of course, a wonderful start for the historian. The "BSC Account" also names Fight for Freedom as a front. But since the British intelligence files are still closed and American intelligence—FBI, army intelligence, navy intelligence, and the CIA—will release little, the task of tracking the particulars of front group operations would, at first, seem formidable; fortunately, however, the Fight for Freedom Papers at Princeton contain a wealth of correspondence, which allows the researcher to establish a paper trail for many events.

This most prominent of the BSC fronts went through several name changes during its eighteen months of existence, but is best known as Fight for Freedom. Initially it was known as the Miller Group because it first met (on Dunkirk weekend, June 2, 1940) at the Fairfax, Virginia, home of Francis Pickens Miller. Miller was the organization director of the Council on Foreign Relations in New York. The nine people present were Miller and his wife, Helen; the man who had called the meeting, Baltimore attorney Richard F. Cleveland;[5] Stacy May of New York; Winfield Riefler of Princeton; Mr. and Mrs. Whitney Shepardson of New York; Edward P. Warner of the Civil Aeronautics Board; and M. L. Wilson of the Department of Agriculture.

"The sense of doom was so strong," wrote Miller later, "that we began our consultations by considering what the United States should do in view of the appalling catastrophe that had just befallen the French and British armies on the continent." The group thought "there was a desperate need for someone to speak for America. Why should not we?"[6]

The result was that at Miller's urging, British intelligence "collaborator" Whitney Shepardson took a pen and sat down at a desk and wrote a statement titled "A Summons to Speak Out." The key paragraph reads: "The United States should immediately give official recognition to the fact and to the logic of the situation—by declaring that a state of war exists between this country and Germany." Because of the prominence of the people who affixed their names to this, the story was given large play in the *New York Times* and the *New York Herald Tribune* and other major news outlets.[7]

The Miller Group progressed during the summer of 1940 into the Century Group—named for the exclusive Century Club in New York City where it met. By the spring of 1941 this had evolved into what appeared to be a national organization, Fight for Freedom, but in reality the core of activist members remained the same East Coast elite and the headquarters remained in New York City.

Mark Lincoln Chadwin in his major study of these "Warhawks," as he calls them, has identified the activist members who dominated the Miller Group/Century Group/Fight for Freedom. The most prominent members will be examined more closely in the next chapter, but here is a simple list:

- Francis Pickens Miller, executive director of Century Group
- F. H. Peter Cusick, Fight for Freedom office manager, executive secretary, day-to-day policy maker; later described as a "shadowy figure"
- Dr. Henry P. Van Dusen, faculty member, Union Theological Seminary, member of the policy committee of the White Committee (CDAAA)

- Lewis W. Douglas, head of Mutual Life Insurance Company, member of the executive committee of the CDAAA
- Ulric Bell, Washington correspondent of the *Louisville Courier-Journal*; replaced Miller in October 1940, became executive chairman of Fight for Freedom in April 1941; according to Chadwin Bell was "leading actor" in Fight for Freedom
- Ward Cheney, head of Cheney Brothers silk fabric maker, quiet financial angel for Century Group
- Herbert Agar, editor of *Louisville Courier-Journal*, signer of "A Summons to Speak Out," prominent speaker and policy maker for Fight for Freedom
- Geoffrey Parsons, chief editorial writer of *New York Herald Tribune*; wrote the foreign affairs part of Wendell Willkie's acceptance speech
- John Balderston, journalist screenwriter; in late summer 1940 directed the British-founded front William Allen White News Service
- Joseph Alsop, journalist, relative of Franklin Roosevelt
- Elmer Davis, CBS newsman, only Midwest native active in Fight for Freedom
- Will Clayton, founder of world's largest cotton-trading firm, vice president of Export Import Bank, assistant to Nelson Rockefeller at Rockefeller Office, which worked with BSC blacklisting operations
- Whitney H. Shepardson, in 1940 coauthor of Council on Foreign Relations series *The United States in World Affairs*
- James P. Warburg, banker, writer
- George Watts Hill of Durham, North Carolina, active in banking, cotton manufacturer, signer of "A Summons to Speak Out"
- Dean G. Acheson, international lawyer, with offices in New York and Washington
- Allen W. Dulles, lawyer, intelligence operative

By the last quarter of 1941, Fight for Freedom closely resembled the central propaganda agency Bill Morrell had envisioned: "The most effective of all propaganda towards the US would be through a unified organization which could be used to attack the isolationists, such as America First, on the one hand, and to create a Nation-wide campaign for an American declaration of war upon the other."[8]

Though it does not name Fight for Freedom specifically as a British intelligence front group, *The Hawks of World War II: The Interventionist Movement in the U.S. Prior to Pearl Harbor* by Mark Lincoln Chadwin supplies a wealth of information showing its interaction with both British intelligence and the Roosevelt administration. Indeed one of the "Warhawks" who worked closely with British intelligence, Lewis Douglas, was considerably disturbed by Chadwin's research.

In a 1968 letter to British intelligence operative Sir John Wheeler-Bennett, Douglas wrote: "…Mr. Chadwin called me on the phone…. He indicated that he had some written evidence that you and Mr. Morgan [British propagandist] had been in touch with one of the groups [Century Group/Fight for Freedom]. I told him…I thought as a matter of discretion he should delete references to you and Aubrey Morgan…."[9]

What, if anything, Chadwin cut because of Douglas's objection is not known. He wrote: "…Bell [chairman of executive committee] and Cusick [executive secretary] continued and expanded their relationship with Aubrey Morgan and John Wheeler-Bennett of the British Information Service, talking with them by telephone once or twice a week. On several occasions during the following year, Bell and Cusick were even asked to be present at the BIS office in Rockefeller Center while the British agents received confidential telephone messages from officials in London about which they wanted the Warhawks immediately informed."[10]

Douglas need not have worried. American historians barely noticed that British propagandists who worked with and for British intelligence were suggesting activities for Fight for Freedom. Douglas was much more discreet; his relevant correspondence is missing. As for Professor John Wheeler-Bennett, he appears repeatedly as a coworker when British intelligence decisions are being made. He admits in his autobiography to having been "one of the earliest workers for the secret propaganda unit, Department EH which was amalgamated into Special Operations Executive."[11]

In 1942, after the secret Political Warfare Executive (PWE) was separated from Special Operations Executive (SOE), Wheeler-Bennett became head of the New York office. The purpose of this office was to maintain liaison with the American Office of War Information. "The reason for this appointment," writes Wheeler-Bennett, "was that I alone, of the staff of the Mission had any knowledge at all of the United States....Moreover, the leaders of the O.W.I. in New York were all personal friends of mine, especially James Warburg and George Backer, who had been firm friends of Britain in the 'Fight for Freedom' movement."[12]

Although he had technically been employed by the British Information Service—whose head, Sir Gerald Campbell, worked "hand in glove" with Bill Stephenson—in Rockefeller Center in 1941, Wheeler-Bennett has this to say about British Security Coordination: "...S.O.E. had established an office in New York under the direction of Bill (later Sir William) Stephenson....I had known many of them from pre-war days...[and] I had maintained a fairly close contact with them."[13]

There was also a close connection between Professor Wheeler-Bennett and President Franklin Roosevelt. From the fall of 1938 to the spring of 1940 the professor taught a class in international law at the University of Virginia. The students included later novelist Louis Auchincloss; Tony Bliss, later of the Metropolitan Opera; Marshall Field, son of the rich interventionist of the same name; Larry Houston, later deputy director of the CIA; and the most immediately important of them all, Franklin Roosevelt, Jr.

One result of the FDR Jr. connection was that Wheeler-Bennett spent a weekend as a White House guest in early 1939. This included a Sunday morning spent discussing international affairs with the president.[14]

These ties were, of course, unknown to the public. Also unknown to the public was the close rapport between Fight for Freedom and the White House—a relationship so close that FFF's New York office spoke by telephone with FDR's assistants Steve Early and "Pa" Watson "at least once or twice a day."[15] This covert White House–FFF connection allowed the White House to coordinate and build a bogus independent demand for interventionist policies that FDR could then follow.

In a March 6, 1941, memo from Peter Cusick to Ulric Bell and William Agar concerning a mass meeting to be held on March 30 at Madison Square Garden, Cusick wrote: "[David] Niles [of the White House staff] will take care of getting all the people that will be needed for the general effect of the presentation.

"Niles is coming to New York this afternoon and wants to talk to Mr. Bell and Mr. Agar and would like to arrange...to go over the details of the financial end of this as it is necessary to put $800 up for the Madison Square Garden binder."[16]

So the White House helped to create the demand for actions the president or his advisers wished to take. Just as SOE agent Bill Morrell had suggested in his memo, FFF was always trying to give the public the impression that important people or a large segment of the public supported the president's interventionist policies.

Not all the cooperation between the White House and FFF was covert. During 1941, Roosevelt met with FFF's Lewis Douglas, Wayne Johnson, and Marshall Field; there were several picture-taking sessions with President and Mrs. Roosevelt in 1941. In 1941, Wendell Willkie, Secretary of the Navy Knox, Vice President Wallace, and even Mrs. Roosevelt spoke at Fight for Freedom rallies.[17]

On May 7, 1941, presidential assistant Lowell Mellett wrote asking for help in placing an article attacking Lindbergh's analysis of the German air force. A week later the president requested that Fight for Freedom advise Director of Civilian Defense Fiorello La Guardia "in regard to the whole subject of effective publicity to offset the propaganda of the Wheelers, Nyes, Lindberghs, etc." The result was that FFF's Peter Cusick went to Washington during May and June 1941 to work with La Guardia.[18]

Since the leaders of Fight for Freedom had always demanded a declaration of war against Germany, they were always willing to prepare the public by advocating extreme positions toward which the president could work, in his cautious, even devious way. Once when Warhawks wondered whether they would offend FDR with their charges against the administration, Ulric Bell went to the White House and read the questionable text to the president. "If you're going to give me hell," he said, "why not use some really strong language? You know, 'pusillanimous' isn't such a bad word."[19]

Fight for Freedom's location in Rockefeller Center, the home of numerous British organizations and British Security Coordination, was convenient and efficient. The Rockefellers provided the rent-free space for BSC and FFF. Moreover, Laurance D. Rockefeller also made an arrangement for FFF's expenses at the Rockefeller Center Club.[20]

Laurance Rockefeller, Republican congressman Lucius Littauer, and Mrs. David K. Bruce (wife of the later London OSS chief and ambassador to Britain) were among those who gave $10,000 or more to Fight for Freedom. Most of the other significant donors to FFF seem to have had the deep pockets necessary for such generosity: movie men Darryl Zanuck and Jack and Harry Warner; Mrs. Harry Payne Whitney; Mr. and Mrs. Marshall Field; Mr. and Mrs. Frank T. Altschul. One donor listed by Chadwin as particularly generous, Dr. Max Ascoli, a dean at the New School for Social Research, was also working for British intelligence through his Italian-American Mazzini Society.[21]

Labor and labor unions, many with close Communist connections, presented the British and the White House with some of their greatest concerns during the period of the Hitler-Stalin Pact, 1939–41. Fight for Freedom claimed great success in bringing unions into the interventionist cause. This triumph, though, may have been caused as much by the German invasion of the Soviet Union as by the efforts of Fight for Freedom. Ernest Cuneo writes: "…I was…FDR's personal liaison with the United Automobile Workers, United Aircraft Workers and the United Farm Machinery workers.…There was damn little to do after Hitler attacked Russia. Before that, there was tough going. The Communist-led unions were doing as much damage with strikes as a couple of U-Boats in the Atlantic."[22]

David Niles of the White House staff (Ernest Cuneo's intelligence contact at the White House) and Isador Lubin, the commissioner of labor statistics, successfully promoted Abe Rosenfield to organize Fight for Freedom's labor division. That Cuneo was "in the loop" with Fight for Freedom and David Niles is evident from a telegram from Fight for Freedom's Peter Cusick to David Niles at the Carlton Hotel in Washington, D.C.: "Hope that you can talk to Ernest Cuneo today in Washington. He is at the Anchorage [Cuneo's apartment] for the Day is Anxious to talk to you."[23]

Fight for Freedom made a major effort to reach unions by publishing advertising in local papers and by its weekly *Labor News Service*. This "news service" consisted of five legal-size pages of short items for shop stewards and union newspaper editors.

Typically the articles told of yet another union leader or union that had decided to back President Roosevelt's foreign policy or, in the words of the man behind the front, SOE's Bill Morrell, "provide evidence that the U.S. public is eager for action": "NINETY-NINE A.F.L. AND CIO LEADERS URGE FULL MEASURES TO DEFEAT AXIS MENACE.…We say to you, Mr. President, Go forward. Go forward boldly, uncompromisingly. We know you love liberty as we do. We will support you completely till tyranny is erased and liberty wholly victorious"; "CLEVELAND FEDERATION SUPPORTS F.D.R., AMALGAMATED APPROVES ROOSEVELT ATTITUDE ON DEFENSE STRIKES."[24]

The central theme of these notices and news items was that President Roosevelt and Britain were good for workers—"PROVIDE BRITISH FOR POST-WAR SOCIAL SECURITY PENSIONS: FIRST LADY REFUSES TO STRIKE-BREAK WITH WHITE HOUSE LAUNDRY" and that the Nazis were bad for workers, particularly unionized workers—"NAZIS ARREST UNION LEADERS IN NORWEGIAN ROUND-UP." Also typically present was an article attacking pacifists or isolationists: "WHEELER HAILED IN AXIS PAPERS; MONTANA SUPPORT DWINDLES."[25]

Fight for Freedom made at least one humorous faux pas for an intelligence front group. *Labor News Service* sometimes carried a personality profile or puff piece on a union man who was a close ally of Fight for Freedom. The December 6, 1941, issue ends with this: "Note to Editors: Through an unfortunate typographical error the story appearing in last week's labor news service on Emile Rieve, president of the Textile Workers Union of America, C.I.O., said, 'He was an international spy.' The sentence should have read, 'He was *no* international spy.'"[26]

It was on the labor issue that Fight for Freedom intertwined with another of Bill Morrell's fronts, the American Labor Committee to Aid British Labor (ALCABL).

This front was tied to the American Federation of Labor. The honorary chairman was William Green, president of the AFL, but the real driving force was chairman Matthew Woll, the third vice president of the AFL. Woll was in turn also president of yet another of Morrell's fronts, the League for Human Rights.[27]

Woll is most likely the "permanent official" with whom British intelligence had contact. The ALCABL was organized in early March 1941, as Woll wrote Franklin Roosevelt, "to mobilize sympathies and resources of organized labor in this country to help relieve sufferings of British Labor fighting heroically against dictators." It was formed during the visit of Britain's Sir Walter Citrine to the United States in response to the CIO's Communist-influenced opposition to aid for Britain.[28] The tactic of British intelligence was to find people with useful views, then fund them, counsel them, guide them, and promote them. These people, given the proper guidance and proper coordination, were then used to attack Britain's enemies, namely the American isolationists, and move the United States toward war.

Though the committee was only formed in March 1941, Woll and Green had been hostile to Hitler since at least 1933. At that time they had reported on Hitler's crushing of the German labor movement, and they had quickly followed by pushing through a resolution boycotting German goods and services.[29] At that time, before the Germans' June 22, 1941, attack on the Soviet Union, Woll had shown another endearing attribute: he was strongly anti-Soviet.

The CIO, on the other hand, had a number of influential Communists, usually referred to as the "left wing," and its local unions were, until June 1941, a real problem. In May 1941, Abe Rosenfield of Fight for Freedom's labor division contacted another BSC front, the League for Human Rights: "We are preparing a statement exposing the 'National Labor Committee Against War' as a Communist front for Tuesday's papers. Won't you please secure names of A.F. of L. and C.I.O. leaders in New York City who would lend their names to such and phone them to me immediately."[30]

Woll contacted the White House at least two more times, first asking for a presidential endorsement of his organization and then for the president's press statement on "Aid British Labor Week." In return he received a letter of encouragement and one letter of support, which he was "at liberty to release" to the press.[31]

On the occasion of American troops occupying Iceland on July 7, 1941, Woll was quoted in Fight for Freedom's *Labor News Service* under the headline "CIO, A.F. OF L. LEADERS APPROVE OCCUPATION OF ICELAND": "In making this move as a measure of vital national defense and not as an act of aggression, the President deserves the wholehearted support of the entire nation."[32]

Another of BSC's fronts, Friends of Democracy, was, if anything, even tougher and more aggressive than FFF. Friends of Democracy, whose national director was a Unitarian minister, the Rev. Leon M. Birkhead, had been formed in Kansas City, Missouri, in 1937. On its stationery it still listed Kansas City as headquarters and persisted in this practice until at least 1951. By 1940, however, it operated from its "Eastern Regional Office" at 103 Park Avenue, New York City. According to Fight for Freedom and OSS executive Francis P. Miller, Dr.

Birkhead "is a grand person who has organized the best private agency in this country for collection of information regarding Nazi activities."[33] Friends of Democracy specialized in sensational, hard-hitting attacks on isolationists and America First. Historian Wayne Cole rates these attacks as "especially prominent and effective."[34]

As an example of the good works he was directing, SOE black-propaganda specialist Bill Morrell included in his memorandum to SOE headquarters a sample of Friends of Democracy's work—a "complete attack upon Henry Ford."[35]

It is certainly that: in a large ten-by-fourteen-inch format with swastikas running across the top, the cover announces, "HENRY FORD MUST CHOOSE." Inside, Ford is labeled an anti-Semite and tied to Hitler and the Nazis. It was also a grab bag of any accusation that might damage Ford's reputation. There was a section titled "T.R. Scores Ford in Last War for Anti-American Propaganda." Another Friends of Democracy project was a similarly tabloid-sized pamphlet, THE AMERICA FIRST COMMITTEE: THE NAZI TRANSMISSION BELT, which labels the committee as a mouthpiece for the Nazis.[36]

As should be expected, these British intelligence fronts worked in concert. Fight for Freedom and the White Committee, for example, distributed Friends of Democracy's pamphlets. Mystery writer Rex Stout, who worked for British intelligence, was an officer of Friends of Democracy and was also a sponsor of Fight for Freedom. Both Birkhead and Stout spoke at Fight for Freedom meetings.[37]

The Rev. Mr. Birkhead wrote to FFF's Ulric Bell in early February 1941: "...we are going to take on about fifteen key anti-democratic leaders and organizations....We hope to do with these organizations and individuals something of the same sort of things we did with Coughlin and McWilliams, and to some extent, with Verne Marshall."[38] Bell wrote back that "if we have anything good enough to destroy the people we are talking about it would be good enough for the White House to spring." He continued that "it will be a simple matter for us to get the material into the proper hands."[39]

When Lindbergh spoke at Madison Square Garden on April 24, 1941, the rally was picketed by Friends of Democracy, which handed out a pamphlet titled *What One Medal Can Do*, referring to the medal that Goering had given Lindbergh on his 1938 trip to Germany. Birkhead announced that this meeting would be "the largest gathering

of pro-Nazi and pro-Fascists…since the American Bund rallies.…"
Fight for Freedom sponsored British intelligence collaborator Rex
Stout and James Warburg in a radio reply to Lindy, and shortly there-
after Birkhead charged that Lindbergh had already "been selected by
Hitler as the 'Fuehrer' of America."[40]

Although Lindbergh's stand against intervention had by 1939–40
alienated his friends, his attorney, and his in-laws in the establishment,
the reaction of the general public is harder to gauge. The crucial event
was his Des Moines, Iowa, speech of September 11, 1941, in which he
mentioned Jews as one group interested in getting the United States
into war. The public reaction, as opposed to the media and intellectual
reaction, at first blush seems to have been mild.

When Lindbergh spoke in the very center of the establishment in
New York's Madison Square Garden on May 23, 1941, he drew twenty
thousand people inside and perhaps another fourteen thousand outside. On October 30, 1941, he spoke again at Madison Square Garden
before nearly twenty thousand, but this may be misleading. As part of
its persistent political warfare and dirty tricks against Lindbergh, BSC
claims to have printed a duplicate set of tickets, hoping to create fights
and turmoil over seating. BSC claims this had the effect of inflating the
attendance when the original crowd proved small and the ushers more
alert then anticipated.[41]

Another BSC front, France Forever, was the American phase of the
British effort to finance and promote Charles de Gaulle as the true
voice of France. Eventually Churchill was to get heartily sick of the
pompous and prickly general, but in 1940–41 he was of major use to
British propaganda.[42]

British intelligence controlled France Forever largely through BSC
agent Sandy Griffith and Market Analysts Inc. In a "Dear Ernie" letter
of August 3, 1940, Griffith wrote to Ernest Cuneo: "I have been asked
to head up a committee of Americans who are in sympathy with the
best of old French ideals and want no traffic with the Vichy France.
This committee will include prominent Harvard and Columbia people
and will be militant. Have you any candidates?"[43]

In the sophisticated public relations form that typified these front
groups, France Forever held its charter signing ceremony at Indepen-
dence Hall in Philadelphia. The president of France Forever, oilman
Eugene J. Houdry, took the occasion to praise de Gaulle and reiterate

the British theme that de Gaulle was fighting for the liberation of France in accordance with France's pledged word.

Another organizer of France Forever, Dr. Albert Simard announced the organization's creed. It incorporated two basic themes of British propaganda: "We are convinced that France and all enslaved European democracies can be freed only by a British victory and that a German victory over Britain will be the signal for an attack on all the Americas."[44]

De Gaulle's London headquarters announced on October 6, 1940, that committees had been formed in nine countries—Brazil, Argentina, Uruguay, Chile, Mexico, Canada, Egypt, South Africa, and the British colony of Mauritius—"to act in close cooperation with the Free French forces." A following *New York Times* article of October 7, 1940, concludes that the headquarters of de Gaulle's followers "is at 8 West 40th Street, New York City under the name 'France Forever.' " By March 9, 1941, the office had been moved to 30 Rockefeller Plaza, convenient to British Security Coordination and Fight for Freedom.[45]

In the Ernest Cuneo Papers is a "Notice of a Press Conference" sent to Cuneo by Francis A. Henson, Sandy Griffith's assistant at Market Analysts Inc. The press conference in Washington's Mayflower Hotel on December 6, 1940, presented "Mr. Jacques de Sieyes, personal representative of General De Gaulle and a founder and member of the Board of France Forever." Also introduced was Dr. Fred G. Hoffherr, the head of the French department at Barnard College of Columbia University. Hoffherr was chairman of France Forever's public relations department. Jean Delattre-Seguy, a Washington representative of France Forever with offices in the Shoreham Building, was also present. On the top of the release, in ink, Henson had written: "Ernie —Stop by If you can—conveniently FAH."[46]

British intelligence exerted covert influence on France Forever in other ways. Always sensitive to the American fear of being bamboozled by clever British propaganda, British Ambassador Lord Lothian had promoted the formation of the Inter-Allied Information Committee (IAIC). This allowed British propaganda to emerge from Czech or Polish or French lips.[47]

The IAIC first met on September 24, 1940, with Robert Valeur, once of the New York office of the French Information Bureau, representing France Forever. Valeur served IAIC in the influential position of director of publications. IAIC's information center was housed—where else—in Rockefeller Center.

The *New York Times* gave good coverage of France Forever's activities—rallies, public meetings, and interviews. As always with British intelligence fronts, the list of outside speakers was impressive and instructive. At a packed December 20, 1940, rally at Carnegie Hall, British intelligence collaborators Robert Sherwood and Clark Eichelberger, executive director of the CDAAA, urged "no appeasement with the appeasers."

Sherwood blamed the war on isolationists and called for the formation now of a union of all the democracies. The president of France Forever, Eugene Houdry, reverberated the propaganda theme the British used in the run-up to Lend-Lease. The claim was that Britain did not need American troops; American supplies were all the British needed to defeat Germany. The claim was false, but deflected isolationist criticism. There was never any hope that the British could invade the continent of Europe without American manpower.[48]

There were also the voices of the administration. On May 27, 1941, Assistant U.S. Attorney General Francis M. Shea told a dinner audience assembled to hear President Roosevelt's radio speech that the United States should fully support the Free French and not "the faithless men of Vichy." Wrote the *New York Times* of the occasion: "Miss [Dorothy] Thompson led the applause during President Roosevelt's speech....At the moment he proclaimed the national emergency she excitedly embraced Edgar Ansel Mowrer....When the President finished she told a friend, 'I am sick with happiness.' "[49]

Edgar Ansel Mowrer, a correspondent for the strongly interventionist *Chicago Daily News* who also spoke at this dinner, has been named as a British intelligence agent. Dorothy Thompson has also been similarly named; see Chapter 3.

At France Forever's Bastille Day event, held at the Manhattan Center, New York City, the administration was represented by that master of personal attack Secretary of Interior Harold L. Ickes. Two thousand people witnessed the speech and many more heard it on radio station WMCA. This station broadcast many interventionist speakers sponsored by British intelligence front groups.[50]

The *New York Times* said Ickes's speech was "one of the most bitter attacks ever made on Mr. Lindbergh by any member of the administration." Ickes called Lindbergh "the knight of the German Eagle" and a "mouthpiece of the Nazi Party line in the United States."[51] Another British intelligence agent spoke at the 1941 Armistice ceremony of France Forever at the Manhattan Center. He was Colonel Rex Benson, whom the *New York Times* identified as the military attaché of the British embassy. Benson was, in fact, a British intelligence agent and an old friend of "C"—Sir Stewart Menzies, the chief of the Secret Intelligence Service (MI-6).[52]

After centuries of conflict with Britain, the Irish could not bring themselves to fight on Britain's side and so declared themselves neutral in World War II. This was much to the consternation of the British, who coveted bases in Ireland to better protect convoys from North America. The British plotted all their tried-and-true stratagems to bring the Emerald Isle to heel. John Colville, Prime Minister Winston Churchill's private secretary, wrote in his diary entry of December 3, 1940: "At dinner he [Churchill] conspired with Cranborne, Rob Hudson, Kingsley Wood and Oliver Lyttelton about means of bringing pressure to bear on Ireland. Refusal to buy her food, to lend her our shipping or to pay her our present subsidies seem calculated to bring De Valera to his knees in a very short time."[53]

In January 1941, Wendell Willkie, who had gone to England at the request of the head of BSC, William Stephenson, made a quick side trip to Ireland to attempt to get the bases. Willkie warned that Ireland's relationship with the United States would be threatened if Britain were not given the bases. This also failed.[54]

At almost the same time, January 23, 1941, Christopher Emmet, Chancellor James Byrne of New York University, and Professor William Agar (brother of Fight for Freedom activist Herbert Agar) sent out a form letter to American interventionists of Irish descent. The results of this ploy were published in March. Byrne headed the list of 129 Irish-Americans who urged Ireland to grant the bases to Great Britain. The Irish were unmoved.[55] If 129 petitioners were of no avail, perhaps a full-blown front group was needed.

SOE documents on the Irish American Defense Association scheduled for release in 1998 give the only extensive inside view of the planning and resources BSC devoted to even its smallest and least successful front. In half of a dozen reports to London, the details of the IADA's plans and ploys are given in detail reminiscent of a major corporate effort to market a new product. The "Index," really a table of contents, to the report of October 18, 1941, lists 123 pages of personnel, activities, and reports: "National Activities Planned, Irish American Opinion Polls (Work in Progress), 'The Case for Irish and American Unity'—First draft of 24-page pamphlet...."

The BSC cover letter to Report number SO/458 of October 18, 1941, says, "Attached is the first report on our activities in connection with the...FORMATION AND ACTIVITIES OF THE COMMITTEE FOR AMERICAN-IRISH DEFENSE....The Report has been compiled by G.112 [Sandy Griffith] and his collaborators....We are subsidizing the MOVEMENT at the rate of $1,500.00 per month..." [about $15,000 per month at 1997 prices].

Sandy Griffith writes in this report: "I have reserved effective control of the organization....the proposed activities have been discussed informally with people in the Administration, with Secretaries Knox and Welles and with Colonel Donovan....We have close friendly relations with the Committee to Defend America and with Fight for Freedom....Erie bases for America are an immediate tangible objective....[as are] anti-Nazi, anti-Coughlin, and other patriotic resolutions."[56]

In another "Dear Ernie" letter of October 2, 1941, on the stationery of Market Analysts Inc., Francis Henson, Sandy Griffith's assistant, wrote: "I enclose some material on an Irish American Unity campaign for which we are working. Some of your State Department friends may be interested. There is to be a 24 page pamphlet out soon with an introduction by Frank Murphy."[57]

The material he enclosed is a "Petition of the Committee for American Irish Defense" with the same street address—8 West 40th Street, New York City—as Market Analysts Inc. and the CDAAA (White Committee). It was not long, however, before the petitions had a new address and a new addressee; it was William Agar, Suite 301, 1270 Sixth Avenue, RKO Building, New York City. Yet another BSC front took up residence close to British intelligence in Rockefeller Center. The press release stated: "Prof. William Agar of Columbia University, distinguished author and scientist and a leader of the Fight for Freedom." The executive committee lists James Byrne as honorary chairman, Rossa F. Downing as national chairman, T. James Tumulty as secretary, and Christopher Emmet as treasurer.[58]

James Byrne was the father-in-law of John F. C. "Ivar" Bryce. Ivar Bryce was a Special Operations Executive agent working for BSC. One of James Byrne's other daughters, Helen, once the wife of *Foreign Affairs* editor Hamilton Fish Armstrong, had been, since March 1938, the wife of columnist Walter Lippmann, who the "BSC Account" says was "among those who rendered service of particular value."[59] Christopher Emmet, the treasurer, worked on many British intelligence projects with British intelligence agent Sanford Griffith and after the war on MI-6 and CIA projects. He was the cousin of Robert Emmet Sherwood.

Christopher Emmet in a fund-raising letter of November 1941 clearly stated the purpose of the organization. The AIDA sought to counter the likes of "America First, Father Coughlin and others still defying the majority verdict" of "an openly and legally recognized Shooting War in the Atlantic."

The AIDA's slogan was, "You can count on the Irish, Mr. President." Emmet also said: "Our first rally was held on Armistice Day at Father Duffy's statue in New York...attended by 6,000 people."[60] All the bandwagon tactics usually so effective—the testimonials by scholars and prominent citizens, the rallies, the petitions, the radio broadcasts—fell flat. The bitter truth was that the president could not count on the Irish.

In the end, the Irish would have none of it; no amount of slick propaganda could convince them that Britain was the last hope of civilization. Mark Chadwin says of the Fight for Freedom interlock with this Irish campaign: "...in one of the few instances in the fall when it seized the initiative and sought to influence diplomatic events concurrently with administrative action, the Century Group failed completely."[61]

For the BSC fronts that specialized in hard-hitting, even malicious, attacks it was an ignominious end. The AIDA was reduced to whining about "vicious attacks by the Coughlinite Irish Organizations and Press." The masters of distortion were left complaining that the Irish had "distorted" AIDA pronouncements.[62]

Lastly, we come to the Committee to Defend America by Aiding the Allies (CDAAA), better known in its day as the William Allen White Committee. This was in fact the second William Allen White Committee. The first White Committee had been the popular name for another interventionist front, the Committee for Concerted Peace

Efforts, and its official name had been just as cleverly and misleadingly contrived: Nonpartisan Committee for Peace Through Revision of the Neutrality Law. These were all interventionist organizations. "The Committee for Concerted Peace Efforts was in effect a front for the League of Nations Association," writes historian Jane Harriet Schwar.[63]

The first William Allen White Committee (WAW I) had lasted only a few weeks in the late summer and fall of 1939. It was of major importance, however, since it marked a "definite shift toward conservatism in the leadership of the interventionist movement." Left-wing radicals had been replaced by pro-British conservatives.[64]

As was true of the other interventionist committees, such as Fight for Freedom, with which it interlocked, half the 550 members of the White Committee lived in the Northeast. One hundred forty-three of these lived or worked in New York City. Fewer than a hundred members lived west of the Mississippi.[65] The dozen men who made the CDAAA run were white male Protestants of largely British descent and old families who had gone to the better Eastern colleges.[66]

One of the White Committee connections to the British was through its William Allen White News Service, launched by the British puppet Inter-Allied Information Committee, also located in Rockefeller Center with numerous other interventionist groups and BSC.[67]

The head of the William Allen White News Service was John Balderston. He had been a war correspondent in the Great War. His highly emotional articles had been favorable to the British, and he had continued in this vein in 1917, when he became director of information in Great Britain for George Creel's Committee on Public Information. He then spent from 1923 to 1931 in London as correspondent for Herbert Bayard Swope's *New York World*. His days with the British in London seem to go with him to Hollywood, where he spent the 1930s as a screenwriter on such films as *Lives of a Bengal Lancer* (British army heroics on the Northwest Frontier of India) and *The Prisoner of Zenda* (Englishman defeats plot against the king of Ruritania).[68]

Like many in the Century Group/Fight for Freedom, he greatly enjoyed his contact with British Ambassador Lothian. Balderston quickly informed Lothian of the Century Group's finances and his own hopes for ties with Clarence Streit's Union Now Movement, which sought to form a union of the United States and Great Britain. He wrote or told

Lothian of the Century Group's efforts to discuss its program with Secretary of State Hull and Secretary of War Stimson and the effort to obtain the cooperation of Republican presidential nominee Wendell Willkie.[69]

In 1940 the British Ministry of Information had been confident enough of its ability to influence the White Committee that it felt the need for a direct telephone link. The British ambassador at Washington, Lord Lothian, ever wishing to use intermediaries and covert links, was horrified: "It would be most disastrous to the William Allen White Committee were it ever to be established that it was communicating and collaborating with any branch of His Majesty's Government."[70]

Most prominent was the energetic leader of WAW I, Clark Eichelberger, the national director of the League of Nations. Quiet support also came from an interventionist group organized around the prominent New York attorney Frederic R. Coudert. Coudert had been a vociferous interventionist before United States entry into World War I and had been legal adviser to the British embassy during that war. Between the wars, Coudert's law firm represented the French government. In this capacity he not only gave advice to the French embassy but made himself useful by writing pro-French articles for American newspapers.[71] The Coudert group invited White to a luncheon on October 20, 1939.

The group had two goals. The first was to repeal the neutrality laws, which were impeding the flow of greatly needed goods to Britain and France. Second, after this effort to get the neutrality laws changed had succeeded, the friends of Britain and France faced up to an even more dangerous problem. They had to make sure that both political parties nominated candidates who supported aid to the Allies. There was great fear that in the heat of the election either party, but particularly the Republicans, might cater to antiwar sentiment. All those present at the April 1940 meeting agreed to try to prevent this.[72] How this second concern was turned into action is the subject of Chapter 8.

Some of those present at this October meeting were official members of the Nonpartisan Committee (WAW I). These would include William Allen White himself, Clark Eichelberger, Frederick Coudert, and Thomas K. Finletter, a member of Coudert's law firm. Others in the Coudert Group who attended this luncheon were Wendell Willkie, the president of the J. P. Morgan–controlled utility Commonwealth and Southern Corporation; Thomas J. Watson, president of IBM and the International Chamber of Commerce and a major factor at radio station WRUL, which British intelligence controlled; Henry L. Stimson, a staunch interventionist active in various pro-intervention organizations; and Frank L. Polk, international lawyer and member of the firm of Polk, Davis, Wardwell—he was acting secretary of state while Wilson and Lansing were at the Versailles Peace Conference. Allen Dulles, a veteran intelligence operative and member of the Foreign Service, may also have been present. The record is conflicting.[73]

By July 1940, charges that the committee was dominated by Wall Street seem to have brought on the formation of an official policy committee, in which the Wall Street connection would be less obvious, to replace the informal relationship with the Coudert Group. To be sure, Frederic Coudert and Thomas W. Lamont, senior partner at J. P. Morgan, continued behind the scenes. However, "committee leaders," writes historian Jane Schwar, "thinking of the possibility of a congressional investigation, prudently did not record Lamont's presence in the minutes."[74]

Though two interventionist committees were named for him, William Allen White, "the Sage of Emporia, Kansas," himself need be examined only briefly, because he turns out to have been anything but a real insider. The ignominious end of White as leader of the William Allen White Committee came when he gave an interview, to Roy Howard of the Scripps Howard chain of newspapers, denying that his Committee to Defend America by Aiding the Allies was interventionist. In a widely published response, White replied: "The only reason in God's world I am in this organization is to keep the country out of war." White went on to say that if he were to make a motto for the committee it would be "The Yanks are not coming."[75]

Clark Eichelberger and several members of the strongly interventionist policy committee of CDAAA were meeting on December 23, 1940, at the home of one of the most deeply interventionist members Lewis Douglas. "We were stunned…" reports Eichelberger. If the committee was "stunned," William Allen White was "very much surprised and hurt at the reaction of members of the committee…." White resigned, but his name was so useful that he remained as honorary chairman.[76]

White gave the impression of having a confused mind, and this was true, but many people would have a confused mind given his circumstances. In his daily life in Kansas the people he met were distanced from the action in Europe, both physically and emotionally. They did not identify with Britain, and they questioned the efforts of White and his Eastern establishment friends to get the United States to abet Britain. The Eastern-based captains of finance and law and intellectual life whose respect White desired were, on the other hand, emotionally committed to a British victory.

CDAAA even moved into the foreign broadcasting business by sponsoring daily shortwave broadcasts in French over the 50,000-watt Station WRUL. Ostensibly these broadcasts were summaries of American press opinion; in reality they were British black propaganda. WRUL was founded to spread "international goodwill," but Montgomery Hyde wrote in *The Quiet Canadian*: "By the middle of 1941, Station WRUL was virtually, though quite unconsciously, a subsidiary of the Stephenson organization, sending out British propaganda in twenty-two different languages and dialects...." The official "BSC Account" says: "Through cut-outs, BSC began to supply it [WRUL] with everything it needed to run a first-class international programme worthy of its transmitting power....BSC subsidized it financially. It recruited foreign news editors, translators and announcers to serve on its staff. It furnished it with material for news bulletins, with specially prepared scripts for talks and commentaries." The man who financed the French broadcasts for the CDAAA was its treasurer, Frederick Chadwick McKee.[77]

Documents that have recently become available confirm Hyde's account and specify how WRUL was controlled by BSC. In his report to London of July 1941 Sydney Morrell wrote: "...WRUL has been the station on which British organizations have concentrated their efforts. This station was privately endowed by the Rockefeller Foundation....A few months ago a new subsidy was paid by S.O.1 to 'France Forever' for separate French broadcasts from WRUL...and another subsidy was paid to the Mazzini Society for Italian broadcasts."

Later in his report Morrell detailed the mechanics of the WRUL operation. "...G.112 [Sandy Griffith]...has set up an office to deal with radio programs....all commentators work receiving their instructions and writing their broadcasts....[these are] approved by the State Department Censor, recorded, sent to WRUL in Boston and then broadcast under the sponsorship of the Fight for Freedom Committee."

The daily *WRUL Broadcast Schedule* from the SOE archives shows the responsibility for running the broadcasts divided between G.112, Sandy Griffith, and G.111, Alexander J. Halpern, once (1917) secretary to the Kerensky government in Russia, now working at BSC, and soon to become the head of its Political and Minorities Section with a new cover symbol, G.400. A note at the bottom of the schedule says, "Where no particular control is indicated we have indirect control."[78]

So the CDAAA was one of many interventionist groups used by BSC to project its interventionist message. It is little wonder then that Fight for Freedom's Francis Miller could later say: "Right-wing 'revisionists' may have grounds to accuse the Warhawks of a 'conspiracy' to involve the United States in a War." The post–World War II revisionists—those who contributed to editor Harry Elmer Barnes's book *Perpetual War for Perpetual Peace* are an example—spotted the gaps and glitches in the standard histories, but their own works, heavy on logic and analysis, unavoidably light on documents, were also vulnerable.

CHAPTER 3

●●●

"Those Who Rendered
Service of Particular Value"

In early 1969 the United States Supreme Court ruled that wiretap re-
cordings must be revealed in open court, even in cases of national security. Ernest Cuneo, once the liaison between British intelligence, the
White House, the FBI, and OSS, wrote a caustic denunciation of this
ruling and sent it to J. Edgar Hoover at the FBI. "Friendly and neutral
powers," wrote Cuneo, "are quaint and laughable terms unrecognized
in the world of international intelligence. Every major nation taps every other major nation, none more than its Allies."

The purpose of these taps, he explained, is "to trace down the foreign country's apparatus in this country. Who is talking to whom is as
important as what is said. To whom each speaks afterward is even more
important, because it leads up to the chiefs in command. The process
of unveiling this is called 'going up the ladder.' "[1]

This chapter reverses the process by going down the ladder to locate
British agents, informers, and collaborators; explore how they helped
to implement British policy; and examine how they helped move the
United States toward World War II and then toward a peace that was
in Britain's interest.

"British Security Coordination (BSC): An Account of Secret Activities in the Western Hemisphere, 1940–45" very explicitly depicts a
number of people as helpmates of British intelligence. The attack on
the American isolationists and defeatists by BSC was a thorough, clas-
sical case of covert political warfare. Of the Americans who aided BSC,
the "BSC Account" says: "The press and radio men with whom BSC

maintained contact were comparable with subagents and the intermediaries with agents. They were thus regarded."[2]

The World War II intelligence community was appalled by the publication of Montgomery Hyde's *The Quiet Canadian* because they
feared that some historian or journalist would use the methodology of
intelligence to track the revealed agents to other and darker operations. Ernest Cuneo wrote to Intrepid's assistant, Dick Ellis: "No great
harm came of it, but Montgomery Hyde broke confidences which I was
assured were inviolate. They involved newspaper friends of mine who
accepted my personal assurances and, indeed, a President for whom I
bore deepest affection."[3]

Who were the newspaper people who were particularly useful to
British intelligence? The "BSC Account" gives a partial list: George
Backer, publisher of the *New York Post*; Ralph Ingersoll, editor of *PM*;
Helen Ogden Reid, who controlled the *New York Herald Tribune*; Paul
Patterson, publisher of the *Baltimore Sun*; A. H. Sulzberger, president
of the *New York Times*; and Walter Lippmann.[4]

The "BSC Account" also lists the Overseas News Agency (ONA),
which was a branch of the Jewish Telegraph Agency. In return for cooperation, BSC began subsidizing ONA in April 1941.[5] Jacob Landau
had founded the Jewish Telegraph Agency during World War I. The
headquarters, first in London, was soon moved to New York; branches
were established in Paris, Berlin, Warsaw, and Jerusalem. The money
to run this news agency came only in part from newspapers; the remainder came from wealthy contributors, the major one being the
banker Felix Warburg.

The ONA evolved from the Jewish Telegraph Agency in the spring of
1940 as an agency to provide news and feature articles on the persecution of minorities. The guiding hand behind this transformation was the
militant interventionist Herbert Bayard Swope, who eventually became
vice chairman of the New York Fight for Freedom Committee. At a
meeting at Swope's home the board of directors was set up; George
Backer of the *New York Post* and Harold Guinzberg of Viking Press, both
leaders of Fight for Freedom, were among the board members. Swope
became "Correspondent and Chairman of the Board," as his business
cards identified him. ONA did well during the war, providing copy in
twenty-eight languages for the Office of War Information. Addition-
ally, it served United States papers with five million circulation.[6]

In the VENONA Project the United States intercepted and then decrypted hundreds of messages between Moscow and its intelligence apparatus in the U.S. Recently released VENONA messages show that Landau was working for the British, but alas the VENONA messages reveal this because Soviet secret intelligence, the NKVD, had so thoroughly penetrated BSC and its offspring OSS.

On September 8, 1943, one of the Soviet agents within British Security Coordination, UCN 9 (probably Cedric Belfrage), reported of the Overseas News Agency: "On instructions of the British, LANDAU left for the 'COUNTRYSIDE' [Mexico] to meet 'TYuLEN' [Soviet ambassador to Mexico Konstantin Umanskij]." Landau was in Mexico City for two months and had several meetings with the Soviet ambassador.[7]

To this list we should add—as the "BSC Account" does—the names of two columnists to whom Cuneo had undoubtedly given his solemn word that their ties to British intelligence would remain secret, Walter Winchell and Drew Pearson. Cuneo (code name Crusader) writes on Pearson and Winchell: "...I controlled the world's largest newspaper and radio circulation, centering on Walter Winchell and his near 1,000 papers and the only near approach was Drew Pearson's Washington Merry-Go-Round. Drew had been my instructor at Columbia, and for the next half century we were the closest of friends....From 1933 on, we were intent on bringing down Hitler/Mussolini and along with Franco had been waging all-out journalistic and legal war on them."[8]

Other BSC ties to the world of media were columnist Dorothy Thompson, journalist Edmond Taylor, movie mogul Alexander Korda, presidential speechwriter Robert Emmet Sherwood, and mystery writer Rex Stout.

Rex Stout was not only an officer in the BSC front Friends of Democracy and a major spokesman for another BSC front, Fight for Freedom, he also admits to working directly for BSC agent Donald MacLaren. In the fall of 1941, MacLaren recruited Stout, George Merten (from BSC's George Office economic warfare operations), and syndicated *New York Post* economic columnist Sylvia Porter to write a propaganda booklet titled *Sequel to the Apocalypse: The Uncensored Story: How Your Dimes and Quarters Helped Pay for Hitler's War*.[9]

As in the case of front groups, there were often several British intelligence agents, subagents, and collaborators working the same organization. There is another tendency that should be noted about these competent and trustworthy agents and collaborators who worked closely with British intelligence in the 1939–41 period. They frequently reappeared in Donovan's Coordinator of Information intelligence service or his Foreign Information Service propaganda arm run by British intelligence collaborator Robert Sherwood. There is nothing very unusual here; this was merely the very human tendency to hire familiar people who had previously served and performed well. The first list of people Sherwood sent Donovan, "for the work we discussed," included Edmond Taylor, Douglas Miller, E. A. Mowrer, H. R. Knickerbocker, and Raymond Gram Swing.[10]

The journalist Edmond Taylor has written me of his cooperation with British intelligence and described the subtlety of the British technique: "What they did more often, especially before Pearl Harbor and in the early months of the war, was to connive, usually as non-committally as possible, with Americans like myself who were willing to go out of regular (or even legal) channels to try to bend U.S. policy towards objectives that the British, as well as the Americans in question, considered desirable."[11]

In fact, the New York office of Donovan's organization, run by Allen Dulles, was Room 3663, 630 Fifth Avenue. The address of British Security Coordination was Room 3603, 630 Fifth Avenue. BSC agent Sandy Griffith's man at Fight for Freedom in Chicago joined OSS, as did SOE man and Walter Lippmann brother-in-law Ivar Bryce. Donald Downes was another. In one case—that of George Merten, a German economist who had turned over to BSC evidence that the Schering drug company was Nazi-owned and who had then worked completely for BSC, gathering economic intelligence and planting articles in the press— an entire operation, the "George Office," was unloaded onto OSS.[12]

The British vigorously maneuvered their agents into positions in Donovan's organization and probably other departments as well. Remember that Intrepid's assistant at BSC, Dick Ellis, was the person really running William Donovan's COI office.

To be sure, there were degrees in the anglophilia of Donovan's personnel. Here is Ernest Cuneo, a powerfully built former NFL football player, on an agreement he had worked out on the fate of Italy: "I went to the O.S.S. Office in New York. De Witte Poole, the assistant to Allen Dulles, hailed me. 'Oh Mr. Cuneo,' he said, 'That Italian Treaty is off! Cancel it!' I said, 'Mr. Poole, the President has approved it. There were some minor things which have to be ironed out, but it's been finally approved by the President.' He said, 'It doesn't matter. Sir Ronald Campbell just called. He doesn't want it so it's off!' I simply lifted him from his seat and slapped his face back and forth and threw him back in his chair."[13]

Among Donovan's papers is a four-page memo. Handwritten across the top is "Provided WJD-by Bill Stephenson (Pre C.O.I.)." It is titled "British Recruitment and Handling of Agents." Though it warns that "definitions of the term 'agent' vary considerably" and that its "discussion is in terms of normal, not wartime, intelligence operations," this memo still serves as a guide to the world of recruiting intelligence agents. It also helps to explain the origins and rationale of the CIA recruiting practices that have come under such close scrutiny in recent years. "Such persons are initially recommended to the service either by friends already in the service or by particular alumni of the service designated for this purpose....Both MI6 and MI5 have such former officers appointed for this purpose, particularly those who are connected with British universities....By far the largest number of British agents are not "agents" properly speaking, but voluntary informers...."[14]

The following sketches look more closely at the collaborators, agents, and voluntary informers who, as the "BSC Account" states, "rendered service of particular value" to British intelligence.

George Backer (1903–74). Backer was publisher of the *New York Post*. During the 1930s he worked for the election of FDR. For his work helping Jews escape from Nazism during the 1930s he was made a Chevalier of the Legion of Honor. From 1932 to 1942 he was married to Dorothy Schiff, granddaughter of the legendary German Jewish philanthropist Jacob H. Schiff. In 1939, Dorothy and George acquired the *New York Post*.

Backer helped British intelligence in the numerous ways open to a wealthy publisher. He was a generous donor to Fight for Freedom.[15] As previously mentioned, Backer was a founding board member of the Overseas News Agency, which worked with BSC. Before the United States entered the war he provided journalist cover for Virginia Hall (field name Marie of Lyons), one of SOE's greatest agents in France.[16]

British intelligence agent and propagandist John Wheeler-Bennett counted Backer and James Warburg among Britain's friends in Fight for Freedom. He also worked closely with them in the American Office of War Information.[17]

Arthur Hayes Sulzberger (1892–1968). When Harrison Salisbury published his history of his employer, the *New York Times*, in 1980 he did not have the benefit of David Ignatius's article at the rival *Post*. Though he readily admits that the *New York Times* was used by British intelligence, Salisbury is at pains to convince the reader of the owner's dedication to objectivity. Salisbury writes: "...World War II was to bring to Arthur Hays Sulzberger another concern....Not long after the outbreak of the war Sulzberger learned that a number of these correspondents had connections with MI-6 the British intelligence agency." Salisbury wrote that this revelation made Sulzberger "very angry," but apparently not angry enough to stop it or to fire the culprits. According to one old *Times* staff man, Hanson Baldwin, "leaks to British intelligence through *The Times* continued after U.S. entry into the war."[18]

One of those to whom Sulzberger expressed his anger about MI-6 use of his staff was Scotty Reston. Reston may well have been one of these BSC people himself. When Frank Thistlewaite of Britain's Joint American Secretariat was asked to pass on one of numerous items that the British planted in the American press, he responded that he would ask Robin Cruickshank if "it would be a suitable topic to feed to one of his tame journalists." Cruickshank liked the idea. Historian Susan Ann Brewer identifies the tame journalists as James Reston of the *New York Times*, Geoffrey Parsons of the *New York Herald Tribune*, and Frederick Kuh of the *Chicago Sun*.[19]

Salisbury recorded that Sulzberger had refused the 1942 proposal of Colonel Donovan that the *Times* be at the disposal of the OSS. The presently unanswerable question is whether Donovan was approaching Sulzberger cold or if he thought the head of the *Times* would cooperate with the OSS because he had cooperated with British intelligence. There were also other indications that Sulzberger's cooperation with British intelligence in the 1939–42 period and later with the CIA was not always as enthusiastic as the wholehearted cooperation shown by the *New York Herald Tribune*.

An August 1941 Fight for Freedom internal memo complains: "Here is another example of the same thing. The *Tribune* gives us a break and the *Times* doesn't."[20] Sulzberger's apparent ambivalence might have remained without explanation but for one of the reports found in SOE agent Valentine Williams's personal file in the SOE archives. Williams had been sent out from London under Ministry of Economic Warfare (MEW) cover to advise Intrepid on propaganda matters, promote General de Gaulle, and pick up his old contacts. On September 15, 1941, Williams wrote to his boss Dr. Hugh Dalton: "I had an hour with Arthur Sulzberger, proprietor of the *New York Times*, last week. He told me that for the first time in his life he regretted being a Jew because, with the tide of antisemitism rising, he was unable to champion the anti-Hitler policy of the administration as vigorously and as universally as he would like as his sponsorship would be attributed to Jewish influence by isolationists and thus lose something of its force."[21]

Walter Winchell (1897–1972). In a letter to Sir William Stephenson of January 4, 1988, complaining about the inaccuracies of the book *A Man Called Intrepid*, Ernest Cuneo wrote of Winchell: "My relationship with BSC was one of the many source-relationships I maintained as part of my de facto editorship of Winchell's policies....We 'moved' about 1,200 words a day, six days a week and had also to prepare a Sunday broadcast. For years I did this as a service to FDR. Thereafter, I was paid more than a million and W.W. left me his papers. Unfortunately, there is an overtone that Winchell was a British agent. He was not. He was, in fact, fighting Hitler long before anyone else in the U.S. or Britain. He was a free man, under the control of no one (including himself)."[22]

As Cuneo admits, he was the one actually writing the column and radio show and maintaining contact with BSC.[23] It is also clear from his papers that he was working with British intelligence agents, such as Sandy Griffith, in 1940 and was certainly working for Britain's interest at the outbreak of the war. "I had worked," wrote Cuneo, "on the holding up of the *Bremen* for 24 hours at the beginning of the war, broadcasting her hour of departure en clair so the British Navy could kill her as she cleared Sandy Hook. They couldn't spare the destroyer."[24]

Helen Reid (1882–1970). Born Helen Rogers in Appleton, Wisconsin, she graduated in 1903 from Barnard and went to work as social secretary for Mrs. Whitelaw Reid. From 1905 to 1911, when Whitelaw Reid was ambassador to Great Britain, she divided her time between England and the United States. She married Whitelaw's son, Ogden Mills Reid, in 1911.[25] Mrs. Reid had effective control of the paper not only because she was a strong-willed and talented woman but because her husband, Ogden Mills Reid, had a drinking problem.

According to intelligence historian Anthony Cave-Brown, Whitelaw Reid was a family friend of MI-6 head Stewart Menzies and attended Menzies family functions.[26] No newspaper in the United States was more useful to British intelligence during World War II than the *Herald Tribune*. A description of BSC's work with the *Herald Tribune* fills a dozen pages of the secret "BSC Account."

Dorothy Thompson (1894–1961). During the period under study, Dorothy Thompson exhibited an amazing ability to reflect the British propaganda line of the day. This is one of the few useful conclusions to be gained from reading the hundreds of pages in her FBI file. (A number of paragraphs and several pages were withheld from the 1940s with the "b-1" "national security exemption.")[27] Thompson's diary, kept for only a dozen entries in early 1942, also illustrates her close ties to the intelligence community.

> January 3—Emmy Rado [a refugee working for Donovan's Coordinator of Information] came in the afternoon about Paul.
>
> January 4—Called J. Wheeler-Bennett [as we have seen, a major figure in British Information Service, British intelligence, and Political Warfare]. In the evening I worked on a memo for D. [Bill Donovan, head of COI].
>
> January 5—Went to lunch with Agars, Goldsmiths and George Field....Agreed to organize the "opening" party Jan. 17th. Wrote end of memo to B.D. [Bill Donovan] in afternoon.[28]

Walter Lippmann (1889–1974). Walter Lippmann was a syndicated *Herald Tribune* columnist closely tied to British intelligence. Not only does the "BSC Account" list Lippmann "among those who rendered service of particular value," but he was not only taking advice, he was giving it.[29]

In late winter or early spring 1940, Lippmann even told the British to initiate Secret Intelligence Service operations against American isolationists. His exact thoughts are unknown. His specific ideas were "too delicate" for the British Foreign Office to put to paper, but the idea is quite clear. Lippmann was a heavyweight. His suggestions on how to handle the American public reached as high as the British War Cabinet.[30]

Lippmann's papers also contain remarkable examples of intelligence history as the "missing dimension" in conventional histories. Intelligence history has been so ignored that even first-class historians do not recognize the names of intelligence personnel. In his 1985 book of Lippmann's papers, *Public Philosopher*, editor John Morton Blum identifies the author of a letter to Lippmann thusly: "Ivar Bryce, a personal friend of Lippmann's had written to express his distress about the Darlan deal." That Bryce was a friend was true, but hardly adequate. Ivar Bryce was Walter Lippmann's brother-in-law and he was in fact a Special Operations Executive agent working for Intrepid.[31]

Though Bryce's name is not well known, one of the works he has claimed has a more public persona; in fact, President Roosevelt himself spoke of it in late October 1941.

Just when the administration was making its final push to have Congress repeal the Neutrality Acts, there emerged a most useful and intriguing document. Said FDR: "I have in my possession a secret map, made in Germany by Hitler's Government, by planners of the new world order. It is a map of South America and part of Central America as Hitler proposes to organize it."[32]

Those who heard the president's Navy Day speech were amazed, and none more so than Hitler and his underlings. They were so stunned by it that on December 11, 1941, they cited it as an example of the sort of provocative act that brought on Germany's declaration of war.[33] Reporters were somewhat suspicious about the bogus map, but to little avail.

Lippmann's brother-in-law, Ivar Bryce, worked in the Latin American affairs section of BSC, which was run by Dickie Coit (known in the office as "Coitis Interruptus"). Because there was little evidence of a German plot to take over Latin America, Ivar found it difficult to excite Americans about the threat. In his 1975 memoir, *You Only Live Once: Memories of Ian Fleming*, Bryce wrote: "Sketching out trial maps of the possible changes, on my blotter, I came up with one showing the probable reallocation of territories that would appeal to Berlin. It was very convincing: The more I studied it the more sense it made...."

Were a genuine German map of this kind to be discovered...and publicized among...the 'America Firsters,' what a commotion would be caused."[34]

Intrepid approved the idea. The skilled team at Station M, the phony document factory in Toronto run by SOE's Eric Maschwitz, took only forty-eight hours to produce "a map, slightly travel-stained with use, but on which the Reich's chief map makers...would be prepared to swear was made by them." In Roosevelt's hands the "document" had its desired effect, and Congress dismantled the last of the neutrality legislation.[35]

John F. C. "Ivar" Bryce (1906–1985). Bryce worked for both SOE and OSS. As an SOE agent he had the number G.140; as an OSS man he was 991. Among other jobs for SOE, Bryce describes himself as an agent recruiter: "and to find...[recruits] in Latin America was...my special responsibility."[36]

Bryce wrote to Lippmann in March 1942: "If you felt at all inclined to write anything about the danger to S. America, I could give you any number of facts which have never been published, but which my friends here would like to see judiciously made public, at this point."[37]

Earlier in the same letter he wrote: "I am sending you a copy of my friend Artuco's book, which I think will interest you....Some of it sounds rather alarming & exaggerated but it is much more accurate than most books on South America."[38]

This book, by Hugo Artuco Fernandez, is certainly one of the many planted books written at the behest of British intelligence and propaganda agencies. British propaganda targeted everyone—from the educated classes with their thirst to be informed and in the know to the superstitious lower classes. The lower classes were fed comic books and bogus horoscopes. Ham Fischer, who did the Joe Palooka cartoons, was persuaded to change from a negative to a positive portrayal of the British. This came about when the British embassy became fearful that his cartoons were damaging their image; a British officer was sent to meet Fischer. It worked. In an interview with propaganda historian Nick Cull, Leonard Miall of the British Political Warfare Executive recalled that Fischer was fed pro-British material through the senior OWI officer Lew Cowan.[39]

The "BSC Account" reports BSC's success at planting the fraudulent anti-Hitler predictions of a tame Hungarian astrologer named

Louis de Wohl. BSC even built him up with bogus confirmations of his predictions with planted stories in the legitimate press. "It is unlikely," says the "BSC Account" somewhat condescendingly, "that any propagandist would seriously attempt to influence politically the people of England, say, or France through the medium of astrological predictions. Yet in the United States this was done with effective if limited results."[40]

The educated classes were targeted for this onslaught. They were subjected to an outpouring of books, many for the head and some for the heart. Concocting propaganda books and foisting them onto an unsuspecting public had been a very successful ploy in World War I, with many prominent authors producing the books and Wellington House secretly publishing them under the imprint of recognized publishers. In 1939 the British government again requested the help of its literati. H. G. Wells refused, but the majority of the first seventy authors approached accepted. Thus in World War II, major publishers—Penguin, Macmillan, Harcourt, and Doubleday—and big name authors—E. M. Forster, Somerset Maugham, historian Alan Nevins, Harold Callender of the *New York Times*—helped the British give an "ideological construction" to a war that many Americans were viewing as the same old European land-grab politics.[41]

A book could be used not only to promote a propaganda theme but also to establish an agent. For example, soon after its creation on the perfectly fitting April Fools' Day, 1938, Section D of MI-6 began exploring ways of cutting off Germany's supply of Swedish iron ore. In May 1938, Section D sent one Alfred Rickman (agent number D/1) to Sweden posing as a journalist. Not only did Rickman know nothing of the local languages or of Sweden, he did not know he was employed by British intelligence. After several months, Mr. Rickman was told to write a book on Swedish iron ore. The book, published by Faber & Faber in August 1939, gave Rickman the credentials as an expert on Swedish iron ore and a cover. He was then told that he was working for British intelligence and set up as an importer of machinery, just in time for World War II.[42]

There was definitely a feeling in the Anglo-American intelligence community that this ploy of planting articles and books was worth the effort. Not only had it been very successful in World War I but those Americans who learned their craft from the British certainly preserved the tradition. The CIA carried on as a patron of literature into the 1940s, 1950s, and 1960s.[43]

Though there was little real danger of the Nazis taking over Latin America, here is *Book Review Digest*'s summary of the book Bryce sent Lippmann: "A native Uruguayan, who is a member of the faculty of the University of Montevideo, describes the Nazi infiltration and diabolical workings throughout South America, especially in his own country and Colombia. The author has made many radio addresses attempting to call attention to the Nazi organization in South America...."[44]

Robert Emmet Sherwood (1896–1955). Sherwood exemplifies the way in which many who helped British intelligence were connected to each other and to England by blood, marriage, and residence.

On his mother's side he was a descendant of the Anglo-Irish Protestant hero Thomas Addis Emmet. His mother, Rosina Emmet Sherwood, was a prominent artist, as were nearly a dozen other female relatives. In 1934 his aunt Ellen Emmet painted the official portrait of President Franklin D. Roosevelt. By blood and marriage the Emmets tied together two of America's great banking families: the Morgans of J. P. Morgan and the Aldriches of Nelson Aldrich Rockefeller.[45]

Despite the talented family, Robert was a slow starter academically and received only a certificate of attendance from Milton Academy, near Boston, in 1914. This was not then thought an impediment to further academic work, and he attended his father's school, Harvard, 1914–17. Rejected by the U.S. Army because he was too tall, he joined the Canadian Black Watch. According to one of his biographers, John Mason Brown, Sherwood "loved England, the England he had first known as a boy in its full majesty of Empire, and then in the desperate testing of the war years." Sherwood also had relatives, the writer Henry James being one, who lived in England. From the late 1920s Sherwood resided in England for increasing periods of time. For the twenty-three years after 1932 he lived half or more of the year at his large house, Great Eatron, at Whitley Surrey, England.[46]

By the fall of 1940, Sherwood was helping to write President Roosevelt's speeches, and he habitually showed the important foreign policy speeches to Intrepid before FDR delivered them. When Intrepid was pushing Donovan as Coordinator of Information, he says, he "enlisted the help of several avenues of influence at the White House. Winant and Sherwood were the most persistent and effective, I think." Thus

Sherwood was what intelligence officers call an "agent of influence," a spokesman at the very center of the policy-making process.[47]

Two major purposes of British propaganda were to excite American fears that Hitler would take over the Americas and to discredit isolationists—to paint them as "fifth columnists" and traitors. On June 10, 1940, there appeared in the *New York Times* and other major papers full-page advertisements boldly headlined "STOP HITLER NOW." The CDAAA, the William Allen White Committee, was the listed sponsor, but Sherwood and his first cousin Christopher Emmet (who worked on British intelligence projects with agent Sandy Griffith) were responsible. Sherwood had written the copy and raised the $25,000 for space. Hitler's agents, wrote Sherwood, were already infiltrating the Western Hemisphere. "Will the Nazis considerately wait until we are ready to fight them?…Anyone who argues that they will wait is either an imbecile or a traitor." Among those who gave large sums for this advertisement were Sherwood himself ($5,000); Dorothy and George Backer, owners of the *New York Post* (helpers of BSC); Ward Cheney, a silk manufacturer, also a heavy contributor to Fight for Freedom; Henry Luce; and publisher Harold Guinzburg, who was highly influential in Fight for Freedom and in intelligence circles.[48]

Paul Patterson (1878–1952). Patterson was publisher of the *Baltimore Sun*. In the case of the *Sun* we have a competent if irascible witness to give weight to the claim of the "BSC Account"—prominent journalist H. L. Mencken was on the *Sun's* board of directors and had written for the paper until early 1941, when he stopped because of what he said was the paper's wildly pro-British bias. Intrepid certainly would have been gratified at the testimony to BSC's effect on the *Sun* had he read Mencken's diaries, which are now open. "From the first to the last," wrote Mencken in an October 1945 summing-up, "they [the *Sun* papers] were official organs and nothing more, and taking one day with another they were official organs of England rather than of the United States."[49]

How did the British get Patterson to render the "service of particular value" mentioned in the "BSC Account"? Mencken also wondered about this, so in March 1944 when Patterson "dropped in" for their "long delayed palaver," Mencken let him have it: "I told Patterson that, in my judgment, the English had found him an easy mark, and made a monkey out of him. He…did not attempt to dispute the main fact. In the course of his talk I gathered…that he is entertained while in London by an Englishwoman who is the head of one of the women's auxiliary organizations—perhaps characteristically, he did not know its name. He also let fall the proud fact that she is a countess."[50]

The identity of the "countess," the "head of one of the women's auxiliary organizations," the name of which Patterson professed not to know, was most likely a granddaughter of Queen Victoria, HRH the Princess Alice, Countess of Athlone, commandant in chief of FANY, the First Aid Nursing Yeomanry. FANY was the ladies' auxiliary of the black-propaganda and dirty-tricks organization Special Operations Executive.[51] Alice was married to the Earl of Athlone, Queen Mary's brother.

John Buchan, Lord Tweedsmuir, the governor-general of Canada, was a well-practiced behind-the-scenes operator well connected to British intelligence and propaganda. When he fell in the bath and died in February 1940, there was a need to place a similar person close to the United States. That person was the Earl of Athlone,[52] one of the most powerful patrons of "C," Stewart Graham Menzies, the head of MI-6.[53] Princess Alice of FANY and SOE can be seen, not with a cloak and dagger, but at her fur-coated, smiling best in an October 1940 *Time* magazine photograph showing her and Franklin Roosevelt leaving St. James Church in Hyde Park. *Time* wrote: "After…lunch [Saturday], the President drove the Princess round the estate (the Earl had a cold)….that night the President talked international affairs with the big, bluff, grey Earl; again the next morning after church."[54]

This is the sort of person of whom Paul Patterson seemed so proud. The connection illustrates how difficult it has been, in this world of cutouts and go-betweens, for historians to identify meetings between FDR and British intelligence. *Time*, after all, did not tell its readers that the president spent the afternoon with a woman from Special Operations Executive.

Ulric Bell (1891–1960). Ulric Bell ran the day-to-day operations of Fight for Freedom. Chadwin listed him as the "prime policy-maker as well as the individual responsible for co-ordinating the efforts of the leaders of FFF and keeping in close touch with the administration." In World War I he had been an infantry captain; he was personally close to Secretary of State Cordell Hull, having been Hull's press secretary at the Montevideo Conference in 1933–34. Normally he was Washington correspondent for Barry Bingham's *Louisville Courier-Journal*.[55]

In the early fall of 1940, Bell replaced Francis Pickens Miller at the Century Group; Miller had returned to the Council on Foreign Relations. Bell became executive director of Fight for Freedom when that name was formally adopted in April 1941. Bell's part in the effort to use the movies for interventionist propaganda and then the effort to protect them when Congress started to investigate must have impressed one of the Fight for Freedom contacts, Spyros P. Skouras of Twentieth Century–Fox. After the war, Bell became Skouras's executive assistant.[56]

Barry Bingham (1906–88). Bingham was the son of FDR's first ambassador to England, the outspokenly pro-British Judge Robert Bingham. Barry inherited the paper on his father's death in 1937. He employed both Ulric Bell and Herbert Agar at the *Louisville Courier-Journal* and continued to pay both of their salaries while they helped run Fight for Freedom.[57]

Barry Bingham was deeply involved with intelligence and attacks on the isolationists. From the spring of 1941 he was ostensibly in the navy, but attached to Fiorello La Guardia's Office of Civilian Defense. Bingham became attached to this office about the time his subordinate Ulric Bell was asked by FDR to help organize the office "in regard to the whole subject of offensive publicity to offset the propaganda of the Wheeler's, Nye's, Lindbergh's, etc."[58]

From the over one hundred surviving pieces of correspondence in Barry Bingham's file in the Fight for Freedom Papers it is evident that after Bell went back to Fight for Freedom, Bingham organized these anti-isolationist speakers for Fight for Freedom. Here are two typical examples of cables to Bingham at the Office of Civilian Defense from George Havell of the FFF speakers' bureau. The first is dated September 22, 1941:

UNABLE TO CONTACT WILLIAM YANDELL ELLIOTT HERE. PLEASE PUT ALL POSSIBLE PRESSURE ON HIM FOR PITTSBURGH DINNER OCTOBER 13TH. UNDERSTAND HE DID A SWELL JOB ON AMERICAN FORUM LAST NIGHT AGAINST FISH.

The second is from September 26, 1941:

ANY PROGRESS ON PATTERSON OR FORESTAL FOR CLEVELAND EARLY IN OCTOBER. WILLIAM YANDELL ELLIOT DARIEN CONNECTICUT

OCTOBER 17TH, SENATOR PEPPER FOR DAYTON, OHIO EARLY
OCTOBER. WILL APPRECIATE WORD FROM YOU.

There is also an interesting letter from his brother Robert, who was
visiting New York from his home in England: "I shall try to arrange for
Scudder to see Raymond Gram Swing sometime this week, as I saw
him myself on Friday. I will tell Herbert's [Herbert Agar's] brother
what happened as it is the same matter he has been working on. I think
it is unwise to write letters about this."[59]

There are also strong indications that Barry Bingham was not only
paying the salaries of two of the British intelligence front's executives
and recruiting speakers for it but was working directly with intelligence, particularly British intelligence.

In a letter of September 12, 1941, from Ulric Bell's secretary: "...I
am enclosing a letter received today from Bishop Henry E. Hobson
regarding his nephew George C. Mackenzie's desire to be of service in
Intelligence work."[60] Another sign of Barry Bingham's direct work
with British intelligence is also from the Fight for Freedom Papers.

Donald MacLaren was a British intelligence agent working for BSC.
In the fall of 1941, MacLaren was arranging for Rex Stout, George
Merten, and Sylvia Porter to write a BSC propaganda booklet, *Sequel to
the Apocalypse*, as part of the attack on Standard Oil of New Jersey. In
the middle of November, MacLaren was apparently staying in Louisville, Kentucky, with his brother-in-law Robert F. Crone. From the
telegrams and messages it is clear that Barry Bingham was trying very
hard to make contact with MacLaren either at the Crone residence or
at the Carlton Hotel in Washington, D.C.[61]

F. H. Peter Cusick (1910–82). Cusick was a native of California, an
advertising executive, a close adviser to Wendell Willkie, and executive secretary of Fight for Freedom.[62] During World War II he was
decorated with the Croix de Guerre by General Jean LeClerc of the
Free French. At the time of his death he was a member of the Council on Foreign Relations and a private consultant on government and
foreign affairs.

While they have not been named as British intelligence agents and
were not permanent officials of a front group, the next four men
worked so closely with British intelligence and propaganda and were so
prominent in Fight for Freedom that they should be mentioned.

Marshall Field (1893–1956). Field was born in Chicago but grew up and was educated in England at Eton and Cambridge. As the United States entered World War I he enlisted in the Illinois Cavalry as a private; he rose to captain. Field's Aunt Ethel married Arthur Tree and had a son by him, Arthur Ronald Tree; Marshall and his cousin Ronald were raised together. Ronald Tree, the classic example of the Anglo-American gentry, became a member of the British Parliament and performed various propaganda functions in the United States.[63] Working closely with the Roosevelt administration and Fight for Freedom, Marshall Field started the *Chicago Sun* in October 1941 to counter Colonel Robert McCormick's isolationist *Chicago Tribune*. According to Field's editor, Turner Catledge, "It was early in 1941 that Field resolved to start a newspaper....Roosevelt was trying to move the nation toward support of England...and Colonel McCormick was fighting him tooth and nail....The *Tribune's* influence on the American heartland was great, and to Field and others who thought the United States must fight Nazism, McCormick's daily tirades were agonizing. All this contributed to the haste with which the *Sun* was started."[64]

Marshall Field's biographer Stephen Becker is more specific about the origins of the final effort that gave Field the resolve to fight isolationists and help Franklin Roosevelt in Chicago. Becker says that Field's determination to start the *Sun* came from his "attendance at a meeting of the Fight for Freedom Committee at the Town Hall Club in New York on the evening of April 30, 1941."[65]

The man who plotted the Fight for Freedom attacks on the *Chicago Tribune* was BSC agent Sandy Griffith's man at the Chicago FFF headquarters, Albert Parry. It was the scholarly Parry (later Chairman of Russian Studies Department at Colgate and Slavic Studies Department at Case Western Reserve) who devised the slogans: "Millions for defense, but not two cents for the Tribune" and "What Chicago needs is a morning paper." The campaign against the *Tribune* must have been important enough to leave Parry in place despite BSC's need for the Russian-born Parry's language and editing skills in subverting Boston shortwave radio station WRUL—one of Sandy Griffith's projects. A cable from Chicago Fight for Freedom to FFF headquarters in New York says: "WIRE FROM PARRY'S BOSS SANFORD GRIFFITH...SAYS...NEED YOU BEGINNING COMING WEEK FOR IMPORTANT SHORTWAVE EDITORSHIP...

PLEASE TELEPHONE GRIFFITH AND ASK POSTPONEMENT OF PARRY'S COMING TO NEW YORK...."[66]

One of the White House's contributions was to use the FBI to call on small-town editors and urge them to support Field's bid for a coveted Associated Press franchise. In the circular world inhabited by those attempting to help the British in their hour of need, Field also turns up as a major financial backer of Ralph Ingersoll's newspaper, *PM* (Dorothy Thompson was another one of the original financial backers). *PM* never attracted enough circulation to make money, but it was a wonderful propaganda vehicle despite its small circulation. In September, Field bought out the other backers for twenty cents on the dollar. Ingersoll and his paper were also among those listed in the "BSC Account" as "among those who rendered service of particular value."[67]

Guinzburg, Harold (1899–1961). Guinzburg was a Jewish native of New York City. He received his bachelor's degree from Harvard in 1921 and then attended Columbia Law School, but dropped out after two years. In 1925 he became cofounder (with George S. Oppenheimer) and president of Viking Press. According to Chadwin, Guinzberg was consulted on "day-to-day policy by Bell and Peter Cusick at Fight for Freedom headquarters." Viking Press published a number of books by interventionist writers of the late 1930s and early 1940s.[68]

In Guinzburg's FBI file is a letter from J. Edgar Hoover of March 12, 1942, saying Guinzburg "is presently employed by the Office of Coordinator of Information, New York."[69] After the United States entered the war, he went to work for Elmer Davis at the Office of War Information. At first he worked with the overseas branch; in 1943 he was put in charge of the Domestic Bureau of Publications; then in 1944 he was sent to London to direct the publications to be sent into liberated areas. Curiously, his entries in *Who's Who* and *Current Biography* make no mention of Fight for Freedom.

Writing forty-five years after the events, Jerome Weidman, author of *I Can Get It for You Wholesale*, may have garbled the sequence of events, but the basic information rings true. Weidman writes that he accompanied the drama critic Leonard Lyons, a favorite of William Stephenson, to plays on Friday nights because Mrs. Lyons, a deeply religious woman, would not accompany her husband the night before Jewish holidays.[70]

In the lobby, during the first intermission, at the opening of Robert Sherwood's play *There Shall Be No Night*, Weidman encountered Harold Guinzburg. Said Guinzburg: "Instead of going back for the second act, I wonder if I could persuade you to take a walk with me?... Willie Maugham suggested we have a talk....No matter what you decide about what I tell you," Harold Guinzburg said, "I must before I say a word have your promise that you must not repeat any of it."[71]

Weidman says that Guinzburg was recruiting him for Robert Sherwood's section of Donovan's Coordinator of Information office. But the time is wrong. The COI did not organize until the summer of 1941, and Sherwood's *There Shall Be No Night* had two openings—April 29, 1940, and September 9, 1940.[72]

Henry Luce (1898–1967). Henry Luce was born in Tengchow, Shantung Province, China, to missionary parents and educated at Hotchkiss, Yale, and Oxford. His mother was Elizabeth Middleton Root, a relative of the more famous Root family; Oren Root was the promoter of the Willkie Clubs.[73] He was a second lieutenant in field artillery in World War I. As publisher of *Time*, *Life*, and *Fortune* magazines, Luce was the only client for the Roper public opinion polls until Roper went with William Donovan as his deputy director.

Luce was very generous with his leaves of absence. In 1940 one of his vice presidents of *Time*, C. D. Jackson, took a leave to organize an anti-isolationist propaganda group called the Council for Democracy. After the war, Jackson, as editor of *Fortune*, brought together the prominent Americans who allowed their names to be used by the CIA front National Committee for a Free Europe.

Luce had been one of the founders of the Century Group/Fight for Freedom. It is correct that he did depart, but so did a number of others—among them Whitney Shepardson and Allen Dulles. Two of these, Shepardson and Dulles, heavily involved with intelligence. The newsreel offshoot of Luce's *Time/Life*, *The March of Time*, was under the direction of Louis de Rochmont, who produced the pro-British anti-Nazi film *Inside Nazi Germany—1938*. When Luce opened an office in London, Britain's heroic struggle became a major theme of *The March of Time*. Luce's London operation was in fact intricately tied to British propaganda.[74]

Luce also was not averse to requesting advice from British intelligence. One of Intrepid's people was the philosopher Alfred Ayer,

G.426, an officer in the Political and Minorities Section of SOE within BSC. In his memoirs, *Part of My Life*, Ayer wrote of Luce's close adviser Raimund von Hofmannsthal: "When I met him he was working for the Time-Life organization, which had offices in one of the other buildings in Rockefeller Center....he was...concerned with its editorial policy. He used to consult me on questions of world politics...."[75]

Luce had made himself so congenial to British intelligence that when, in June 1941, Ian Fleming, working for BSC's naval intelligence section, wrote a proposal for Donovan's Coordinator of Information office, he proposed Luce to run the foreign propaganda section. Because Fleming was under urgent time constraints to finish this proposal, Luce must have been the first name that came to mind: the obvious man.[76] When the choice of Luce did not work out, Robert Emmet Sherwood, a man we can now see was a staunch collaborator of British intelligence, took this post.

The warm feelings did not last. The British soon found themselves in conflict with Henry Luce. His global internationalist vision of the "American Century" and his ability to publicize that vision were very useful when the British were trying to involve the United States in international events. But they became a threat to the British vision of the postwar world after Pearl Harbor. By early 1943, Henry Luce was on the list of "enemies" who endangered the British Empire.[77]

Dr. Henry P. Van Dusen (b. 1897). Henry Van Dusen was born in Philadelphia. He graduated from Princeton, Edinburgh, and Union Theological Seminary. His years as a student at Edinburgh and his participation in international religious meetings had given him a large number of friends in both Britain and the United States.[78]

Dr. Van Dusen was a member of the policy committee of the CDAAA (White Committee). Particularly on the sensitive issue of food for starving Europe, proxy propagandists such as Van Dusen and Bishop Henry Hobson were extremely useful. They protected the integrity of the British blockade, piously explaining why the Europeans needed to be starved for their own good, while allowing the British to stay undercover. Dr. Van Dusen even helped British propagandists by arranging for Sunday radio talks by leading British churchmen.

Van Dusen was also helpful in promoting Britain's black propaganda. For the British Ministry of Information he compiled a mailing list of prominent American churchmen, who then received, apparently from a publisher unconnected to the British, a British propaganda publication named the *Christian Newsletter.* The Ministry of Information was grateful for "an extremely valuable piece of propaganda...very much welcomed by the people to whom it is sent."[79]

Alexander Korda (1893–1956). Alexander Korda (*The Lion Has Wings, That Hamilton Woman*) was a bona fide British intelligence agent, and several other prominent movie producers were working with the British.[80] Ernest Cuneo included Korda in "the Club," the intelligence people who gravitated to Bill Stephenson's suite at Claridge's in London.[81]

In *Secret Intelligence Agent*—according to Bill Ross-Smith, once of BSC, a more candid book than *The Quiet Canadian* and more reliable than *A Man Called Intrepid*—H. Montgomery Hyde wrote that Alex and Vincent Korda were "secret service agents." On a trip to see Korda in 1941, Hyde says he gathered "that at Churchill's suggestion endorsed by Stephenson, Korda...had taken an office ostensibly as a motion-picture headquarters but which really served as a clearinghouse for British intelligence." The eastern branch office of Korda's intelligence cover–filmmaking enterprise was, once again, in Rockefeller Center, New York City.[82] This gave him ready access to BSC head William Stephenson. Elinore Little Nascarella, then a Stephenson secretary, remembers Korda as regularly "in and out" of Intrepid's office.[83]

Alexander Korda had been working for British intelligence since the 1930s. After Munich, Admiral Sinclair, the head of MI-6, fearing that his organization had been penetrated in the field, created a parallel organization called the Z Network under "Uncle Claude" Dansey, the ruthless former Passport Control officer in Rome. The Kordas worked for Dansey. Alexander Korda recruited agents, and his London Films organization was used by Dansey as cover for Z agents in Europe. After the war started, and after many hours of consultation with Churchill and British intelligence, Alex was sent to the United States "to make major films that would subtly represent the British point of view...in a way that would seem patriotic but not propagandistic."[84]

When the Films Division of the British Ministry of Information sent the prominent film executive A. W. Jarratt to Hollywood, it was Alexander Korda as the leader of the pro-British filmmakers who hosted a magnificent dinner in November 1940 so that his friends could hear of Britain's needs. Present were Harry Cohn from Columbia, Sam

Goldwyn from MGM, Arthur Kelly from United Artists, Sidney Kent of Twentieth Century–Fox, Hal Roach, the brothers Warner, Darryl F. Zanuck, and representatives from Paramount, RKO, and Universal. Louis B. Mayer seems to have spoken for the moguls when he said that the British could "count on the producers of Hollywood doing everything possible to help the great cause for which the British empire was fighting." The promises were not only made but were followed by prompt action.

Alex Korda's efforts were appreciated by Churchill and rewarded, even if the reward baffled outsiders. Korda was knighted in the King's Birthday Honours List in 1942. Many questioned how it was that a divorced Hungarian Jew who had escaped the dangers of the European war, to live safely in the United States had become the first person in the movie industry to be knighted by the British king. After the war, Alex Korda hired British intelligence agent and later Stephenson biographer Montgomery Hyde as his legal adviser.[85]

There were other movie men who also helped the British. Fight for Freedom's Walter Wanger was one. Wanger was born in San Francisco, in 1894, to Jewish parents, but by World War II he was an Episcopalian. His higher education had been at Dartmouth, Heidelberg, and Oxford. Wanger was versatile; he had been an attaché at Versailles and a motion picture director with Paramount Studios. He saw the movies as a powerful instrument for educating the public.[86] He was trusted enough that British operative John Wheeler-Bennett was sent to Hollywood by Lord Lothian to discuss making pro-British films with him.[87] Wanger produced two blatantly anti-Nazi films in the summer of 1940. In collaboration with the English director Alfred Hitchcock he made *Foreign Correspondent*, which Hitler's Dr. Goebbels pronounced "a masterpiece of propaganda."[88]

So BSC had available, willing, and powerful agents, subagents, and collaborators at the very nerve centers of American politics, news, and entertainment.

CHAPTER 4

•••

The Voice of the People

The World War II public opinion polls are widely used by historians. They are so convenient and the numbers so crisp and credible. Occasionally, it is true, some historian will point out that poll questions were "loaded," or that "the right questions were not asked." Despite these flaws, historians continue to employ them, often feeling, as one wrote recently, that "flawed polls are preferable to none."[1] Few seem to wonder about the depth or the source of the defects.

The first thing to know when reading the public opinion polls commonly cited from 1939 to 1942 is that none of them was produced by disinterested seekers of truth. The most prominently published polls were all under the influence of British intelligence, its friends, employees, and agents. At the very best, when questions of the war or international relations are considered, the major polls should be thought of as what modern critics call "advocacy polls."

Advocacy polls are polls that are used as a means to reach some predetermined end. Their purpose, says polling expert Irving Crespi, "is to influence policy makers by claiming that the public wants a course of action espoused by the sponsoring group to be adopted." Unfortunately, Crespi goes on to say that advocacy polls are suspect because their "intent is always apparent."[2]

The intent of these polls was not apparent. They purported to be the scientifically, objectively gathered voice of the people. Unknown to the public, the polls of Gallup, Hadley Cantril, Market Analysts Inc., and Roper were all done under the influence of dedicated interventionists and British intelligence agents. Moreover, they often were unable to bear close scrutiny or comparison with other polls, even at the time.

The secret "BSC Account" makes three pertinent points about the Gallup polls, which were withheld from Montgomery Hyde's *Quiet Canadian/Room 3603*: British intelligence had "penetrated" the Gallup organization; the Roosevelt administration also had a man named Hadley Cantril at Gallup; and Gallup was dissuaded from publishing some polls considered harmful to the British.[3]

There is considerable testimony corroborating the first two statements. BSC had David Ogilvy, more recently a very successful advertising man, at Gallup. The White House did have Hadley Cantril at Gallup. There is little reason, given the available evidence, to doubt the "BSC Account" on the third point. The polls were another instrument playing the correct notes from the right score in the British orchestrated attempt to move the United States toward war.

By the late 1930s the public opinion polls had become a highly visible barometer of public opinion. In Richard Steele's words, they "became a political weapon that could be used to inform the views of the doubtful, weaken the commitment of opponents, and strengthen the conviction of supporters."[4]

British intelligence agent Sanford Griffith (G.112), who worked under SOE officer Bill Morrell at BSC, clearly recognized the possibility of exploiting the polls. In November 1940, after a failed effort to get rid of isolationist Hamilton Fish, he put his ideas to paper under the title "Recommendations by Sanford Griffith for Hamilton Fish Campaign and Continuation." Among the four pages of recommendations are these thoughts on polling: "Opinion polls are a source of information, a propaganda weapon....Favorable results of the poll are accepted by the newspapers as news and are effective propaganda."[5]

Polls were thus an integral part of BSC's tenacious, and ultimately successful, campaign to damage Fish politically and finally to eliminate him. In February 1941, Elmo Roper released a poll undermining Congressman Fish's opposition to Lend-Lease. The poll of Fish's constituents said that 70 percent of them favored the passage of Lend-Lease. This blatant attempt to hamstring Fish in the congressional debates was at least modestly successful, according to his biographer.

The poll had ostensibly been done for one of Fish's constituents, James H. Causey, president of the Foundation for the Advancement of Social Sciences, tied to the University of Denver.[6] Fish, irate at these tactics, called for a congressional investigation.

The man in the White House, Franklin Roosevelt, was more subtle than Fish, but he was also subjected to heavy doses of interventionist opinion, of which the polls were a significant part. In FDR the British and their interventionist allies were confronted with a president who was, in his own devious way, extremely sensitive to public opinion and would not move without it.[7]

The group of devout Anglophiles who had gathered at the Virginia home of Francis and Helen Miller on Dunkirk weekend, June 2, 1940, were anything but cautious in their pronouncements. They had quickly published "Summons to Speak Out," demanding an immediate declaration of war on Germany.[8] These elitists who were to form the core of Fight for Freedom knew what they wanted and were impatient with the president's concern for public opinion.

The British and their allies sought to eliminate obstacles to presidential and congressional actions that would prepare and speed the United States toward war. The president, though by nature a procrastinator, was just as anxious to aid the British as they were to gain the aid; corroborative public opinion polls would help get needed measures through Congress or, as in the case of the Destroyer Deal in September of 1940, make the legislators feel they lacked a mandate to stop actions already taken. Author G. F. Lewis, Jr., writing in the June 1940 *Public Opinion Quarterly*, found that approximately two-thirds of congressmen considered polls in their foreign policy votes, even though they denied being so influenced.[9]

FDR's attempts to gauge public opinion are clearly evident almost from the moment he took office in 1933. Routinely the president had taken the pulse of the people by traditional means: he started off his day by reading several major daily newspapers. These impressions were enhanced by a clipping service organized by his longtime political adviser Louis McHenry Howe, which monitored 350 newspapers and forty-three magazines.[10]

During 1941, FDR received a series of reports from Treasury Secretary Henry Morgenthau's office, analyzing press opinion on

Lend-Lease, taxes, and defense bonds. Other agencies sent similar reports, most of them "liberal interventionist."[11]

Steele gives numerous examples to illustrate the strong interventionist bias in these Treasury Department reports to the president. There is a replay effect at work here. Not only were the report writers biased, but so were their sources of information. The reports were based on material from the *New York Times*, the *Washington Post*, the *New York Herald Tribune*, the *New York Post*, and the *Baltimore Sun*—the very places BSC was most successfully planting articles.[12] Once again, sections of the orchestra were working harmoniously to produce the interventionist music.

In May 1941, the president read: "the impact of events abroad has produced a mass migration in American opinion....Today's isolationist follows the precepts of yesterday's interventionist." In June the president was congratulated: "decisive Administration measures 'have had an inspiring effect.'" In August: "...the degree to which the American press has enlisted in the war against Nazism is graphically illustrated by its reaction to the British invasion of Iran." In September: "The newspapers want a final showdown on foreign policy." Steele is quite correct that the purpose of these reports was to correct "Administration timidity."[13]

In this circuitous world of intrigue and manipulation it is often difficult to distinguish when others were attempting to correct the administration's "timidity" and when the administration has already planted a feigned public outcry to which it could then seem grudgingly to respond—calling it "the will of the people." In September 1941, the William Allen White Committee "initiated" a letter and telegram campaign to Hull and Roosevelt calling for the rejection of any compromise with Japan that would not fully uphold American principles respecting China. There had been no real public outcry. The impetus for this action had come from within the administration itself.[14]

The president also used visitors and correspondents to flesh out the views he and his wife, Eleanor, gathered in their travels. One of those who reported to him on a regular basis was John Franklin Carter (1897–1967), a syndicated newspaper columnist and radio commentator who worked under the name Jay Franklin. "In 1941," writes historian Richard Steele, "Carter's services to the White House were expanded to include various clandestine operations—the kind of secret agent type activities that both he and the President loved." Carter's intelligence-gathering organization included comments on public opinion, "particularly within the New York business community."[15]

Another regular reporter of anecdotal opinion was Morris Ernst. Ernst was a well-known and well-connected trial lawyer and civil libertarian. He apparently reveled in knowing the powerful, because he was also an informant for J. Edgar Hoover. Ernst gathered the sort of gossipy information FDR so loved from the guests at his famous parties. The guests, however, hardly represented a cross section of national opinion. They might well be called the friends of British intelligence: "the publisher of the *New York Herald Tribune* (Helen Reid) and the *New York Times* (Arthur Hays Sulzberger); Henry Luce of *Time-Life-Fortune*; correspondents and columnists Dorothy Thompson, Raymond Gram Swing, William L. Shirer...."[16] Their opinions were invariably little more than reiterations of the basic interventionist British themes—send destroyers, send money, send supplies, help convoy, declare war.

The standing of the "scientific polling organizations" in the eyes of FDR and his minions varied. The White House thought Gallup was a backer of Willkie and was "suspected of coloring his reports." This may well have been correct, though Gallup himself may not have been the one actually coloring the reports, since he appears to have rarely written them.[17]

The "BSC Account" is correct that President Roosevelt had his own interventionist plugged into the Gallup apparatus. That man was Hadley Cantril (1907–69), a social psychologist. With the benefit of Rockefeller money, Cantril ran the Office of Public Opinion Research at Princeton. Cantril had graduated from Dartmouth College and had done graduate work at the University of Berlin before receiving his doctorate from Harvard in 1931; in 1939 he was a major force in the establishment of the Princeton Listening Center to study German radio propaganda.[18]

In the uproar within the intelligence community over the publication of Hyde's *Quiet Canadian*, former BSC officer David Ogilvy, an early wartime assistant to Gallup, wrote a letter for Hyde: "I beg you to remove all references to Hadley Cantril and Dr. Gallup....Dr. Gallup was, and still is, a great friend of England. What you have written would cause him anguish—and damage. One does not want to damage one's friends....In subsequent years Hadley Cantril has done a vast amount of secret polling for the United States Government. What you have written would compromise him—and S.I.S. [Secret Intelligence Service— MI-6] does not make a practice of compromising its friends."[19]

Cantril operated from the assumption that the president needed "an approving body of public opinion to sustain him in each measure of assistance to Britain and the U.S.S.R."[20] Cantril told David Niles of the White House (also the BSC contact at the White House) how it was done.

While analyzing Gallup results in 1943, Cantril came up with the startling observation that FDR's prospects for the presidency were inversely related to the prospects of peace. If peace was at hand in 1944, FDR would have serious trouble getting reelected. Niles asked if the results could be suppressed. Telling Gallup what not to publish had never been his style, Cantril told Niles, "but I have tried to influence poll results by suggesting issues and questions the vote on which I was fairly sure would be on the right side." All of this was strictly confidential and beyond the grasp of prying congressmen and Cantril's business and academic associates.[21]

British intelligence claims to have been less shy, and there is no reason to doubt the "BSC Account" claim that BSC persuaded Gallup (or more likely someone in his organization) to drop the results of questions that reflected poorly on the British cause.[22]

Scattered through the literature are numerous footnotes and scholarly asides suggesting that there was something wrong with the 1939–44 polls. Typical is this comment by scholar Jane Harriet Schwar on the Destroyer Deal the British were so desperate for: "Of those expressing an opinion, 61% supported the sale of destroyers. It should be noted, however, that the questions asked were heavily loaded in favor of the destroyer transfer."[23] Despite these suggestions there has been little systematic, coherent analysis of them. This seems strange given the many ways polls can be influenced once you have someone on the inside.

In *Lies, Damn Lies and Statistics* Michael Wheeler points out the problem: "Proving that a given poll is rigged is difficult because there are so many subtle ways to fake data...[as easy as faking results but less detectable]....a clever pollster can just as easily favor one candidate or the other by making less conspicuous adjustments, such as allocating the undecided voters as suits his needs, throwing out certain interviews on the grounds that they were with non-voters, or manipulating the sequence and context within which the questions are asked....Polls can even be rigged without the pollster knowing it. If a candidate could get hold of a list of sampling points...[consequently]. Most major polling organizations keep their sampling lists under lock and key...."[24]

The minimum requirement, of course, is that those determined to rig a poll have someone on the inside. This need was clearly fulfilled at Roper and Gallup, the National Opinion Research Center, and Market Analysts Inc.

British intelligence had "penetrated" the Gallup organization; there can be no doubt of this. British intelligence officer David Ogilvy later wrote about his days at Gallup: "I could not have had a better boss than Dr. Gallup. His confidence in me was such that I do not recall his ever reading any of the reports I wrote in his name. Once he had worked out the methodology of the research, he lost interest and moved on to something new." David Ogilvy's revered older brother Francis had been one of the earliest recruits to Lawrence Grand's Section D of MI-6, the black-propaganda and dirty-tricks organization.[25]

Although Ogilvy's autobiography is brief, he drops several august names and emphasizes the intimacy of this Anglophile intelligence world: "J. C. Masterman and R. B. McCalum tried...to teach me history....My other letter of introduction was from my cousin Rebecca West to Alexander Woollcott." One of the first people Woollcott introduced Ogilvy to at his island in Vermont was Robert Sherwood. Ogilvy continues: "I find it difficult to describe my early days in New York without gushing about American hospitality. At the top of my list I put Charles C. Burlingham....Then there were Tom Finletter, who later became Secretary of the Air Force, [and] Tom Lamont, who had been a partner in J. P. Morgan since 1911—I ate my first Thanksgiving dinner under his roof." This was the Thanksgiving of 1938, just after Munich—a period when the British intelligence services were seriously gearing for war.[26]

In a letter he wrote suggesting changes in H. Montgomery Hyde's *The Quiet Canadian*, Ogilvy said that he had started to report to Laurence Grand of MI-6's Section D in 1939. In his autobiography he reveals his dual role: "I had been moonlighting as advisor to the British government on American Public Opinion, but it was time I played a more active part." Bill Ross-Smith, one of Intrepid's assistants at BSC, wrote to Hyde on the publication of *The Quiet Canadian*: "PUBLIC OPINION POLLS—David Ogilvy acted as my sub agent on this for six to twelve months before I brought him in to B.S.C. proper." The work for Ogilvy turned out to be economic warfare from an office in the British embassy in Washington.[27]

There were other polls, to be sure, but almost all of them were controlled by British intelligence and its helpmates. For example, Elmo Burns Roper, Jr. (1900–71), had only one client, Henry Luce of *Time*, *Life*, and *Fortune*. In a 1968 speech to the American Statistical Association, Roper might well have been talking about Luce when he complained about those who employed pollsters but then released only those results that favored their point of view. Henry Luce was notorious for interfering with his writers and arbitrarily slanting the news.[28]

Roper had attended the University of Minnesota and the University of Edinburgh, Scotland. He had gravitated into market research, eventually forming Roper Research. In 1935, Henry Luce hired him to conduct polls for *Fortune*. His work for the interventionist Luce must have marked him as reliable, because he became "a charter member of Donovan's 'brain trust' " and deputy director of OSS. As discussed in Chapter 1, Donovan's organization was a creation of British intelligence really run by an MI-6 officer, Dickie Ellis.[29]

The National Opinion Research Center at the University of Denver was incorporated on October 27, 1941. Denver seems far from the Eastern foreign policy elite and the English, Gallup, and Hadley Cantril. But it only seems that way. The money for this enterprise had come from that prominent Fight for Freedom interventionist Marshall Field III. Field, as we remember, was very close to his first cousin Ronald Tree, the director of British propaganda. Field also financed the stridently interventionist *PM* newspaper.

Field had also founded the *Chicago Sun*, whose purpose was to "end the un-American monopoly" of Colonel McCormick's *Chicago Tribune*. Describing a trip to the United States early in the war, Tree wrote: "I...went down to Long Island to spend the week-end with my cousin, Marshall Field, the proprietor of *P.M.*....Educated from boyhood in England, he wanted to do anything he could to help the British cause."[30]

If the money for the National Opinion Research Center came from Marshall Field, its founder was an Englishman named Harry Hubert

Field (no relation to Marshall Field). Harry Field (1897–1946), a native of Harrogate, England, had served in World War I and had worked with the Young & Rubicam advertising agency; in 1936 he helped George Gallup set up operations in England.[31]

The official history of the founding of NORC says that Harry Field was following "Elmo Roper's suggestion—that a government managed survey organization be established." Hadley Cantril was one of NORC's earliest advisers and directors.[32]

Whatever its original purpose, NORC quickly became the contractor for the U.S. government's Office of Facts and Figures and then the propaganda-producing Office of War Information, testing the attitudes of the common people toward the war. Much was kept hidden from the Congress and the public, particularly studies for the State Department.[33]

In 1940 and 1941, BSC rigged a series of polls, usually with the help of its friends in the Miller Group/Century Group/Fight for Freedom Committee. These polls were done by Market Analysts Inc. at national conventions to project the notion that the members of prominent organizations were pro-British, avidly in favor of intervention, and intensely antagonistic toward America First.

William Stephenson's *A Man Called Intrepid* refers to one of these BSC poll-rigging projects. This was an FFF poll of the membership at the CIO national convention which opened November 17, 1941, at the Moose Temple in Detroit. In what appears to be a direct quote from the "BSC Account," Stevenson says: "Great care was taken beforehand to make certain the poll results would turn out as desired. The questions were…to steer the delegates' opinion toward the support of Britain and the war.…Public Opinion [was] manipulated through what seemed an objective poll."[34]

BSC got just what it wanted—widely distributed front-page news that the delegates were uniformly anti-Hitler, anti-Japanese, and anti–Charles Lindbergh and that "Ninety-four percent of the delegates… thought defeating Hitler was more important than for the United States to stay out of war."[35] The "BSC Account" also states: "The campaign was particularly appreciated by some representatives of the Roosevelt administration who attended the convention as observers." The persistent association of the White House and BSC and its front groups is again clearly evident here. Fight for Freedom's labor division had been organized at the behest of Commissioner of Labor Statistics Isador Lubin and David K. "Devious Dave" Niles of the White House staff.[36] Documents in the Fight for Freedom Papers substantially corroborate the assertions of *A Man Called Intrepid*. There is an FFF telegram to the Statler Hotel in Detroit: "Please reserve Suite of two Bedrooms on the Lower Floor for Fight for Freedom, Inc. Week beginning Sunday night November sixteenth."[37] There is also mention of British intelligence agent Sandy Griffith (G.112):

Ulric [Bell]:—

Abe has probably kept you informed about the plans Sandy Griffith and he are working out re the CIO convention. They look very good.

I think we have an excellent opportunity to break some stories from Detroit.

Would you approve sending Merle [Miller] out for one week? Things are much more likely to go right if he is on the spot than if we do it by remote control.

Bob [Spivak][38]

Fight for Freedom had taken over these polls earlier, but the exact date is not clear from their documents. It is clear that Market Analysts Inc. also did similar polling for the Committee to Defend America by Aiding the Allies. This should not be surprising, given CDAAA's close connections to British intelligence and propaganda agencies.

After World War II, Francis Henson, assistant to British intelligence agent Sandy Griffith, put this in his résumé: "Director of Washington Bureau of Market Analysts, Inc. New York City. The chief client was the Committee to Defend America to Aid the Allies [sic] (the William Allen White Committee); my job was to use the results of our polls, taken among their constituents, to convince on-the-fence Congressman and senators that they should favor more aid to Britain. (1940–42)"[39]

Not every organization was so easy as the CIO. The National Association of Manufacturers banned the interviewing of members between sessions and "also threatened to warn members individually against answering questions by poll takers."

FFF's Dr. Frank Kingdon's telegram requesting NAM to lift its ban on polls is quoted to illustrate the breadth of FFF's polling operation: "Our questionnaire is similar to those used by ourselves at national conventions of *American Legion, National Labor Union conventions* and asked individually of all members of Congress." Kingdon's suggestion that Sandy Griffith was using his polls to influence Congress is born out not only by Henson's résumé but by research done on the Destroyer Deal by British historian David Reynolds. He cites a "provisional poll [of the Senate] by Market Analysts, Inc., forwarded by [White House insider Ben] Cohen and seen by [Secretary of the Interior Harold] Ickes on 8 Aug." Cohen was, of course, working very close with the British on the Destroyer Deal. He and John Foster of the British embassy concocted the legal opinion that, when published in the *New York Times*, served to give a fraudulent legal gloss to the Destroyer Deal.[40]

Sandy Griffith did other, more public work on this project. In his book on the Destroyer Deal, *Fifty Ships That Saved the World*, British MP Philip Goodhart, records that at the 1940 Republican convention in Philadelphia—"according to a public opinion research firm called Market Analysis [sic]"—"some sixty per cent of the delegates favored extensive aid to Britain."[41] Again this is a familiar scenario: a poll at a convention, by a man who was a British intelligence agent, producing results saying clearly that the delegates wished to send "extensive aid to Britain."

Though the technique used at the conventions may have been to load the questions, there are other methods for affecting poll results without directly fabricating them. Leonard Doob in *Public Opinion and Propaganda* notes how he himself "has repeatedly demonstrated how the interviewer, the order of the questions on the ballot, the suggested replies, and the wording of the question *may* affect the results...."[42]

Cornell political scientist Benjamin Guinsberg has written that "polls do more than simply measure and record the natural or spontaneous manifestations of popular belief. The data reported by opinion polls are actually the product of an interplay between opinion and the survey instrument."[43]

In his 1944 book *Gauging Public Opinion*, Hadley Cantril, the interventionist who was working with Fight for Freedom and the White House, gives an example of how answers to one of the most often quoted Gallup polling questions of the pre–Pearl Harbor period was biased by the interviewers. The question was:

> Which of these two things do you think is more important
> for the United States to try to do—
> To keep out of war ourselves, or
> To help England win, even at the risk of getting into war?

It was apparent as early as October 1940 that if the interviewer favored helping England, then 60 percent of the respondents favored helping England. If the interviewer favored keeping out, only 44 percent favored helping England. In a democracy this is a crucial difference.[44]

Cantril also refers to a March 1941 study showing that the social class of the interviewer affected the degree of isolationism that respondents would admit; most interviewers were middle-class. In a test group, working-class interviewers were trained to ask the same questions. The result: "On war questions the working-class interviewers reported more isolationist sentiment than did the middle-class interviewers." From other parts of this study Cantril concluded that "it seems likely that the findings of the working-class group are more representative of the true state of opinion...."[45]

The results of this question concerning the desire of Americans to help England even if it meant the United States becoming involved in the war were used to keep the isolationists off balance.

Cantril's analysis on how poll results could be severely skewed even by the social class of the interviewer was unknown to the isolationists, but they did suspect there was something wrong with the polls. Robert M. Hutchins, the isolationist president of the University of Chicago, chaired a committee that looked at the problem and sponsored a carefully done opinion poll by Samuel E. Gill, a professional pollster from New York. This poll showed only 20.3 percent answering "Yes" to the question "Do you believe that the United States should enter the war as an active belligerent at this time?" The "Yes" percentage rose only to 34.4 percent when a possible British defeat was proposed. At the time these poll results were released, July 14, 1941, the various well-publicized polls into which BSC and the interventionists had their fingers showed 60 to 90 percent of Americans willing to fight if Britain was threatened with defeat. Even if this poll is simply considered an advocacy poll from the other side, it shows the wide variability of results obtainable from "scientific" polling techniques. This episode should also make the historian extremely wary of the opinion polls of the time.

But the Hutchins poll did not disturb the public. The Hutchins group found it almost impossible to get its results published. BSC and its interventionist allies had a lock on the major media outlets. Only *Time* magazine carried a very small, very disdainful mention of the poll; no other national paper or journal even mentioned it.[46]

Another possible ploy, visible only on those rare occasions when the questions are published verbatim, or to the professional investigator with access to the raw data, is the problem that can be caused by the order of the questions.

Rowena Wyant of the Office of Radio Research, Columbia University, wrote an interesting article for the fall 1941 issue of *Public Opinion Quarterly*. Buried deep in her article, titled "Voting via the Senate Mailbag," is a three-pronged attack on the Gallup poll. The problem was the exact order of the questions. She wrote: "...the Gallup poll appears to be unduly weighted in favor of the [draft] bill. These possible sources of bias are...: 1. The question itself, 'Do you favor increasing the size of our army and navy by drafting men between the ages of 21 and 31 to serve in the armed forces for one year?' has the rather obvious defect of not being confined to the issue it is supposedly testing....2. The conscription question was asked immediately after two questions which may be accused of steering the respondents' thoughts in a bellicose direction...." Wyant also found evidence that some of the subjects were afraid to tell the truth.[47]

The draft (selective service) merits a closer examination. Sir William Stephenson's mandate when he arrived in the United States in June 1940 was to bring the United States into the war. One of the predicaments faced very early by the British was that even if the United States could be dragged into the war, its army was far too small to be useful.

If the British were to go back onto the continent of Europe, the number of troops they could muster was simply inadequate. Despite the vigorous denials, there was no possibility for the British to invade Europe without American troops. The polls played their part in this campaign. The polls of the summer of 1940, which seemed to show overwhelming public support for the draft, were in fact running counter to a number of other indicators. Public devotion to the draft was doubtless much thinner than it appeared.

In the published literature there are many references to the involvement of British intelligence in the effort to get President Roosevelt to give or trade Britain fifty destroyers. There is little mention of similar efforts to pass an American draft law. William Donovan's trip to England in July 1940 was promoted by William Stephenson of BSC. In England, Donovan was subjected to a hoax as the British impressed him with a great facade suggesting they were well prepared to resist the Germans.

The startling thing for the researcher reading Donovan's posttrip correspondence with his hosts is the great effort the British intelligence and propaganda chiefs must have made to impress upon him the need for an American draft law. Judging by its frequent mention in the correspondence, the draft must have been the primary topic of discussion. Someone has torn from its bindings Donovan's letter to Sir Stewart Graham Menzies, the head of MI-6. Fortunately the Log of Documents summary survives. It says: "Letter WJD to Col. S.G. Menzies DSO re WJD plans, his efforts to get conscription passed by House and Senate and his efforts to alert the country as to situation in Europe 8/27/40."[48]

Donovan's correspondence with Admiral John Godfrey, the head of the British Office of Naval Intelligence, to Sir Cyril Newall and to Marshall Field's cousin Ronald Tree of British Information Services carry on similarly. To Admiral Godfrey he wrote: "We have been having difficulties with conscription. In my absence I found that resistance had developed in several quarters. However, we have been keeping up the fight and I really believe that we will probably have the bill passed and in effect within the next month. It will not be as complete as I would have liked it, but it will mean that we are going to have men available."[49]

On August 17, 1940, "our man," as British intelligence called Donovan, made a nationwide radio address promoting the draft. He was sponsored by the Century Group.

Another example of the considerable effort British intelligence put into promoting the American draft law can be seen in the work of intelligence agent Sandy Griffith and his polling company, Market Analysts Inc. In a letter of August 3, 1940, Griffith wrote to Ernest Cuneo:

"Enclosed are copies of a release I just made of some preliminary returns. This gain in sentiment for conscription I think is very important." The press release, titled "Big Majority of People Favor Conscription," announced: "Three-fourths (75.6%) of the American people are in favor of 'some form of universal selective service now.' " Sandy also notes the "unbroken rise in public opinion in support of conscription."[50]

The ostensible prime mover for the draft was another major figure in Fight for Freedom, Grenville Clark (1882–1967), Harvard College 1903, Harvard Law School 1906, onetime law clerk with Franklin Roosevelt. His Wall Street law firm, Root Clark, Buckner and Ballantine, was one of the most prestigious in the country, but Clark was unknown to the general public despite his role as a major figure in the Plattsburg Movement of officer training from World War I.

In May 1940 he started the campaign for a draft law. With the help of that irrepressible Anglophile Supreme Court Associate Justice Felix Frankfurter, Clark was able to have the isolationist, antidraft Secretary of War Henry Woodring replaced by the interventionist, pro-draft Henry Stimson. Clark's National Emergency Committee pledged itself to raise $285,000 (more than $3 million in 1997 dollars) in six months for publicity. One luncheon at the Bankers Club on June 7, 1940, netted $30,000.[51]

The public opinion polls whose questions Rowena Wyant found so biased produced spectacularly prodraft results. Of those people Gallup asked whether they would favor one year compulsory military service at age twenty, the yes response in December 1938 was 37 percent; in December 1939, 39 percent; on June 1, 1940, 50 percent; and by the end of June, 63 percent. This had climbed to over 70 percent by late August 1940. Certainly an astounding figure.[52]

Of those men Gallup questioned who would actually be facing the draft shortly if it passed, those between the ages of sixteen and twenty-one, an unbelievable 81 percent were willing. Congressional mail, on the other hand, was running "overwhelmingly against conscription."[53]

In tracking this problem for London, the British Library of Information wrote in its August 14, 1940, "Washington Letter": "Congressmen are frightened by their mail which is overwhelmingly against the bill and they don't trust the straw polls which indicate the country approves. They feel that even if not faked they don't take into consideration the fact that a man sufficiently interested in a public question to write about it, is a man prepared to turn out and vote, while a man who has to be hunted up and asked his opinion by a canvasser is likely to stay home."[54]

Even if they were not fully believable—and they were not—the polls controlled by British intelligence and its interventionist allies served to confuse the issue of public support for the peacetime draft. Without these cooked polls the congressional mail would certainly have killed conscription.

Secretary of War Stimson attributed the imbalance of letters to "Mushroom peace societies" that were better organized and financed than the champions of conscription.[55] Stimson's statement is a complete falsehood. All those who opposed the bill spent less than $5,000 for their campaign. The high-powered prodraft campaign had been run by Pearley Boone, a former *New York Times* journalist who had more recently done the publicity for the New York World's Fair. With his able staff of writers and photographers he easily outmatched history professor Howard L. Beale from the University of North Carolina.[56]

There are others besides Rowena Wyant who analyzed the polls and the issues involved with intervention. A study by Dartmouth psychologist Ross Stagner examined the Gallup polls from April 1937 until February 1941. Stagner chose fifty-nine questions for study because they focused directly on the "problem of intervention against Germany." About one-third had related to the repeal of the Neutrality Act in the fall of 1939.[57]

Stagner analyzed the polls for four types of wording that tend to bias the results. For thirteen of the questions he judged the language to be as impartial as possible within the bounds of plain English. In forty-six of the fifty-nine, however, he found flaws. Since some questions combined these flaws, there were fifty-five "cases of dubious practices." Seven of these he judged to bias the answer toward the noninterventionist camp while forty-eight tended to elicit an interventionist reply.[58]

His example of the effect of injecting prestige-bearing names, such as President Roosevelt's, into the questions is revealing. The week of May 29, 1940, the Gallup's organization for the Princeton Public Opinion Research Project asked: "The United States Army and Navy have about 5,000 airplanes. Would you approve of selling all, some, or none of these planes to England and France at this time?" Forty-nine percent of the respondents were recorded as answering "none." But only 20 percent disapproved of this action a few days later when President Roosevelt's name was injected thus: "President Roosevelt has taken action making it possible for England and France to buy airplanes that were being used by our Army and Navy. Do you approve or disapprove of this action?" The great change was due to the "prestige value of Roosevelt's name," plus the fact that the deal was already done and could not be changed.

An important fact here is that the questions used in the Market Analysts Inc. BSC-rigged polls were very similar to those being asked by Gallup and to a lesser extent by Roper. The Roper polls usually gave a larger choice of answers. Two purported examples of FFF questions were included in the article reporting the refusal of the National Association of Manufacturers to allow its members to be polled by Fight for Freedom: "Which do you consider more important: that Hitler be defeated or that the United States stay out of war?" and "Do you think that we should try to block further Japanese expansion even at the risk of war?"[59]

There is an important issue to note regarding the simple direct question of whether the respondent wished the United States to declare war on Germany and fight against her. The percent in favor never rose above 21 before Pearl Harbor was attacked. It was on tangential, difficult-to-check, often loaded and contrived questions that covered stepping-stone issues that the American public was said to favor policies that would obviously lead to war.

The way that most authors today quote the polls of 1939–42 gives the numbers an aura of hard scientific truth that is little merited. In a recent book review attacking John Charmley's revisionist book *Churchill: The End of Glory*, Louis D. Rubin, Jr., writes: "But public opinion was overwhelmingly on the side of Britain; an opinion poll taken in July 1940 indicated that seven out of ten Americans believed a Nazi victory would place the United States in danger, and so were in favor of assistance to the embattled British."[60]

As with many other ploys worked by British intelligence and its friends, there were people at the time who suspected that there was something wrong with many of the polls being ballyhooed by interventionists. The anti-interventionist problem was how to prove the deceptions, discover who was involved and how the rigging was done, and then get their views published.

The North American Newspaper Alliance sent out a story from Washington on February 8, 1941, saying that Senators McKellar of Tennessee and Holman of Oregon and Representative Walter M. Pierce of Oregon "have resolutions pending, which they say they intend to press cooperatively for an investigation of the Gallup, *Fortune Magazine* and other polls which have been reporting public opinion on the lease-lend bill and other features of the defense program." Whether or not at the prompting of the White House, the administration's spokesman and House Majority Leader John McCormack "said he could not see why there should be an investigation of polls...."[61]

Senator Gerald Nye of North Dakota did no better challenging the major polls. On May 6, 1941, he introduced Senate Resolution 111, "Investigation of Polls of Public Opinion." This resolution was referred to the Committee on Interstate Commerce. It disappeared.[62]

So the polls of World War II should be seen for what they were: at worst they were flatly rigged, at best they were tweaked and massaged and cooked—advocacy polls without the advocate being visible.

CHAPTER 5

•••

G.112—
Lt. Commander Griffith

Sandy Griffith was a British intelligence agent. The archives of Special Operations Executive list him as Lt. Commander Griffith and indicate that he also had an SIS connection.[1] His work and that of his company, Market Analysts Inc., and his closest associates, Francis Henson and Christopher Emmet, allows us to focus on some of those events in which British intelligence actively attempted to alter American public policy. These include the legal/political problems of Hamilton Fish, which drove him from Congress; a series of carefully wrought public opinion polls favoring the peacetime draft, the Destroyer Deal, and America's desire to help Britain; the creation of a number of British intelligence front groups; the BSC attack on Esso; the writing of propaganda radio programs used on shortwave Boston radio station WRUL; and finally the trial and conviction, and retrial and conviction, of George Sylvester Viereck, among other accused seditionists.

Sometime before World War I, Griffith attended Heidelberg University. With the outbreak of the Great War, Griffith joined first the Belgian army for six weeks and then the French army before joining the U.S. Army.

The *American Legion Magazine* of February 1939 carried an article, "They Told All," describing the great success American army intelligence (G-2) had interrogating German prisoners in the World War. Much of the article is on Sandy Griffith. One photograph shows a serious, dark-mustached Griffith staring into the camera. The caption reads: "Captain, later Major, Sanford Griffith under whose direction most of the 48,000 Germans captured by the A.E.F. were subjected to questioning."[2]

At the end of the Great War Sandy Griffith found himself a member of the Armistice Commission at Spa. From 1920 to 1923 he worked in Germany and Rome as a European correspondent for that great friend of British intelligence the *New York Herald Tribune*. From 1923 to 1927 he was based in London representing the *Wall Street Journal* and other Dow Jones publications; his two sons, Sandy and Peter, were born there in 1925 and 1927. From 1927 to 1930 he represented the stockbroker Dillon, Read & Co. in Paris, where his daughter, Brenda, was born in 1929.

During the early 1930s he worked as a broker for Stokes Hoyt & Co. and Otis & Co. In 1924 he had married Katherine Beach Bennett; he was divorced in 1934. Her death in that year left him with the three children.[3]

After a 1938 stint as director of consumer research projects for a company called Miller Franklin, Griffith became, in 1939, president of Market Analysts Inc. In 1939 and 1940, this company worked from a summer office at the New York World's Fair. There Griffith functioned as a consultant to companies wishing to brighten up their booths at the fair—Borden, Addressograph Multigraph, IBM.[4] By 1940 his polls for the Committee to Defend America by Aiding the Allies—the White Committee—were becoming a major focus of his efforts.

Bill Ross-Smith, assistant to Intrepid at British Security Coordination, remembers Griffith: "Sandy was a cheerful confident American utterly devoted to awakening American Opinion. He lived near Lloyd's Neck Long Island, where I once visited him for Sunday lunch."[5]

There was another connection between BSC and Sandy Griffith, the particulars of which are not clear. According to Sandy's son Peter, "Dick Ellis came out to the house a number of times in 1940. His son Olic Ellis, whose mother was Russian as I recall, spent several weeks with us at that time. He was fourteen or fifteen, the same age as my older brother, Sandy. I believe Ellis was divorced from Olic's mother at the time." Ellis was, of course, the number two man at BSC and the man who actually ran "Wild Bill" Donovan's COI/OSS from its start in 1941.[6]

According to his second wife, Sandy Griffith joined British intelligence in "the late 1930s—'38 or '39." Most likely this was the black-propaganda and dirty-tricks group, Section D of MI-6, which underwent tremendous expansion during this period. BSC officer Bill Ross-Smith also remembers: "When [Bill Morrell] first arrived at BSC he worked in my section for a while & did excellent, he soon moved on to dealing with press, radio, black propaganda & anti British pro-German organizations. For instance he coordinated Sandy Griffith's work."[7]

Sidney "Bill" Morrell (SOE code number G.101), who "coordinated Sandy Griffith's work," had been European correspondent for Lord Beaverbrook's *Daily Express*, had married Beaverbrook's secretary, and, according to a later employee, had been recruited into British intelligence by "the Beaver himself."

Morrell had been the only reporter who had been present at all of Hitler's great triumphs of the 1930s. The resulting book, titled *I Saw the Crucifixion*, charges that British Prime Minister Neville Chamberlain was wrong at Munich. William Shirer mentions Bill Morrell several times in *Berlin Diary*: "Prague, September 12 [1938]....I listened to the broadcast of the [Hitler] speech in the apartment of Bill and Mary Morrell overlooking Wilson station. The smoke-filled room was full of correspondents—Kerr, Cox, Maurice Hindus, and so on."[8]

In much the same way that Stephenson had lent Dick Ellis to help organize Donovan's Coordinator of Information office, Intrepid also lent Bill Morrell to Robert Sherwood for Sherwood's Foreign Information Service. With Morrell at Sherwood's office we should not be surprised to find Market Analysts Inc. also working with Sherwood's people. Judging by the closing lines of a report to Ernest Cuneo from Sandy Griffith's assistant, Francis Henson, Market Analysts must have been in close touch with Sherwood: "The primary purpose of this letter is to urge you to call and go out to lunch with Mrs. Mildred 'Pat' Allen, who is now secretary to Robert Sherwood, assistant to Donovan ...she is dying to meet you—after I tooted your horn for you."[9]

Sandy Griffith's helpers on these projects were Christopher Temple Emmet and Francis Henson. Christopher Emmet is a classic example of those who ran the British intelligence fronts before and during World War II and who, having proved themselves faithful and competent, went on to help run the CIA/MI-6 fronts of the Cold War. The Eastern establishment ties of family and school are also well exemplified in Christopher Emmet. Emmet was born in 1900 in Port Chester, New York, into a prominent Protestant Irish patriot family—one of whose members, Robert Emmet, had been hanged by the British in 1803. In 1968 *Life* magazine did an article titled "America's 'Grandes Dames.'" Christopher Emmet's mother merited a full-page photograph captioned, "Alida Chanler Emmet, 94, of Stony Brook, Long Island, is a grandniece of Mrs. William B. Astor and one of only two or three ladies now living who made their debuts at her great-aunt's 1892 ball, the ball of the original Four Hundred."[10] His father, sisters, and kin were prominent artists.

The catalog of a recent art exhibit gives a taste of the Emmets' prominence. "New York society stampeded the opening tea for the Arden Gallery's 1936 fall exhibition, 'Paintings, Drawings and Sculptures by Five Generations of the Emmet Family.'" The ties of blood and marriage to both the banking Aldrich and Morgan families are evident in the names of some of the exhibitors. There was not only Rosina Emmet Sherwood, the mother of Pulitzer Prize–winning playwright Robert Sherwood, but also Elizabeth Winthrop Emmet Morgan, Jane Grenville Lapsley, and Mrs. Nicholas Biddle, Jr.[11]

One in-law, Margaret Chanler Aldrich, had won a Congressional Medal for her work as a nurse during the Spanish-American War.[12] This connection, of course, tied Christopher to the Aldrich/Rockefeller clan. Emmet's first cousin was playwright, FDR speechwriter, and British agent of influence Robert Emmet Sherwood, with whom he worked so closely.

Emmet attended Harvard (1919–20) before going on to "several universities in Germany" during a six-year study and writing odyssey. He returned to the United States in 1933. By 1938 he was secretary to the Volunteer Christian Committee to Boycott Nazi Germany. In 1940 he became chairman of the Committee to Aid Britain by Reciprocal Trade and helped Sandy Griffith and Francis Henson found France Forever. He became vice president of the latter, which was a British intelligence front group whose purpose was to promote Charles de Gaulle as the true voice of France.[13]

In 1941 he was treasurer and major force in the British intelligence front group Committee for American Irish Defense. It had the same street address, 8 West 40th Street, as Sandy Griffith's Market Analysts Inc. The ground floor of this building was occupied by the New York chapter of the CDAAA, of which Emmet was a member of the executive committee; in July and August 1941, Emmet played a major role in the amalgamation of the New York chapter with Fight for Freedom. According to his obituary, Emmet worked during World War II for a "Freedom lobby to defeat 'isolationist' congressmen who had opposed American involvement in the European War."[14]

Later during the Cold War when the British and American intelligence assets were used to prevent the Russians from dominating the continent of Europe, Emmet manned a slew of front groups in the CIA/MI-6 political warfare against the Soviet Union. These included chairman, Committee Against Mass Expulsions; treasurer, Committee for a Fair Trial for Draja Mihailovich; organizer, Committee for a Just Peace with Italy; member board of directors, Common Cause (this is not today's Common Cause, but according to author Christopher Simpson was the prototype for the CIA-sponsored National Committee for a Free Europe); executive vice president, American Council on Germany; member of executive committee, American Friends of Vietnam; and chairman, American Friends of the Captive Nations.[15]

Another who helped Sandy Griffith was his assistant, Francis Adams Henson (1906–63). Fortunately, Henson was a prolific correspondent. He was sent by his family to Lynchburg College in Virginia because they considered it to have "a good safe Christian atmosphere." By graduation in 1927, he had done very well and had even edited the school paper. His family's hopes had not. "I had...become militantly pro-labor and in general a socialist," he later wrote. From 1927 to 1932, Henson worked for the YMCA in New York and Connecticut and moved farther left. From early 1933 until 1936, Henson writes, "I was a fellow traveler of the CP [Communist Party] under various disguises and serving in many capacities."[16]

From 1932 Henson was in turn "executive secretary of the National Religion and Labor Foundation, founded by Jerome Davis of Yale"; an organizer of "the American League Against War and Fascism and...its first co-secretary with Donald Henderson"; "Secretary of the International Student Service in the United States," and "secretary of the Emergency Committee to Aid Refugees from Germany."

In 1935, Henson became treasurer of the Committee on Fair Play in Sports, which opposed American participation in the German Olympics. When this group lost its fight he represented the committee in Germany. There he "sought to convince American and other newspaper men that the Nazis were using the Olympics as a facade to hide ugly Nazi realities."

After a short stint as campaign manager for the Committee to Aid Spanish Democracy, Henson became, in 1937, administrative assistant to the president of the United Auto Workers Union, which was within the CIO. By this time, he says, he believed that the Communists were a menace to labor. He says that John L. Lewis saw to it that he was fired for this belief. Henson then went to Washington in 1939 to become a freelance writer for the New Deal—mainly writing for Commissioner of Education J. W. Studebaker.

In 1940 he went to work for Sandy Griffith at Market Analysts Inc. "My job," wrote Henson after the war in his résumé, "was to use the results of our polls, taken among their constituents, to convince on-the-fence Congressmen and Senators that they should favor more aid to Britain."[17]

One of the first published references to Market Analysts Inc. is in British MP Philip Goodhart's book on the Destroyer Deal, *Fifty Ships That Saved the World*.[18] Goodhart cites Market Analysts to the effect that "some sixty per cent of the delegates [to the 1940 Republican convention in Philadelphia] favored extensive aid to Britain." In the two-page copy of the results of this poll sent to Ernie Cuneo appear the topics important to the British:

> I. If Germany wins a decisive victory over France and Britain, do you think that we will be endangered in the U.S.? Yes 60% No 37.6%

> IV. If you think we are endangered, do you favor our helping the allies with everything (check as many as necessary) a/ short of war.... 65.4%

Please note that the 65.4 percent who wished to give the Allies everything necessary short of war is actually 65 percent of the 60 percent in Question I who believed the United States would be endangered by a German victory. In short, only 39 percent of the delegates questioned actually wished to give the Allies (a loaded word to be sure) "everything short of war."[19] Questions II, III, IX, and X played on one of the major themes of British propaganda—namely, that once the Allies were beaten, Hitler would very quickly attack the Western Hemisphere:

II. Do you think that our armed strength will be sufficient for us to defend the U.S.?

III. If Germany wins do you think we can defend the Monroe Doctrine in the Americas?

IX. If Germany were to set up a puppet government in the Americas, would it be a threat to American Security?

X. If yes, would you favor U.S. military intervention there?

This was repeated at the July 1940 Democratic convention. "Dear Ernie: Enclosed are the final results of our opinion poll. We got good play throughout in the *Chicago Daily News*, the *New York Times*, and a couple of the agencies....Sandy."[20]

The *Chicago Daily News* was passionately interventionist with several reporters who worked closely with British intelligence and the British Information Service. The result of this poll sponsored by the White Committee was to soften the impact of the rather isolationist platform the Democrats had adopted. "A wide disparity," says the press release, "exists between the Democratic Platform and the opinions of the individual delegates, as revealed in a very complete poll." According to this poll, 85 percent of the delegates thought that a British defeat would endanger the United States, and of these 59.7 percent thought Hitler would give us "no time at all" to arm after he had defeated Great Britain. Sixty-five percent thought that Germany already threatened the United States.

Griffith and Henson also provided investigative services at the conventions. Later that same day, July 22, 1940 another informative letter was sent to Cuneo: "Enclosed are some rough notes on the activities of the pacifist organizations at the two conventions....Sandy." In nine typewritten pages these notes identified how the isolationists had succeeded in getting their way on the platform committee at the Democratic convention, identified the principal pacifist organizations, and gave the results of interviews with them.

For example: "*National Council for Prevention of War.* Frederick J. Libby, the Executive Secretary of the Organization,...is a Quaker with an abnormal amount of religious fanaticism and an anti-English hate which goes back to the time he was snubbed as a student at Oxford.

He…has…persecution mania which leads him to see spies and mysterious influences everywhere—in this case English ones."[21]

Paranoid Libby may have been, but he was not wrong—they were after him. It is one of the tricks of fate that he shared his suspicions of lurking English agents with a genuine British intelligence agent. Griffith went on to interview Dr. Dorothy Detzer, national executive secretary of the Women's International League for Peace and Freedom, and somehow acquired from her a copy of the memorandum on lobbying, titled "Peace Pressure Primer," which was also sent to Cuneo. This investigative work was carried out under cover of a company called Information, Inc. "*Confidential Research for the Facts You Seek*," says the letterhead, giving Francis Henson's Washington, D.C., address at the National Press Building.[22]

Also on August 9, 1940, Griffith continued his efforts to have Cuneo use his influence to have Market Analysts Inc. become the pollster for the Democratic National Committee; Cuneo had served the committee as attorney: "Dear Ernie: Enclosed is a brief outline of the kind of nation-wide job we can do on opinion polls. You can get me at my number at the Fair. I am anxious to see you on this and on the general situation.—Sandy." The eight-point outline claimed that Market Analysts Inc. had in both 1939 and 1940 made "all of the attendance analysis for the New York World's Fair," that it did work for the "foreign government exhibitors" and conducted a variety of "local and national political surveys." Sandy further claimed "225 interviewers in all parts of the country" and said that a "rush job…can be done in 48 hours" and that he could "insure full privacy."[23]

Henson, as Sandy Griffith's Washington representative, continued, during the fall of 1940, to supply Cuneo with information on the front group France Forever, which he and Sandy and Christopher Emmet had created to generate support for Charles de Gaulle. "I want to continue to run errands for you etc.," wrote Henson in a letter of October 1, 1940. They also continued to supply Cuneo with intelligence.[24]

In Cuneo's Henson files is a report on an interview with William R. Castle on November 19, 1940. Castle was a retired diplomat with close ties to former President Herbert Hoover.[25] Castle was of interest to British intelligence because he was a member of the national committee of America First, the leading isolationist group in the United States. The interviewer was Francis Henson. Once again the target suspected that the interviewer was a spy, but he was not suspicious enough: "Castle was very cordial," wrote Henson, "and talked with me for about one hour and a half. When I left and gave him my card and the Washington office address of M[arket] A[nalysts Inc.] he said, 'So you are not a spy of the White Committee.' I answered, smiling, 'If I am I am a very open spy, don't you think?' He smiled."[26]

One other British project Henson worked on should be mentioned before returning to Market Analysts Inc.'s polling endeavors. British propaganda both overt and covert was very diligent, from the late 1930s, in trying to get the United States to accept its responsibilities as a world power, a world power guided by the more mature, surer hand of the British, but still a country with global political commitments.

One aspect of this project was to subject American schoolchildren and their teachers to good healthy doses of internationalist propaganda. The thought was that this could be done cheaply via radio. Historian Susan Ann Brewer tells of the unforeseen problems: "W. M. Newton, the B.B.C. representative in Chicago, was stunned to discover that there was no federal or hardly even a state authority for education. The decentralization of the American System made it difficult for the British to pursue this method."[27]

By 1943, "Teachers (especially history)" made the British "enemies list." American anticolonialism was blamed on American teachers. Graham Spry, a Canadian journalist and onetime executive of Standard Oil of California, told the Law Committee: "What was taught was the doctrine of American nationalism." The British propagandist proposed improving the American curriculum and textbooks.[28] It is not surprising that working as closely with British intelligence on covert propaganda as Francis Henson did, he helped fill this British need: "Dear Ernie—...Chet Williams wants you to have Winchell plug the 1st of his new books. How about something like this: 'The U.S. Commissioner of Education, J. W. Studebaker and his No. 1 man on the Public Forums, have struck a new blow to the solar plexus of the dictators....These books, for 6,250,000 high school youth, tell how we came by American freedom...it leads a procession of scores of books being brought out this fall by Row, Peterson & Co under the trademark 'Unitext'...the kids are going...to know why this country is worth fighting for...and my guess is that the adults will find them useful as first class brickbats to throw at Fifth Columnists.' I think the books are fairly good because I helped ghost write them. This, of course, should not be mentioned. Ever—Francis Henson."[29]

One of Griffith's most effective polls was done at the American Legion convention, September 15, 1941. This poll received two days of big play on the front page of Secretary of the Navy Frank Knox's *Chicago Daily News*. Question: "In view of the dangers from continued widespread Nazi and Fascist agitation in the United States, do you favor our breaking off of diplomatic relations with Germany-Italy, Yes 67.8%." Slightly more than 55 percent thought that Hitler would attack the United States if he defeated Britain and Russia. The poll results were used to promote a Legion resolution removing all geographical limitations on the movement of American armed forces. (Draft proponents had been forced to accept limitations which would have kept U.S. troops from Europe in order to get the Conscription Law passed in 1940.)

The *Chicago Daily News* story by Clem Lane said when this resolution was proposed: "In this recommendation the Legion leaders are simply following the wishes of the rank and file, and are not leading them into war, as the isolationists charge. This is borne out by a sampling poll, the results of which were made public today, in which it is indicated that 40 per cent of the Legionaries want the United States to enter the war now."

In a Sunday, September 21, 1941, article in the *New York Times*. Washington reporter Arthur Krock gauged the impact of the American Legion resolution, promoted by Griffith's poll, on Congress: "Definite signs are beginning to appear that what may be called the anti-war involvement group in Congress had lost its solidarity...defections have begun to show....the reasons are not hard to find...the resolutions adopted by the American Legion...are another factor in the shift."

As Krock wrote, this British intelligence poll was a stunning reversal, for the Legion "has long argued against another war adventure abroad." Not everyone was convinced by this poll. The *Chicago Tribune* took its own poll of the Legion delegates and found 70 percent against sending troops to Europe.[30] But this hardly mattered in the developing culture of belligerence that Arthur Krock detected in Congress. Sandy Griffith and his BSC polls helped to create the illusion of public support on which Franklin Roosevelt could base his moves toward war. He was only following the will of the people.

The principle was enunciated by Christopher Emmet in a letter to Griffith when Sandy was in Milwaukee preparing for the American Legion convention: "…this sort of effort where we are going after people who are on the fence requires the most careful possible preparation before publicity in order to get as much of a 'band wagon' psychology as possible."[31]

This devious tactic of running spurious polls at the conventions of various high-visibility organizations worked quite well at numerous conventions including that of the CIO. By purporting to represent the interventionist sentiments of the CIO rank and file at the convention, this poll circumvented one of the great leaders of the CIO, John L. Lewis, who was completely antiwar. Robert Spivak got out the good word to his press contacts. David Stern of the *Philadelphia Record*, Victor Riesel of the *New York Post*, Harold Levine of *PM*, Bruce Bliven of *The New Republic*, Freda Kirchway of *The Nation*, and Bruce Bliven, Jr., of *the New York Post* were sent a cover letter for the poll that said in part: "I think you will find interesting the fact that despite the official attitude of the C.I.O. on the captive mines situation, delegates are very determined to defeat Hitler and to protect the United States."[32]

As far as the objectivity of the poll, Spivak gave assurances on that subject also: "The Poll was conducted for us by Market Analyst, Inc. a private polling organization without any viewpoint that it is trying to foster." One may wonder if he smiled when he typed "without any viewpoint."

Some of these polls were organized by the militant New York Fight for Freedom/Committee to Defend America and its activist chairman, Frank Kingdon; we will see more of Kingdon in the next chapter on the effort to remove isolationist Hamilton Fish from Congress. Kingdon ran into problems with the National Association of Manufacturers. The usual trick of polling the rank-and-file members and then reporting interventionist poll results to undercut the mandate of the organization's isolationist leadership did not work because the leadership refused Kingdon's request to "permit the polling of its members on questions of vital national policy."[33]

Griffith and Henson worked on other British intelligence projects after Pearl Harbor. British Security Coordination waged not only political warfare against Britain's enemies (this included those wishing to be neutral), but also economic warfare against German companies and

American companies that had ties to them. Since America was technically neutral before Pearl Harbor, these business relationships between
German and American companies were often legal.

BSC nevertheless attacked them in several ways. One of the targets,
Schering, the giant drug company, is typical. BSC collected the evidence from spies it had planted within the company and then "both the
Department of Justice and the press were supplied with full particulars.
...the press campaign was taken up throughout the country by more
than a thousand papers [Winchell's circulation] as well as by many
magazines...."

As a result, Schering was convicted of conspiracy, its board of directors was purged, and it was fined for antitrust violations. Much of the
evidence for this was manufactured by BSC, planted in Schering's European mail, and then conveniently confiscated by censorship examin-
ers in Bermuda and sent back to the United States for use as evidence
by United States authorities.[34]

Not all aspects of this political/economic warfare against American
companies with ties to German companies went well. Sandy Griffith
and Francis Henson had the misfortune to run one campaign against a
company that was too big a fish for even BSC to boat easily. That company was Standard Oil of New Jersey, now called Exxon.

The campaign against Standard Oil of New Jersey was really only
one phase of the campaign against what was, in 1940, probably the
world's largest corporation, *Interessen Gemeinschaft Farbenindustrie
Aktiengellschaft*, better known as I.G. Farben. The campaign against
I.G. Farben was in turn one of the projects being run by Intrepid's
assistant John Pepper through the "George Office," directed by
George Muhle Merten.[35] The attack on Schering was one of the
projects run by "George."

Merten left Schering in March of 1941 and became an economic
consultant with offices in—where else—Rockefeller Center. In September 1941, Merten's offices became a British Security Coordination
front called the Western Continents Trading Corporation.[36]

Part of this project against Jersey Standard was run by British intelligence agent Donald MacLaren, who assisted Merton and was later
transferred to William Donovan's COI/OSS, where he was put under
Francis Pickens Miller, whom we previously met as a major figure in
Fight for Freedom.[37] In the fall of 1941, MacLaren put together a team

to write a booklet to attack I.G. Farben and American companies that did business with the chemical giant.

Several of the talented people who toiled on this BSC project were public personages in their own right. One was Rex Stout, the mystery writer and interventionist who had worked long and diligently with the BSC front Friends of Democracy. Stout "pledged full cooperation." Screenwriter, FFF activist, and head of the William Allen White News Service John L. Balderston was another. Sylvia Porter, the popular writer on money matters, then working for one of BSC's friends, George Backer at the *New York Post*, was one more.

Most of the work was done by British agent Donald MacLaren and Sylvia Porter. Rex Stout wrote the foreword and thus became the only recognizable name associated publicly with the project. The putative author, one John Boylan, did not exist. Titled *Sequel to the Apocalypse: The Uncensored Story: How Your Dimes and Quarters Helped Pay for Hitler's War*, it went on sale in March 1942. According to Stout's biography, done with his "full cooperation," the booklet's "distribution in the United States was facilitated by the energetic efforts of Nelson A. Rockefeller...[the] Coordinator of Inter-American Affairs."[38]

Beginning in the 1920s, Standard Oil of New Jersey had entered into a series of global agreements with I.G. Farben. These covered the exchange of patients and research and a strategic agreement that Standard summarized: "...the I.G. are going to stay out of the oil business and we are going to stay out of the chemical business...."[39] The exchange of information BSC was trying to stop had continued after the war began in Europe. The major subject of contention was the German and American process for making synthetic rubber.

In 1941, encouraged and provided information by BSC, Thurman Arnold, the crusading antitrust chief of the Justice Department, brought antitrust suits against Standard Oil. These were accompanied and driven by a typically ferocious media campaign of planted material and by a contentious minority stockholders' group. Francis Henson wrote to Ernest Cuneo: "Here is something hot for Walter [Cuneo wrote Walter Winchell's column and radio show]...on the Jersey Company....We have been working on this project for a long time, as you know, first for some individuals in the Fight for Freedom Committee and now in cooperation with William Floyd, II who is chairman of the Minority Stockholders Committee of the Standard Oil company of

New Jersey....I am asking Mr. Floyd to enclose with this letter an outline of what he hopes Winchell will say."[40]

In his letter to Cuneo, Floyd suggested his material go in Winchell's "column in the *Mirror* or his Sunday broadcast." One of Floyd's suggestions for a lead was "A stockholder's group wants to make Standard oil come all-out for the War."[41] This was just one more item in the British intelligence campaign against I.G. Farben and Standard Oil, but outsiders, even very astute outsiders, failed to see the wire-pullers.

I. F. Stone, columnist for *The Nation*, attended the Standard Oil of New Jersey 1943 stockholders' meeting in the Flemington, New Jersey, Grange Hall. Stone reported: "A committee of five minority stockholders with 744 shares among them managed miraculously to roll up 228,759 share votes for a resolution which would have pledged the management not to resume its cartel with I.G. Farben after the war."[42]

One should not be too hard on Mr. Stone; he was dealing with professional intelligence agents. Only with our present knowledge does it appear that he should have been more suspicious of the "miraculous" performance of the five minority stockholders. Sandy Griffith, the one-time European correspondent for the *Wall Street Journal* and Wall Street stock market operator, was perfect for this operation.[43]

Things did not end very well for either side in this confrontation. Walter Teagle, who as president of Standard Oil of New Jersey made several of the deals with Farben, and his successor, Texan Bill Farish (Teagle became chairman of the board), were both broken by the accusations of treason. Farish soon died of a heart attack. Teagle "lost all his customary confidence, became nervous and fumbling," according to author Anthony Sampson.[44]

Jersey Standard was not without defenses. According to one BSC document, one-time Standard Oil attorney and later head of the CIA Allen Dulles, then part of Donovan's Coordinator of Information, intervened on behalf of Standard Oil and I.G. Farben. The document explains that in March 1942, Dulles and someone else in COI "expressed their desire to have our propaganda action in the U.S.A., as far as I.G. Farben is concerned, discontinued. Their explanation of this was that this might involve large American companies like Standard Oil of New Jersey, etc., thereby perhaps impairing the war effort."[45]

In later years, Sandy Griffith also told his wife, Valerie, that Pinkertons hired by Standard Oil circulated the story that he was a Communist.

This made life quite difficult for him; there is some confirmation in this story because of similar problems that plagued others involved in this operation. Francis Henson's letters to Cuneo after the war are filled with requests for testimonials to refute charges that he was a security risk.[46]

In 1975, Drew Pearson's successor on the "Washington Merry-Go-Round" column revealed that newly opened State Department files listed Rex Stout as a "tool of Communist Agents" because of his part in writing *Sequel to the Apocalypse*.[47]

As bad as things turned out for some of the exposed participants, they could have been much worse. In the summer of 1943, Francis Henson, by then in the army and stationed at Camp Lee, Virginia, wrote a two-page single-spaced letter to Sandy Griffith in greatest secrecy.

While in a bar in Washington he had happened upon a drunk and talkative "J.B. Matthews, brain trust of the Dies Committee"—the Special House Committee for the Investigation of Un-American Activities. Matthews told Henson that he had been shipped around and unable to get ahead in the army "because of the dirty work you and Griffith did." Griffith, said Matthews, "acted as a British and French agent...." He further claimed, wrote Henson, that "all of the telegrams to and from various people have been surrendered to the Dies Committee, under subpoena, by WU [Western Union] and PT [Postal Telegraph-Cable]."

Matthews seems to have had a good idea who had been involved. He listed John Hunter, the English actor who helped run Fight for Freedom; (Henry) Hoke, who worked with BSC to stop isolationist propaganda from being mailed postage-free; and "Agar"—both Herbert and William worked for BSC fronts. He also mentioned Eugene Houdry of France Forever.

Although the chief counsel of the Dies Committee knew a great deal, particularly about how the Justice Department had worked with BSC to attack Standard Oil, he admitted that getting the information out to the public faced two obstacles, wrote Henson: "M.[atthews] says that this would have come out before—especially re game of the Justice Department and Thurman Arnold, if the Senators were not so scared of being labeled pro-Esso." Matthews also admitted to Henson that he could not "get to first base with the present administration." Henson closed, noting to Sandy that their problems were "Certainly as much excitement as a Graham Greene novel...."[48]

Little of this evidence gathered by the Dies Committee ever disturbed the public. The administration, as pointed out by Matthews, had a firm grip on the Democratic Congress. For more than half a century the clerk of the House of Representatives repelled all attempts to look at these files.

Neal Gabler in his book *Winchell* recounts his failed four-year quest for the Dies Committee files on Walter Winchell, who worked so closely with BSC. Gabler writes: "Donald Anderson, the House clerk, has refused on the ground that it would not serve the national interest. An archivist, however, has told me that the file is roughly two inches thick."[49]

With the mid-90s change in party control of the House and additional pressure from Congressman Sharrod Brown, the Dies Committee files were finally opened in mid-1996. The drunken J. B. Matthews had spoken correctly. The investigators had everything: Market Analyst Inc.'s checking account records, duplicate ledger cards from MA's bank account, nearly thirty pages of long-distance telephone records, and hundreds of copies of telegrams.

Three things are clear in going through this trove. The committee had stumbled on Sandy Griffith by accident. They did not know quite what to make of his extensive operations. Without the administration's iron grip on the House leadership, all these operations could have easily blown up in hearings with sworn testimony.

Committee investigator Robert E. Stripling wrote to Congressman Dies: "In checking on one Francis Henson, member of the Board of Directors of the Union for Democratic Action...we found that...[he] was the Washington representative of a corporation known as 'Market Analysts,' which is headed by one Sanford (Sandy) Griffith....Committee agents subpoenaed the telegrams for 'Market Analyst' and Sanford Griffith...and they reveal an amazing conspiracy...which has been carried on...by Sanford Griffith...certain high officials of the Anti-Trust Division of the Department of Justice...to smear and discredit the Standard Oil Company of New Jersey."[50]

To a large extent the BSC cut-outs held. The investigators traced the money for Sandy's operations against Standard Oil to the great flows of funds from Eugene Houdry's Catalytic Development Corporation. They seem not to have made the immediate connection that Houdry was a major player in France Forever. The investigators also noticed

Sandy's creation of the Irish American Defense Association. But again, the go-betweens held at least temporarily. In a memo to Dies a staffer wrote: "…Sanford Griffith set up an organization known as 'American-Irish Defense Association.'…it is my opinion that Griffith undertook this project at the request of…certain Jewish leaders in an effort to solidify Irish in this country behind the war effort. It is my understanding that this enterprise flopped for the reason that it was discovered that there were more Jews in it than Irishmen."[51]

Part of the genius of British intelligence in the United States during World War II was its ability, with the help of its American friends in the White House and media, to evade the legal and political consequences of its disruptive actions while making sure that every possible penalty was heaped upon its enemies.

The case of German propagandist George Sylvester Viereck illustrates how BSC was able to help the Justice Department obliterate competing voices. Propaganda thrives best if there are no competing expressions of opinion to disturb the audience.

George Sylvester Viereck had registered as a representative of the German newspaper *Muenchner Neueste Nachrichten* and the German Library of Information. Given that the German propaganda effort was a only a small fraction of the British propaganda machine (for instance, after 1938 interventionists had the radio commentary and radio drama and the movies to themselves), Viereck did strike some painful blows. In December 1940, Senator Ernest Lundeen of Minnesota formed a Make Europe Pay War Debts Committee under encouragement from Viereck. At this delicate time, when Britain was nearly bankrupt and about to push for what became Lend-Lease, His Majesty's Government did not need anyone harping on the embarrassing fact that Britain had not paid her World War I debts. This committee proposed that European debtor nations cede their islands in the Western Hemisphere as payment, thus the eventual name change to "Islands for War Debts Committee."[52]

Viereck also took over a small publisher named Flanders Hall and over the course of eighteen months published twenty titles. The most popular title unfavorably pointed out contradictions in statements made by British Ambassador Lothian under the title *Lord Lothian Against Lord Lothian*. Although Viereck wrote this, the putative author was Senator Ernest Lundeen. Viereck also wrote a foreword to this work under the name James Burr Hamilton. In the summer of 1941 that close friend of British intelligence Drew Pearson wrote an article exposing Viereck, *Lothian Against Lothian*, and Flanders Hall. This was followed by the impaneling of a grand jury, in September 1941, to examine the prevalence of Nazi agents in this country. Viereck was questioned by this grand jury and indicted. One of the charges was that Viereck had used fictitious names to conceal from the American public the true names of the authors. The British were never charged with this offense, though they were doing the same thing, many times more prolifically and successfully.

At 8:00 A.M. on October 8, 1941, seven agents of the Justice Department called on Viereck's residence, arrested him, and without a search warrant searched his home and office and took away his canceled checks and numerous papers and books. Bail was set at $15,000, about $150,000 in 1998 dollars. The presecuting attorney, William P. Maloney, told the press that George Viereck was "the head and brains of an insidious propaganda machine, engaged in sabotaging the President's efforts to arouse the American people to their danger." Viereck's biographer says that the truly damaging evidence against the defendant was supplied by the British censor in Bermuda, specifically by one Nadya Gardner.[53] BSC agent and author Montgomery Hyde, who had worked as part of this censorship unit, writes in his memoir, *Secret Intelligence Agent*: "I proposed that she should go to Washington as soon as possible to testify....Her sensational evidence changed the whole atmosphere."[54]

Prosecutor Maloney helped his own cause and made Viereck appear intensely devious by quoting out of context from Viereck's books. The judge upheld the prosecutor's objections to the defense witnesses and disallowed other key parts of the defense as irrelevant. On March 5, 1942, the jury returned a verdict of guilty. The judge imposed maximum sentences on the three counts. On September 21, 1942, the court of appeals denied a retrial. But on appeal to the Supreme Court the conviction was overturned 5–2 with Justices Black and Douglas dissenting (Jackson and Rutledge not participating).[55]

In his majority opinion the conservative Chief Justice Harlan Fiske Stone judiciously stated: "...men are not subjected to criminal punishment because their conduct offends our patriotic emotions...." But then Stone became specific. He said the district court judge had erred in his charge to the jury. If that were not bad enough for the prosecution, Stone's "haymaker landed." Speaking of prosecutor Maloney, Stone wrote: "He may prosecute with earnestness and vigor—indeed, he should do so. But, while he may strike hard blows, he is not at liberty to strike foul ones."[56]

In his history of the United States Supreme Court, *Nine Young Men*, Wesley McCune writes that "the freeing of Viereck was a bitter blow to lawyers for the administration...."[57] This was probably even more disconcerting for British intelligence, but both BSC and the Roosevelt Justice Department were equal to the task. Viereck was retried and convicted in July 1943. Once again British intelligence supplied prize witnesses—Nadya Gardner who had appeared before, and now also BSC's Sandy Griffith. Viereck's biographer describes Viereck's reaction to Sandy Griffith's damaging testimony: Viereck in an unusual letter to the judge "reiterated his charge that the testimony of Sanford Griffith was untrue. Griffith had claimed he overheard Viereck at a meeting of the Overseas Press Club, saying that the German government was prepared to 'spend plenty of money' to get accurate analysis of American public opinion polls and that he could obtain and had obtained money from the German embassy."[58]

Montgomery Hyde says that for his efforts in helping to get this conviction "I was personally thanked by [Attorney General] Francis Biddle." The prosecutor also sent a letter thanking Hyde for his efforts and saying, "Miss Gardner deserves great credit both for the quality of her work and her shrewdness as a witness."[59]

That one or both British intelligence agents may have committed perjury is not surprising. Intelligence agencies are instruments of a government's foreign policy. The loyalty of British agents was not to the integrity of the American legal process, but to the needs of British foreign policy.

British intelligence influence comes into play here in other incremental and technical ways. In July 1942, while Viereck had been appealing his first conviction under the Foreign Agents Registration Act, a grand jury in the District of Columbia indicted him and twenty-seven others for sedition and conspiracy under the Smith Act. Prosecutor Maloney's first indictment was so dubious that a second was drawn up in January 1943 widening the charges and adding five defendants. And even this indictment was supplanted by a third, which added five

German-American Bund members, thirty-five organizations, and forty-two publications.

Attention should be paid to a small item on page 11 of the August 16, 1944, *New York Times*: "Ben Lindas, Government-appointed and un-paid attorney for George Sylvester Viereck, a defendant in the mass sedition trial, today asked Justice Edward C. Eicher to consider his contention that publication of a book called 'Blackmail,' by Henry Hoke, was prejudicing his client's case. 'Hundreds of thousands of cop-ies of this book are being sold in the country,' he said, describing it as giving alleged evidence against the defendants which the prosecution has not yet introduced."

With delays and a mistrial—the judge died—the trial went on until June 1947. As will be shown more completely in the next chapter on the travails of Congressman Hamilton Fish, Mr. Hoke, who ran the *Reporter of Direct Mail Advertising*, was one of those working with In-trepid to destroy isolationism and chill the climate for those who op-posed America's global mission as defined by the British and their American sympathizers. Viereck was unable to reconcile with his wife, who had sold most of their assets and given the money to charity; his reputation was destroyed.[60]

The drunken J. B. Matthews of the Dies Committee was certainly correct when he told Henson: "Griffith is as guilty as Viereck...." He was also correct when he told Henson that Henry Hoke was working with Griffith.[61]

After the war the emerging Cold Warrior Christopher Emmet wrote Sandy Griffith: "We got in some good blows against one form of totalitarian aggression and if we can't do likewise against the other form of the same danger, perhaps that was too much to expect."[62] Sandy Griffith went into the resort hotel business with a place called Holiday Lodge at Northport, Long Island. He remained active in the nether world of the intelligence business.

CHAPTER 6

•••

Destroying
Congressman Fish

In the fall of 1940, BSC agent Sandy Griffith and his trusted coworkers Christopher Emmet and Francis Henson were in Poughkeepsie, New York, running the Nonpartisan Committee to Defeat Hamilton Fish. In a letter to interventionist attorney Charles C. Burlingham, thanking him for his financial assistance, Emmet pronounced the essence of the entire British intelligence campaign against the isolationists: "If...we can defeat Fish, who has been considered invincible for twenty years, we will put the fear of God into every isolationist senator and congressman in the country."[1]

This was the road to the bipartisan internationalist United States foreign policy that shaped the world after World War II. The joint British intelligence–Roosevelt administration effort to rid the Congress of Hamilton Fish, an influential isolationist from Franklin Roosevelt's home district, was not unique. Given that the "BSC Account" says William Stephenson declared "a covert war" on the isolationists, it is not surprising that other isolationist congressmen had similar problems.[2]

For example, isolationist senators Wheeler of Montana and Nye of South Dakota met defeat in campaigns that bear a striking resemblance to the problems that defeated Fish—great flows of outside money and assistance for their opponents; surprise charges of wrongdoing just before election time; virulent attacks untraceable to anyone; the distribution of books in their districts charging them with disloyalty.[3]

In his farewell address to the United States Senate on December 19, 1944, Senator Nye remarked ruefully on the tactics that had defeated him: "Propaganda sponsored by irresponsible forces outside the state, plus propaganda the source and responsibility for which could not be traced to anyone, had many honest North Dakotans convinced that if I was not actually on Hitler's payroll, I should have been."[4]

The elimination of Congressman Hamilton Fish is closely examined here because it exhibits a wide range of the classic political warfare tactics British intelligence used to defeat the isolationists. These attacks on the isolationists not only preceded Pearl Harbor but continued afterward, because the British needed the United States to accept its responsibilities as a world power. The war was rapidly exhausting Britain's resources. Only if the United States could be wed to the British cause could Britain look forward to prosperity and success in an unstable and dangerous postwar world. Scholar Susan Ann Brewer argues persuasively that the historical foundation of this wedding, the "special relationship" between the United States and Britain, was, in its origins, largely a myth created by British propaganda to help fulfill Britain's needs for a strong partner.[5]

The dissenting voices of the isolationists were delegitimized, and, as individuals, they either turned around, as did Senator Arthur Vandenberg of Michigan, or they were largely driven from office. J. G. Donnelly of the Foreign Office summed up the success of British intelligence and propaganda in August 1945: "The Americans, without necessarily knowing it, are bound to continue to see the world in large measure through the British window."[6] This was possible because Fish and those like him who proposed that Americans view the world through other than "the British window" had been driven from office and respectability.

Hamilton Fish was born on December 7, 1888, in Garrison, New York. He outlived almost all his adversaries, dying on January 18, 1991, at 102 years old. His father, another Hamilton Fish, had been in Congress, and his grandfather, yet another Hamilton Fish, had been President Grant's secretary of state. His son, yet a fourth Hamilton Fish and also a congressman, but more liberal, died in July 1996.

The Hamilton Fish of our interest was first elected, as a Republican, to Congress in 1920 from a New York district that included Dutchess, Orange, and Putnam counties; thus he was President

Franklin Roosevelt's congressman. By the late 1930s, Hamilton Fish was causing problems for the administration and the president. He had become the ranking Republican on the House Rules Committee and the House Foreign Affairs Committee.[7]

On a trip to Europe in the summer of 1939, the very eve of World War II, Fish met with officials of several governments. For these meetings President Roosevelt wanted to prosecute Fish under the Logan Act, for meddling in foreign affairs, and if that proved impossible to have some congressman attack him. The prosecution did prove impossible, but Congressman Clifton Woodrum of Virginia certainly warmed FDR's heart with a wonderfully uninhibited ad hominem attack on Fish.[8]

By 1940, Fish was being lumped together with two other isolationists, Congressmen Joseph W. Martin, Jr., of Massachusetts and Bruce Barton of Connecticut, in the president's cadenced refrain "Martin, Barton, and Fish." Though British intelligence and the administration may have been after him earlier, the concrete evidence of their concerted efforts to relieve Fish of his seat begins in the fall of 1940.

The Nonpartisan Committee to Defeat Hamilton Fish operated in October and November 1940. It had an extremely small base, and little of that was from Fish's district. Only ninety-five contributors gave the $4,616.95 (about $50,000 in 1998 dollars) collected for the campaign. The largest contribution, of $1,000 or $500, depending on the set of accounts, came from Sidney Spivak. Frank Kingdon, the head of the militant New York chapter of the White Committee, gave $250, and Frederick McKee of Fight for Freedom gave $500. McKee, remember, was also the conduit for British intelligence funding for its control of Station WRUL. Francis Henson gave $200, a rather hefty amount in 1940.[9]

Offices for this campaign were at 100 Broadway, Newburgh, New York, and 8 West 40th Street, New York City; the latter address housed the League of Nations Association, the William Allen White Committee, and Sandy Griffith's Market Analysts Inc. The chairman of the Nonpartisan Committee to Defeat Hamilton Fish was the Rev. Leon C. Birkhead, who was also the head of the British intelligence front group Friends of Democracy. Christopher T. Emmet was secretary and treasurer.[10]

Sandy Griffith's assistant Francis Henson wrote Ernest Cuneo a letter on October 18, 1940, from the Campbell Hotel in Poughkeepsie,

New York: "I enclose some very interesting material issued in connection with the 'Stop Fish' campaign. Sandy and I are in Poughkeepsie working on the matter and will probably be here until election day." There is a piece of the literature the Nonpartisan Committee put out for the campaign in Drew Pearson's papers. The cover of the four-page pamphlet has photographs of Hitler, German Foreign Minister von Ribbentrop, and Fritz Kuhn of the German-American Bund.

One picture showing Kuhn and Fish together looks very incriminating. It is labeled "Hamilton Fish inspecting documents with Fritz Kuhn (jailed ex-Bund leader), who was Fish's invited guest at State Constitutional Convention. The caption of the map (on the table) indicates that it shows locations of Nazi Units and Camps." The headlines say "VOTERS OF DUTCHESS, ORANGE AND PUTNAM COUNTIES IS HAMILTON FISH PRO-NAZI?" The rest of the material is a wild array of charges and out-of-context quotations.[11]

Fish later explained that the photograph of Kuhn and himself had been taken in 1938 when Kuhn appeared uninvited before Fish's committee of the New York State Convention in Albany, which was investigating the advisability of a proposed ban on the drilling and arming of paramilitary groups. Fish said that the photograph was taken while he was talking with Kuhn.[12]

Henson continued in his October 18, 1940, letter to Cuneo: "I suggest you call this campaign to the attention of friends in Washington. I also hope that you will suggest to Walter [Winchell] that he put something into his column about the matter and give us a plug over the radio on Saturday night."[13] Cuneo also may have been the connection to Drew Pearson in 1940, though by 1942 it is clear that Sandy Griffith was sending material directly to Pearson. The number of those strongly enough opposed to Fish to contribute money was small—only eighty-four people gave $10 or more, and none of these had an address in Fish's district. Seventy-four of those who contributed $10 or more gave New York City addresses.[14]

The opening salvo at Fish came from the *New York Times*, one of the newspapers that greatly assisted BSC. In early October 1940, the *Times* took an editorial stand supporting the movement to defeat Fish and in the process put forth a striking metaphor. If Willkie was elected, said the *Times*, Fish "would be an albatross around Willkie's neck."[15]

Fish also had local problems when the usually Republican *Middletown Times Herald* urged a vote for his opponent, and the Poughkeepsie Trade and Labor Council charged that Fish's policies "can only be interpreted as direct aid to the dictator nations."[16]

The real "October Surprise," however, came on October 21, 1940, with a "Washington Merry-Go-Round" column by Drew Pearson and Robert S. Allen. These columnists suggested the Nazis were subsidizing Fish through inflated rents they were supposedly paying him for property. The charge was false but could not help but erode voter confidence in Fish.

Had all this effort by Sandy Griffith and his helpers Emmet and Henson had any effect? Fish, after all, survived this 1940 onslaught, but by only nine thousand votes, less than half his margin of victory in 1938 and his smallest margin in many years.[17] This was a very small margin for an incumbent Republican in a Republican district.

Sandy Griffith wrote to Ernest Cuneo after the election: "Francis probably reported to you on the Hamilton Fish fight. Our size-up of the situation was correct—that $2,000 or $3,000 additional a week or two ahead would have been sufficient to put it over. The local Democratic machine in the district was of practically no help."[18]

Agent Griffith also wrote a four-page memo titled "Recommendations by Sanford Griffith for Hamilton Fish Campaign and Continuation," dated "November 1940 (upon conclusion of campaign)," which examined the congressman's weaknesses and spelled out the best methods to attack him in the future.[19] Griffith wrote: "Only those items are included as could relate to campaigns against other congressmen."

To read Griffith's "recommendations" is to review the "political difficulties" not only of Fish but of numerous isolationists who in their temerity ran afoul of the political warfare tactics of British intelligence.

It is little wonder that historians have had difficulty seeing the hidden strings or the puppeteers behind the curtains. A number of times in Section III of his memo, Griffith emphasizes that attacks must appear to be spontaneous, with the organizers staying offstage:

III. *General Strategy Against Fish*
(a) Make attacks from all sides, particularly from own district.
    Keep as far as possible an indirect approach and avoid any suggestion of central planning.

Emphasize spontaneity.

Keep in background any protests emanating from New York City, and protests from Jewish and foreign groups.[20]

In Section IV, Griffith puts forth the basic British intelligence tactics for black propaganda—propaganda that seems to be emanating from independent sources. Also he recommends creating media tie-ins for attacks on Fish, even if there are no real events that lend themselves to the task:

IV. *Dissemination*

(a) Make selections from material to supply specific needs of individual editors, radio commentators and columnists.

Use personal approach through best existing contacts to a large number of newspaper people rather than using broadside *routine* releases or giving news exclusively with a single paper.

Tie-in attacks with current events. Study, and where necessary create, incidents which give sufficient news pegs on which to hang a story....[21]

Sandy Griffith had a number of specific recommendations based upon the above principles. All of them involved staying out of sight and letting others make the publicly visible maneuvers. His recommendation that Fish should be given the impression that he was a lame duck who did not represent his constituents had almost immediate consequences in the Lend-Lease debates of early 1941.

On February 17, 1941, Henry Luce minion and *Fortune* pollster Elmo Roper released a public opinion poll of Fish's constituents done at the request of James H. Causey.[22] According to Roper, only 20 percent of the voters in Fish's district agreed with their congressman's foreign policy views. Even more significantly and conveniently, 78.6 percent of those polled favored the Lend-Lease bill, while Fish himself had stated that his mail was heavily against Lend-Lease.

Fish's biographer Richard Hanks writes of this poll that: "it probably forced Fish in subsequent debates into a more moderate position on foreign policy issues than he might otherwise have been inclined to follow."[23] The validity of these polls should be judged against the fact

Sandy Griffith sailing in the 1930s. *Photo courtesy of Brenda McCooey.*

Sandy Griffith with his children after the death of his wife. The New York license plate is from 1935. The Griffith children (left to right) are Peter, Brenda, and Sandy. *Photo courtesy of Brenda McCooey.*

Francis A. Henson was agent Sandy Griffith's principal assistant at Market Analysts Inc. from 1940 to 1942. *Photo courtesy of Stephen R. Farrow.*

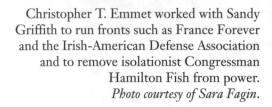

Christopher T. Emmet worked with Sandy Griffith to run fronts such as France Forever and the Irish-American Defense Association and to remove isolationist Congressman Hamilton Fish from power. *Photo courtesy of Sara Fagin.*

Dr. Albert Parry was British Intelligence agent Sandy Griffith's man at the Committee to Defend America/ Fight for Freedom office in Chicago. In a classic intelligence odyssey, Parry went on to the OSS and then to the CIA fronts of the 1950s and 1960s. A Russian expert and prolific writer, he taught at Northwestern, Colgate, and Case Western Reserve universities. *Photo courtesy of Thomas Parry.*

John Hunter, shown here as a captain in Patton's Third Army, was American born but spent most of his life in England. An experienced scriptwriter, he worked in Sandy Griffith's stable of scriptwriters for Boston radio station WRUL. Hunter also worked on the opinion poll–rigging side of the operation. He appears to have been an MI-6 man assigned to Griffith.
Photo courtesy of Brenda McCooey.

Richard Julius Maurice Frederick Carl Wetzler Coit (G.100)—a name to be reckoned with and certainly not to be taken in vain, despite his cherubic looks. A banker by profession, Dick Coit (or "Coitus Interruptus" behind his back) was chief of staff to William Stephenson at BSC. *SOE Archives.*

President Franklin D. Roosevelt aboard Vincent Astor's yacht S.S. *Nourmahal* on March 27, 1935. FDR, with his characteristic cigarette holder, is in the center, looking down. Vincent Astor and his friends in the Room, later code-named The Club, acted as an intelligence-gathering agency for FDR. During World War II, Astor was also FDR's area coordinator for New York intelligence.

Vincent Astor, the Duke of Kent, Lady Clifford, FDR, and the Duchess of Kent aboard Astor's yacht *Nourmahal* on March 27, 1935.

Matthew Woll is second from left. To his left is William Green, president of the AFL. Woll was the driving force for BSC's anti-Nazi labor fronts. After the war both Woll and Green were major figures in the Cold War anti-Communist crusade. Beside Green is Alexander Kerensky, who held power in Russia briefly in 1917 before the Bolsheviks pushed him out. *George Meany Memorial Archives.*

Picketers from the BSC front Fight for Freedom outside an America First rally in September 1941. Driving isolationists such as Congressman Hamilton Fish from public life was a major BSC objective. *Princeton University Libraries.*

David K. Niles was the White House contact for British Security Coordination and the BSC front Fight for Freedom.

Robert Emmet Sherwood worked closely with BSC head William Stephenson, even showing him President Roosevelt's speeches before they were delivered. *Franklin D. Roosevelt Library.*

Walter Winchell's column and radio show gave him the largest following of any American news commentator. Winchell had been working against the Nazis since the 1930s. Winchell and his ghost writer Ernest Cuneo worked closely with BSC.

Wendell Willkie, an active Democrat and a man who had never held public office, was suddenly and unexpectedly nominated by the Republicans in 1940, thus depriving the voters of any real choice on international policy in the November 1940 elections.

Celebrated political columnist Walter Lippmann, shown here with his wife Helen Byrne Armstrong Lippmann, was one of the prominent journalists who helped BSC. Mrs. Lippmann's father was a highly visible member of the BSC front, the American-Irish Defense Association. Her sister was married to BSC agent Ivar Bryce. *Yale University Library.*

On November 30, 1946, Sir William Stephenson received the Medal of Merit, America's highest civilian award, from his World War II collaborator William Donovan, the wartime head of the OSS. Looking on are Donovan's OSS assistant Col. G. Edward Buxton and Lady Stephenson. This photo and the accompanying article in the *New York Times* give away a great deal to the careful reader or those in the know. *AP/Wide World Photo.*

Ernest Cuneo was the liaison between BSC, the White House, the FBI, the Treasury, and the OSS. He is shown here with BSC staff member Margaret Watson, who became his wife. *Photo courtesy of Jonathan Cuneo.*

John D. Rockefeller, Jr. (left), and banker Thomas Lamont of J. P. Morgan raise a glass at the Associated Canadian Organization of New York dinner, June 18, 1941. Lamont was a major force in the BSC front, the Committee to Defend America by Aiding the Allies and in the creation of Wendell Willkie. The Rockefellers were major contributors to Willkie and to BSC and Fight for Freedom. *Baker Library, Harvard Business School.*

that despite U.S. entry into World War II and a ferocious campaign against him, Fish survived the election of 1942, and it was only on the third try in 1944, abetted by a redistricting, that the administration and British intelligence were able, narrowly, to rid the Congress of him.

V. *Specific Activities Recommended*
(a) *Local:*
   Keep alive the several volunteer anti-Fish committees in his district.
   …let the local committees pass resolutions and communicate them to the local press. Let them register in a variety of ways that Fish does not represent opinion in his district and that he went back to Congress a lame duck. Let local Legion Posts keep alive his obstructionists record on conscription.

Griffith's thoughts on action to be taken in Washington propose "ganging up on Fish" with the administration. He was a pollster, and public opinion strategies seem to have rarely been out of his mind. Since Ernest Cuneo was always kept abreast of Henson and Griffith's activities, this coordination was relatively easy. Franklin Roosevelt absolutely delighted in the thought of "Cooking Ham Fish's Goose":

(b) *In Washington*
   Whenever Fish pushes into the news provide the Press with data showing Fish up as out of step with his constituents.
   Pin on the pro-Nazi and obstructionist labels. Cooperate with the Administration and hostile colleagues to assure their ganging up on Fish whenever he obstructs.

But more than one can play this polling game, even if not as effectively. While the interventionists could hide behind the names of "scientific" polling organizations and get their polls wide dissemination, the isolationists were more restricted. But Fish as a method of self-defense did make an effort by promoting his own advocacy poll. On June 18, 1941, Fish mailed 107,000 franked letters to his constituents. Accompanying the letter, which warned of the dangers of war, was a stamped return postcard; it allowed the voter two options: "I am opposed to the United States entering the war," or "I am in favor of the United States entering the war." Soon the results began to flow back to

Fish, and even he professed to be amazed by the 9–1 vote for staying out of the war: "I want the people to know the facts and not be fooled. I was fooled myself. I thought there was a much greater desire in my district to get us into war. I would not have been surprised if the poll had shown as high as one-third of my district for war, yet when the votes are counted, it discloses 9–1 among the plain people."[24]

The bureau of publicity of the Democratic National Committee responded quickly, if circuitously, by sending a "suggestion" to various Democratic newspapers calling Fish's poll a "naive enterprise" and saying that if the poll had been differently worded the response would have been "overwhelmingly to the contrary."[25] This may well have been true. As mentioned in Chapter 4, interventionist pollster Hadley Cantril emphasized the importance of the wording when he wrote David Niles at the White House of his efforts to suggest questions to Gallup that would get the desired interventionist answers.

Sandy Griffith had a number of other suggestions. They all relied on the ability to manipulate the press and to give the impression the movement against isolationists like Fish was nationwide:

(c) *Smoke him out in advance:*
    1) By having the newspapers send around reporters to interview him.
    2) By having patriotic committees send around delegations accompanied by reporters to report on the interview.
    3) Where possible link Fish in with the most disreputable leaders in the movements he sponsors.
    4) On his specific obstructionist stands get people from several parts of the country to write him protest letters....[26]

There were other harsh suggestions made by agent Griffith, and most of them happened to Fish over the next four years as his political career lurched from one disaster to another. Some of Sandy's strategies were based on legal harassment: "Where Fish makes libelous statements about others, give the injured party able counsel and try to get litigation started as a peg on which to hang further publicity."

Others were more overtly political: "Engineer...debates" while offering "able speakers to rebut him." "Opinion Polls are a source of information, a propaganda weapon..." and "are accepted by the newspapers as news and are effective propaganda." Griffith also suggested a "Combat Fund" of at least $5,000 ready "at all times for anti-Fish activity."[27]

In August 1941 there was more trouble for Fish in his 26th Congressional District. More than five hundred citizens of the town of Warwick signed a letter charging that Fish's activities were aiding Hitler. The upshot was the scheduling of a debate. And there was no respite for the beleaguered congressman. Within days after the first challenge, another group, in Amenia, New York, asked Fish to debate Lewis Mumford; the Mumford debate took place on August 30, in the local high school. The New York City press was well represented.

Mumford had been one of the original members of Sandy Griffith's Nonpartisan Committee to Defeat Hamilton Fish. Mumford was also one of the sponsors of Fight for Freedom.[28] The *New York Times* reported that among the throng of spectators were Mrs. Franklin Roosevelt and Mrs. Henry Morgenthau; Herbert Agar and Christopher Emmet had traveled from Connecticut. Agar, we have seen earlier, was one of the leading lights of Fight for Freedom.[29] Emmet was secretary and treasurer of Sandy Griffith's committee against Fish.

Mumford promoted the standard Fight for Freedom position that Hitler threatened everything America stood for, that the United States should immediately declare war on Hitler, and that Fish's isolation aided the Nazis. Fish talked about the costs of war in terms of money and lives and about how those wishing to get the United States into the war were dominated by Communists, refugees, international bankers, and interventionist newspapers.[30]

Fish barely had time to recover from the tumultuous gathering at Amenia when on September 19, 1941, he debated Harvard professor of government William Yandell Elliot at Warwick, New York. Professor Elliot went right to the heart of the matter, saying Fish was a "dupe of Nazism." He drew cheers for his sly play on Fish's fellow isolationist Senator Burton Wheeler, saying that Fish was not a fifth columnist, just a fifth-Wheeler.

The *New York Times* reported that the crowd was mostly interventionist. Although there was not a "good radio tie in" as Sandy Griffith had suggested, Fish was persuaded to do the debate with Elliot over again two nights later for a national radio audience. It should be made clear here that Hamilton Fish was not an admirer of Adolf Hitler, was not an anti-Semite, and was not pro-Axis. He was vociferously opposed to all dictatorships and had consistently spoken out against anti-Semitism.

Congressman Fish had little rest. By the summer of 1941, British Security Coordination had organized a well-executed campaign against the free use of the mails—the franking privilege—by isolationist congressmen.[32] Interestingly, Sandy Griffith had mentioned the possibility of attacking Fish on the franking issue in his November 1940 "Recommendations" but thought it would be difficult because an attack on Fish would "threaten prerogatives of all members."

British intelligence officer Montgomery Hyde's *The Quiet Canadian,* **which contains about 35 percent of the secret "BSC Account,"** gives this background on the franking privilege controversy: "Early in 1941, a friend of Stephenson [Intrepid], who was in the advertising business, drew his attention to the fact that certain isolationist congressmen were using the 'frank' for distributing free through the mails not only their own isolationist speeches but others that had been specially written by Nazi propagandists."[33]

The original "BSC Account" amends this slightly to say that Stephenson had a friend in the direct mail business. This "friend of Stephenson" was undoubtedly Henry Hoke (1894–1970), the publisher of the *Reporter of Direct Mail Advertising.* The Dies Committee had also spotted Hoke's work for British intelligence, its drunken and talkative chief investigator, J. B. Matthews, told Francis Henson in 1943.[34]

This franking controversy was not Hoke's first attempt to stem the flow of German mail propaganda. A year before he had appealed to the Post Office to issue a fraud order to prevent the German Library of Information from mailing, to 100,000 readers, its eight-page "Facts in Review," edited ably, perhaps too ably for his own good, by propagandist George Sylvester Viereck. Hoke had on that occasion also demanded that the bulletins distributed by the German Railroads Information Bureau be censored to prevent the country from being flooded by German propaganda.[35]

Hoke's June 1940 call for censorship had come at a time when the British were desperate to stem the flow of German propaganda and improperly interpreted news. Given proper news management and spin, even military disasters like Dunkirk could be portrayed as victories of a sort. But these wordy edifices constructed by British propaganda were not very sturdy, and the last thing they needed was comparison with objective fact, to say nothing of contrary propaganda. At the time of Dunkirk the German news was actually much more straightforward and factual than the British. Stopping the flow of untimely news and film from Europe was a major British challenge in June 1940.

Henry Hoke authored two books of interest here: *Blackmail* (issued in 1944) promised "the inside story of the conspiracy to disrupt America"; *It's a Secret* (1945) laid bare subversive organizations and their activities. This is the book that German propagandist George Sylvester Viereck's attorney said was prejudicing the jury against his client. These books were written under the auspices of an obscure group that had Hoke as executive chairman, the Graphic Arts Victory Committee.[36]

In the franking controversy the charges against Fish were just part of British Security Coordination's campaign to attack prominent isolationist members of Congress. The campaign kicked off in May 1941 with an open letter from Henry Hoke accusing Senator Burton Wheeler of misusing the franking privilege.[37]

By July 25, 1941, this campaign merited two columns above the fold on the front page of the *New York Times*: "Stimson Accuses Wheeler of Actions Near Treason, Citing Anti-War Cards Franked to Soldiers by Senator...." Hoke's charges against Wheeler are mentioned in a story tagged on to the Stimson charges. Fish became embroiled in the controversy over misuse of the franking privilege on August 26, 1941. This charge dogged him for the rest of his congressional career.

The first accusation came in the form of a press release from Fight for Freedom accusing Congressman Fish of allowing William C. Pelly, an anti-Semite and leader of the fascist Silver-shirts, to use his frank. Fish's franked envelope addressed to "FIGHT FOR JEWDOM COMMITTEE" (which still resides in the FFF Papers at Princeton) contained advertising for such anti-Semitic works as the "Protocols of the Learned Elders of Zion" and a magazine named *Liberation*. FFF also wrote in its press release that when reached by telephone, Fish said: "But it doesn't bother me any.... There's been too much Jewism going around anyway...."[38]

Fish responded immediately in a press release of his own. His version of the telephone interview differed notably from the Fight for Freedom version; he wrote: "No American in public life has made more speeches against religious and racial persecution in Germany,

Romania and at home than I have. I was the author of the Zionist Resolution for a Homeland for the Jewish people in Palestine that passed Congress in 1923. I challenge anyone to show one single utterance of mine that was anti-Semitic during the twenty-one years that I have been in Congress."[39]

The clarity of Fish's very positive record on Jewish issues and issues of discrimination is undoubtedly the reason that only *PM* printed Fight for Freedom's accusations.[40] Though he was able to deal with this accusation rather easily, it was not the end of his troubles.

The episode had begun when isolationist Prescott Dennett, the chairman of the Islands for War Debts committee, became alarmed that the contents of his office were about to be subpoenaed. Twenty mailbags were then transferred by truck from Dennett's office to Fish's. But Fish's office refused to accept the bags. After some confusion, eight of these bags were left outside Fish's storage room and the remainder were sent to the office of America First.

This "was observed," writes Montgomery Hyde in *The Quiet Canadian*, "by one of Stephenson's agents who had been keeping watch." This suggests that Intrepid had someone in Fish's office, or that there was a telephone tap. The *Washington Post* and *PM* conspicuously carried the story, and with much fanfare; the *PM* headline read "HAM FISH SNATCHES EVIDENCE WANTED IN U.S. NAZI HUNT."

This became a continuing story in both papers. The *Washington Post* reporter, Dillard Stokes, opened the mailbags, though he had no permission to do so. Both the *Washington Post* and *PM* were able to obtain inside information on the supposedly secret grand jury proceedings for their stories.[41]

It finally came out that Fish's clerk George Hill was the guilty party, and he was convicted and sentenced to two to six years for lying under oath about the franked mail, his relations to German propagandist George Sylvester Viereck, and $12,000 he had received. Prosecutor William Power Maloney, who worked with British intelligence on this prosecution, also got in some good political blows in early 1942, when he finally got Hamilton Fish on the witness stand in the trial of George Sylvester Viereck.

Fish admitted he knew Viereck, though he had not seen him in a year and a half, but denied that any Nazi propaganda had gone out of his office with his "consent and approval." Prosecutor Maloney asked if

Fish had read a Viereck book on German propaganda. "Isn't it a co-incidence," asked Mr. Maloney, "that the views on Nazi propaganda expressed in that book are similar to those you have held as a Congressman?" Mr. Fish, leaning forward in the witness chair, retorted hotly: "The man who made that statement lies." "Are you referring to Mr. Viereck?" inquired the prosecutor. "I am referring to you," Mr. Fish shot back.[42]

Wrangling with a Justice Department prosecutor was not a good way for Fish to start an election year, but British intelligence's Sandy Griffith and the Justice Department also had an interesting "October Surprise" ready for him. The administration and British intelligence and its fronts gathered to finish Fish.

They were all back in 1942 working under the name Independent Committee of the Twenty-sixth District, certainly a wonderful name for an organization run by an intelligence agency. The chairman was James Causey, who had put forth the early 1941 public opinion poll that had thrown Fish off balance during the Lend-Lease debate.

As might be expected with such a carefully organized campaign, there was also an "August Surprise" five days before the August primary. On this occasion, Dillard Stokes, who had written the *Washington Post* articles in BSC's campaign against misuse of the franking privilege, charged Fish with income tax evasion. Fish, wrote Stokes, had never declared $25,000 he had received from Rafael Trujillo, the Dominican Republic dictator. Caught off guard, as was surely intended, Fish said he had lost $12,500 of the money, along with some of his own, in an oil investment. He had returned the rest.

He said that he had consulted the Internal Revenue Service concerning this transaction and had been told he need not declare nor pay taxes on this money. What Fish said may have been true, but the exposure of his dealing with a man such as Trujillo left many wondering about his judgment.[43]

Despite the best efforts of the Independent Committee of the Twenty-sixth District and all those who harassed and vilified Fish, the candidacy of the major contender, Republican Augustus W. Bennett, was a dismal failure. In the August 11, 1942, Republican primary, Fish overwhelmed Bennett by two and a half to one. Fish had a plurality of two to one over the combined votes of the other three contenders for the nomination.

128 ••• DESPERATE DECEPTION

Publicly undaunted, the anti-Fish forces announced that they had just begun to fight. Very quickly they met to map out strategy and unite behind the Democratic candidate, Hoyt. The Independent Committee of the Twenty-sixth District, run by agent Sandy Griffith and Intrepid's "friend in advertising" Henry Hoke, disbanded in mid-August 1942. But Griffith and Hoke were not quitting. They moved on to produce similar tough attacks in the autumn under the banner of the Hoyt for Congress Committee of Putnam Valley Democratic Club, Inc.

Fish confronted numerous attempts at character assassination in September and October, all of them the managed events in which British intelligence specialized and which Sandy Griffith had recommended. In an open letter to Republican voters, Bennett, whom Fish had just trounced in the Republican primary, announced that he was endorsing the Democrat Hoyt.[44] The national magazines *Collier's* and *The Nation* carried articles suggesting that the country would be better off without Congressman Fish.[45] Fish also found himself opposed by the CIO and, for the first time in his career, the AFL locals in his district.

Though these problems all fit into Griffith's overall list of recommendations, their exact origins are not clear. In the case of the "October Surprises," there is unequivocal documentation linking British intelligence agents and the political bombs bursting over the Fish campaign; Drew Pearson kept all the pertinent correspondence, which now resides in his papers at the LBJ Library in Austin, Texas.

Here are the highlights of a letter from Intrepid's friend Henry Hoke to Drew Pearson. Attached to the letter are samples of the literature the committee was releasing, tying Fish to the Nazis. The major purpose of the letter, however, was to prepare Pearson to deliver the "October Surprise" the British agents hoped would be fatal to Fish.[46]

Hoke points out that Franklin Roosevelt's Justice Department was the secret source that had supplied the British agents with the ammunition with which to prompt Drew Pearson: "...so far as I know now, we are not supposed to reveal the source of our information, but the following five checks were issued by Henson Sturm to Hamilton Fish, and the Department of Justice has the checks....You can check with Sanford Griffith on Henson's record as a wholesaler of Nazi propaganda....Sanford Griffith claims that Sturm was one of the chief payoff men for the Nazi government....Sanford Griffith has reams of reports on both Sturm and Henson, but those reports aren't available today....I am told that Fish could not possibly sue for Libel....I am sending you, Drew, tear sheets of the second ad we ran on Fish in the *Putnam Valley Courier*....I am sending you also a photostat of the map-chart that will appear in the third ad...."[47]

The tear sheets Henry Hoke enclosed with his letter include a blatant full-page picture-and-captions layout featuring short biographies of seemingly every Nazi or Nazi sympathizer who could remotely be tied to Hamilton Fish: "Prescott Dennett has been indicted...had nearly daily contact with George Hill in Hamilton Fish's office...; William Griffin recently been indicted...; Caviar Auhagen is now in jail...; Charles Hudson was recently indicted for sedition...; Fritz Kuhn leader of the Bund...." Twenty of these vignettes certainly give the impression that Fish associated with few people who were not Nazis or under indictment or in jail.

The second "ad" shows an outline map of the United States with Nazi propaganda going to Viereck and from Viereck to Fish's office from which the map shows the propaganda being distributed to various people, most of whom were under indictment, already convicted, or, in the case of Father Coughlin's *Social Justice*, banned.

Drew Pearson, who is listed in the "BSC Account" as one of BSC's friends in the press, made the charges in his October 26, 1942, "Washington Merry-Go-Round" column that Congressman Fish had received $3,100 from German propagandists in the Romanoff Caviar Company. Fish was incensed by this "despicable eleventh hour attack" and did what Sandy Griffith had hoped for in his "Recommendations" back in November 1940—he laid himself open to the lawsuit that Griffith had always hoped to entangle him in.

Henry Hoke rushed the good news to Drew Pearson in a note and a letter, both dated October 29, 1942: "Dear Drew, Just a note. Sandy Griffith just told me that he thinks you have a darn good case for a libel suit against Fish. It would be a wonderful case of man bites dog."[48] In his longer letter, Hoke was more specific: "I am rushing to you by air mail, something you should see if you haven't seen it already....notice that Mr. Fish says of you:—'Drew Pearson, in my opinion, is the most contemptible, dishonest, and dishonorable smear propagandist in America and by inference the most colossal liar in the nation.' When I got word yesterday of the Fish statement about you, I went over to Sandy Griffith's office and he let me see all of the de-

tailed report on Sturm, Mack, Fish and Von Gienanth....Since Fish
was claiming that Sturm was a good American citizen, I figured we
would have to get some sort of quick action to have Sturm put on the
pan. So, I called Bill Maloney and gave him a summary of all the reports. Bill then decided to issue his subpoenas (there wasn't any
chance to get an indictment before the election). Confidentially,
Sandy Griffith is making up a full report of the Mack angle for Bill
Maloney. He is sending the report tonight....The thing is loaded
with dynamite and I think it is a much better story than the Westrick
affair of some time back."[49]

Hoke's mention of "the Westrick affair" also marks him out as an
insider, because the Westrick affair was from start to finish a British
intelligence operation. Dr. Gerhard Westrick was thought by BSC to
be a high-grade German agent, though he was registered with the U.S.
State Department as the commercial counselor at the German embassy
in Washington. Westrick had disturbingly good contacts in American
business circles, particularly at ITT and Texaco Oil Company. These
facts were written into news stories and placed in BSC's favorite newspaper, the *New York Herald Tribune*, with headlines such as "HITLER
AGENT ENSCONCED IN WESTCHESTER."

Westrick was "deluged with abusive letters and telephone calls." The
angry crowd that gathered outside his home led his landlord to ask
Westrick to leave. BSC-instigated action also led to Westrick's losing
his driver's license and finally his recall to Germany. One upshot of this
operation by Intrepid's people was that the *Herald Tribune* was nominated for the Pulitzer Prize for these planted articles.[50]

As for Congressman Hamilton Fish, the voters, of course, were in-
nocent of the coordination between British intelligence agent Sandy
Griffith and Special Assistant to the Attorney General William Power
Maloney and columnist Drew Pearson. What the public saw was the
headlines of October 29, 1942: "U.S. JURY CALLS 2 N.Y. EXECUTIVES
TO EXPLAIN CHECKS FOR REP. FISH" or "TWO SUBPOENAED IN FISH
INQUIRY."[51]

There was more to come for the harried Fish on the Monday before
the election. That morning the five-column headline in the *Beacon
News* of Beacon, New York, in Fish's district, announced: "WRITER
SEEKS $250,000 LIBEL DAMAGE FROM HAM FISH; 'LIAR' REMARK IS BASIS
OF LAWSUIT."[52]

This was a bold and imaginative effort by British intelligence and the White House as they pursued their mutual goal of relieving Ham Fish of his congressional seat. Immediate results, however, were rather disappointing. Ham Fish defeated his Democrat-American Labor Party opponent, Ferdinand A. Hoyt, by 4,000 votes out of a total of approximately 100,000.

In *Second Chance: The Triumph of Internationalism in America During World War II*, historian Robert Divine calls this 1942 election a "jolting setback" for Roosevelt and the internationalists. "The election," he writes, "created widespread gloom. English observers feared that the United States would once again repudiate its responsibilities as a world leader...."[53]

The Hoyt for Congress Committee, however, did not seem publicly discouraged and continued to try to damage Fish as much as possible by emphasizing the large number who voted against Fish and by continuing to tie him to the Nazis: "The 44,691 citizens in the Twenty-sixth District saw the defeat of Hamilton Fish as a matter of national importance. They properly construed the broadcast from Berlin in August, praising the renomination of Fish, and the broadcast from Tokyo Sunday night, 1 November, urging his re-election, as signs which lent weight to their opinion."[54]

In a letter dated November 7, 1942, G. F. Hansen-Sturm, assistant treasurer of the Romanoff Caviar Company, wrote to Drew Pearson denying most of the "facts" in the article, starting with the misspelling of the family name and pointing out that the payments allegedly made to Fish were made before the United States entered the war and had actually gone to the National Committee to Keep America Out of Foreign Wars, which included fifty congressman, one of whom was Fish as chairman. This letter must have prompted Pearson to call Sandy Griffith, because at the bottom of the letter, in what appears to be Pearson's hand, is Sandy Griffith's address and phone number.[55]

Drew Pearson wrote two pertinent letters on November 12, 1942, one to Henry Hoke, the other to Sandy Griffith. To Sandy Griffith he wrote: "...also, I would appreciate a little advice as to whether I should go ahead with this Ham Fish suit or not. Personally I am inclined against it. I have enough to do writing the column, and the less I see of the courts the better."[56]

To Henry Hoke, Pearson wrote about the failed campaign against Fish: "Thanks for your good letter. I sure am sorry we didn't put things across, but we did the best we could. Anyway it was a good race." Pearson wrote further that he would be willing to take the libel case against Fish to trial if there was anything to gain. Sandy Griffith wrote back to Pearson on November 19. He had "discussed your problem with a couple of wise lawyers," who feared that in a trial Fish's attorneys might be able to prevent Pearson from making "Fish's Nazi affiliations" the major issue. "But dragging the case out indefinitely might have some value...it would offset any capital Fish might make of your dropping the case."[57]

Pearson wrote back agreeing with Sandy and his wise lawyer friends. Fish was to be left with the suit hanging over his head as a distraction.[58]

In *The Hawks of World War II*, author Mark Lincoln Chadwin identifies members of the executive committee of Fight for Freedom who were the most popular speakers: Herbert Agar, Alexander Woollcott, Rex Stout, and Wendell Willkie. Of these we have a good record of Wendell Willkie, the nominal leader of the Republican Party, and his work with President Franklin D. Roosevelt to dispose of Republican Congressman Fish.

A February 21, 1942, note from President Roosevelt inviting Willkie to lunch says: "By the way, it seems to me that the problem of Fish is just as much a problem as it was when we talked it over many months ago. I have various recommendations for candidates."[59]

Roosevelt suggested Warren Lawes as Fish opponent. Roosevelt to Willkie April 15: "I did enjoy that little party the other night a lot. We did not get very far on the Ham Fish Matter." Willkie reported back on April 27, and then on June 2 he reported the death of Dan Gleason, who had been helping against Fish—"since which time the whole matter has been in some confusion."[60]

That the anti-Fish effort consumed considerable effort and time is also recorded by FDR's assistant William Hassett: "July 11, [1942,] Saturday: Told me Wendell Willkie was coming up from New York to see him—state and congressional politics. The Boss and Wendell Willkie have this in common: they both hate Ham Fish and Tom Dewey."[61]

The British had high hopes that Willkie could help them eliminate American isolationism. Historian Christopher Thorne is certainly correct on British hopes for the Hoosier: "...Wendell Willkie, on whom considerable thought and care was already being focused by Whitehall …and who, it was hoped, could help prevent his party [the Republicans] from adopting an isolationist attitude after the war."[62]

The Foreign Office and the British ambassador in Washington were in turn working closely with Intrepid and BSC. In his foreword to the secret "BSC Account," the "Bible," Sir William Stephenson writes: "…one feels impelled to make specific mention of the close cooperation afforded BSC by H.M. Embassy in Washington—without which much that was achieved could not have been. Lord Lothian's intimate concern in the early days proved invaluable; and so, too, did the unfailing support subsequently given by Lord Halifax."[63]

According to the notes of Willkie's extremely friendly biographer Ellsworth Barnard of the Lord Halifax file in Willkie's papers: "Shows W.[illkie] was working very closely with the British embassy early in 1941 getting confidential information for use in his speeches about aid."[64]

This cooperation extended into 1942, and it specifically concerned Willkie's efforts to get rid of the isolationists, Fish in particular. Isaiah Berlin was the political commentator in the British embassy in Washington. To wit:

> March 20, 1942—Willkie, whom I saw a few days ago, is doing all he can to prevent the inevitable reaction against the Administration in forthcoming congressional elections from accruing to benefit of isolationists groups who are active underground.

> 4 June 1942—Willkie told a member of my staff recently that he thought the extreme isolationists would be gradually eliminated from the Republican Party in the course of the primaries.…Fish would probably not be nominated though there might be a hard fight for this.…Willkie expects the Republicans to lose fifteen to twenty in the House when the election takes place.[65]

So here again was the three-cornered relationship that made so many of these operations a success and moved the United States irrevocably into the international arena—British Security Coordination, the Anglophile elite, and the White House.

Fish was finally defeated in 1944, but then he was faced by an additional burden, which when coupled to his other problems proved to be more than he could overcome. This problem was created in 1942. It was then that the New York state legislature chopped Fish's district—Orange, Dutchess, and Putnam counties—into three pieces. Putnam and Dutchess counties were linked to other counties already having representatives. Since he lived at Garrison in Putnam County, Fish would have been stuck in a race against an incumbent. To avoid this, Fish announced, in early 1942, that he would be moving his residence to Newburgh in Orange County, the 29th Congressional District, which would not have an incumbent. Although this change of residence avoided the race against an incumbent, it placed him at a disadvantage and opened him to ridicule by his opponents.

Other problems continued to dog the congressman. There was an old familiar one over Fish's misuse of the congressional frank. This variant of the problem apparently had its origin in 1942 when a booklet was published—by the Seventeenth District American Legion Americanism Committee of California—making the standard charges of misuse of the franking privilege.

Since Fish, a well-decorated officer (Silver Star, French Croix de Guerre) of World War I, had been active in American Legion affairs, this was a serious blow. But far worse was a resolution passed at the 1943 annual Legion convention in Omaha, Nebraska, charging that Fish had allowed the misuse of his frank for subversive and un-American activities. This sorely distracted Fish, who felt obliged to make a lengthy defense of himself at Indianapolis, Indiana.

Only in May 1944 did the Legion announce the report of a special committee that exonerated Fish completely. But this was late in the game, and though false, the charges had taken their toll in time and travel and added to the incremental damage that all the charges had recorded.[66]

As in the past, Fish had several visible and vigorous antagonists in this election. Probably the most visible was New York governor and presidential aspirant Dewey. He was under great pressure from the internationalist Willkie wing of the Republican Party to endorse a postwar international organization and to attack Fish. As late as July 26, 1944, he refused four times in one day to comment on Fish's reelection. Eventually Dewey came out against Fish.

The other antagonists were Helen Hayes, one of the leaders of the theater, radio, and arts division of Fight for Freedom,[67] playwright Maxwell Anderson, and Rex Stout, who had participated in other BSC fronts and had worked directly for BSC on the anti–I.G. Farben book *Sequel to the Apocalypse*. Anderson dredged up all the old charges and ran them in advertisements in several papers and even published a poem, "Mr. Fish Crosses the River," in *The New Yorker*, ridiculing Fish's change of residence.[68]

The breaking up of his district and the incessant charges—usually false or wildly misleading—all took their toll. In the election Fish was defeated by five thousand votes. Historian Richard Hanks in summing up this defeat has written: "Fish lost the election because of his own errors of judgement and because of the swirl of controversy that descended around him—whether the charges had substance or not. He was a part of another era in American history and his removal from the Congress, while hardly an enthusiastic endorsement of internationalism, was a notification that the electorate was moving into a new age with new expectations."[69]

I would argue that it would have been difficult for any one person to have the judgment and political acumen necessary to long survive the incessant, constantly shifting, all-pervasive political warfare directed against Fish by British intelligence with the connivance of the White House. At that, it took three major efforts by his foes finally to defeat him. Christopher Emmet's words before the election of 1940 bear repeating, for they are the very essence of what the defeat of Fish meant: "If...we can defeat Fish, who has been considered invincible for twenty years, we will put the fear of God into every isolationist senator and congressman in the country."[70]

Given the collective forces aligned against him and their ruthless tactics, the duration of Fish's survival is a tribute to his tenacity and energy and perhaps even to his inflexibility. We will now examine a senator who, by demonstrating greater flexibility, enjoyed more survivability.

CHAPTER 7

•••

Uncle Arthur

There is no question that the British planted Kay Summersby, the British WAC, on Eisenhower, and there was the neat way in which the British foisted Mitzi Sims, wife of the Canadian counselor, on Sen. Arthur Vandenberg and later, the attractive British widow, Mrs. Paterson [sic].

—Drew Pearson[1]

British intelligence operations on Senator Arthur Vandenberg were based on a very simple human assumption—those who are sleeping with a senator are most likely to have his ear. In recent years the American public has been treated to a catalog of hairdressers, movie stars, models, and would-be models whose liaisons with statesmen and would-be statesmen have enlivened the pages of the national press. There is a major difference, however, between the amorous revelations of the recent past and those of this account of the World War II era.

With the possible exception of Judith Campbell Exner, John F. Kennedy's paramour, who acted as a courier between Kennedy and the Mafia, none of these recently revealed lovers was the emissary of a great power. They were, by most accounts, independent and unaffiliated United States citizens, not special pleaders for a foreign power. Their endeavors posed little threat to the political direction of the state.

The bedmates discussed in this chapter are something quite different: they were the covert intelligence agents and lobbyists of a foreign power. Although other high officials and even office workers were

137

targeted for similar attention by British intelligence, this chapter explores the efforts made to track and influence Senator Arthur Vandenberg, Republican of Michigan.

Senator Vandenberg's disposition toward the British was extremely important to them during the period 1939–49, and had he won the Republican presidential nomination in 1940, it would have been even more important. Certainly his attitude toward Great Britain would not be allowed to dangle on mere chance or personal whim, particularly when there were such fine opportunities to give chance and whim a nudge.

To some extent these women operated as moles, ferreting out information from Senator Vandenberg and his colleagues, but far more important, they were "agents of influence." Ernest Cuneo, code name Crusader, the liaison between British intelligence, the White House, OSS, the Treasury, and the Justice Department, was quite correct when he wrote: "An Agent of Influence is rated far above even the mightiest of Moles."[2]

Historians have long noted that Vandenberg, a prominent isolationist in the late 1930s, had a surprising change of heart in the mid-1940s. Thereafter he helped champion the legislation that involved the United States in the affairs of the world and prevented it from retreating into itself after World War II. In a 1962 article in *The New Yorker*, Richard H. Rovere wrote: "It was Vandenberg's conversion from isolationism…that made him a large figure in the postwar world. Without his help, it is at least conceivable that Roosevelt and Truman would have suffered the fate of Woodrow Wilson."[3]

Before recent times the private adventures of prominent politicians were not seen as fit subjects for the legitimate press. *New York Times* political reporter R. W. Apple, Jr., told of the old journalistic ethic in a 1987 article: "In early 1963, for example, a fledgling reporter for this newspaper was assigned to patrol the lobby of the Carlyle Hotel while President Kennedy was visiting New York City. The reporter's job was to observe the coming and going of politicians, but what he saw was the coming and going of a prominent actress, so that was what he reported to his editor. 'No story there,' said the editor, and the matter was dropped."[4]

Both Arthur Krock of the *New York Times* and syndicated columnist Drew Pearson knew of Senator Vandenberg's fondness for women.

Playing on the name of one of those women, wags in Washington apparently called Vandenberg "the Senator from Mitzi-Sims" or "the Senator from Mitzi-gan." Neither Krock nor Pearson mentioned this in public print for two decades. Both writers do say they questioned Vandenberg.

Vandenberg died on April 18, 1951. Two days later, Drew Pearson wrote a diary entry on the senator. Part of it reads: "I recall vividly two conversations with Vandenberg: one was when he returned from Detroit in the spring of '48, and I told him half-jokingly that some of his friends in Michigan had quoted him as saying that he would not run for President because if he did 'Drew Pearson would bring out the facts regarding the "Senator from Mitzi-Sims." ' I told Vandenberg: 'Senator, I would not write that story....' "[5]

Arthur Hendrick Vandenberg was born into a solidly middle-class family in Grand Rapids, Michigan, on March 22, 1884. Unfortunately his father lost everything in the panic of 1893; young Arthur was forced to work: "I had no youth. I went to work when I was nine, and I never got a chance to enjoy myself until I came to the Senate."[6]

He attended the University of Michigan briefly, 1900–1901, to study law. Soon out of money, he returned to Grand Rapids, to his girlfriend and to employment in the newspaper business. By 1906 he was managing editor of the *Grand Rapids Herald* at the then munificent salary of $2,500 a year. As editor he fell into the mold of progressive Republicanism, advocating "moderate and practical reforms" on the domestic front. World War I and Wilson brought out his patriotism, but by the time of the vote on the League of Nations he was a reservationist.

By 1928 the man who had dropped out of college for lack of money was a millionaire. His diligence had made him board chairman of Federated Publications, which published not only the *Grand Rapids Herald* but the *Battle Creek Enquirer and News* and the *Lansing State Journal.* Now he could afford the political career he had long wished to pursue.

Vandenberg became senator from Michigan on the March 1928 resignation and death of the incumbent, Woodbridge N. Ferris. After some arm-twisting, Governor Fred W. Green finally kept his political promise to appoint Vandenberg to the remainder of Ferris's term.[7]

The new senator soon acquired the reputation that historians have passed down. Fred Rodell styled Vandenberg as "more like a strutting, orating, Claghornesque caricature than any Northerner in history."

The comment that he was "the only Senator who can strut sitting down" was to be repeated over and over for the rest of his career. The *Chicago Tribune*'s well-connected reporter Walter Trohan writes: "I knew Vandenberg quite well. I was paid, in part, to know him. I confess I was not fond of him.... Politicians as a class are vain but he was vain beyond most of the tribe. His chief conversation was on his last speech or the one he had in preparation.... I remember seeing him when he had moved into William Borah's office after the latter's death [January 19, 1940] and gloated in calling it to my attention as though he had inherited Borah's role of spokesman on foreign policy, at least for the GOP."[8]

This was a typical male view of Arthur Vandenberg; however, given the testimony of one of the British women involved with the senator, this must still be considered a one-dimensional perspective of Vandenberg.

Lady Cotter—Mrs. John F. Paterson during the time of our interest—remembers Arthur Vandenberg as "delightful—interesting and amusing...kind and generous...no bad attributes...[from him she received] tremendous friendship and understanding."[9] Other qualities not mentioned by those put off by the senator's vanity were his willingness to work and his great drive to succeed.

Although he became a friend and in many ways a protégé of isolationist William Borah, Vandenberg was a supporter of President Hoover's emphasis on restrained American involvement in world affairs. But the Depression closed in on the Hoover administration, and the focus of his successor, Franklin Roosevelt, was on domestic policy.

One piece of domestic legislation fostered by Vandenberg is especially interesting because it illustrates not only his intelligence and diligence but the deftness of FDR and his smooth publicity machine. In 1933, Vandenberg managed to push through federal insurance on bank deposits over the strong objection of Franklin Roosevelt. Indeed, Vandenberg has been called the father of the FDIC. Once the legislation proved itself popular and successful, the White House took pains to deny that Vandenberg had anything to do with the law. Judge Samuel I. Rosenman, FDR's speechwriter, listed the FDIC as one of FDR's great accomplishments. Raymond Moley noted that FDR, "despite his last-ditch opposition, in later years claimed credit for the Legislation."[10]

In 1934, Vandenberg was one of the few Republicans who was returned to the Senate. In fact, for the first two years of the New Deal, Vandenberg's conciliatory performance marked him as a "New Deal Republican." Perhaps this was the key to his survival. The "Second New Deal," starting in mid-1935, was quite another case, however, and Vandenberg fought that vigorously on the basis of constitutionalism.

Arthur Vandenberg's reputation as an isolationist undoubtedly had its origins in his sponsorship, with Gerald Nye of North Dakota, of Senate Resolution 206, to investigate the munitions industry. His work on the Nye investigation convinced him that the United States' entry into World War I had been a mistake.

A trip to Europe in the summer of 1935 further strengthened these feelings, and by 1936 Vandenberg supported the isolationist position advocated by Senators Nye and J. Bennett Clark of Missouri.[11] 1936 was not a good year for the Republican Party; Franklin Roosevelt had a 523–8 electoral college victory over Alfred Landon, and only seventeen Republicans remained in the Senate after the election.

Vandenberg was disturbed by these political disasters, but for him personally there had been positive developments. He had often been mentioned as a possible presidential candidate in 1936 and could easily have had the party's nomination for vice president. After the party's defeat, Vandenberg was considered the leader of the Republicans in the Senate. According to Vandenberg biographer David Tompkins, "during 1937 most opinion polls rated him as the Republican voters' first choice for the nomination." Lord Beaverbrook, the Canadian publisher friend of both Churchill and BSC head William Stephenson, pronounced Vandenberg the "next president."[12] Vandenberg publicly denied any presidential aspirations. But his high rankings persisted.

Ominous events in Europe were also afoot. In March 1936, Britain increased its defense budget in response to international tensions. Germany, citing danger from the recent Franco-Soviet alliance, reoccupied the Rhineland. In October 1936 the Rome-Berlin Axis was formed.

This was the unstable background of world tensions and Arthur Vandenberg's personal prospects that underlay the developing relationship with the socially adept Simses—Mitzi and Harold. Mitzi Sims is probably the woman to whom *New York Times* correspondent Arthur Krock was referring when years later he wrote: "Vandenberg's romantic impulses led to gossip at Washington hen-parties, where the hens have teeth and the teeth are sharp, that Vandenberg had been 'converted' from isolationism by the pretty wife of a West European diplomat, a lady of whom, as the saying goes, he saw a lot."[13]

One of Mitzi's nieces told me in a 1987 telephone interview: "Aunt Mitzi was a jet-setter before there were jets. She and Harold ran around with the Duke of Windsor and that crowd....Mitzi had lots of beaus—why, Arthur Vandenberg was one of her beaus—you aren't going to print that, are you?" Few entries in Mrs. Vandenberg's diary mention the Simses until a dinner in April 1937; then in May 1937 the Vandenbergs drove the Simses back from a party to the Wardman Park Hotel, a residential hotel where both couples lived. Invited up to the Simses' apartment, the Vandenbergs stayed until 5:00 A.M. and had, according to Mrs. Vandenberg's diary, "Some Eve."

It is clear from Mrs. Vandenberg's diary entries of 1937 that she and Senator Vandenberg knew the Simses casually, but the entries are formal and their full names—Mitzi Sims, Harold Sims—are usually written out.[14] They are clearly not the "Mitzi" and "Harold" that were soon to dominate the Vandenbergs' social life until Harold's unexpected death in May 1940 and Mitzi's departure on February 11, 1941, just days before British intelligence's most adept and famous agent, Betty Pack, "Cynthia," appeared.

Harold Haig Sims was born in 1880 into what the *Montreal Star* said years later was "an old established" Montreal family. His father had been a prominent manufacturer in that city. He was educated at Bishops College School, Lennoxville, and then McGill University. He worked in banking in London before returning to Montreal, where he worked in the insurance business. In 1917 he became "associated with the British Government." He went to Washington with the British War Mission and afterward was appointed an attaché at the British embassy.

As a wealthy man, Harold Sims worked "in a commercial and diplomatic capacity," without compensation. As was fitting for a man of wealth and social position, Harold belonged to the St. James Club, Royal Montreal Golf Club, Montreal Racket Club, Montreal Hunt, and Zeta Psi Fraternity.[15]

His obituary in the *Washington Post* supports the statements of Harold's nieces in a series of telephone interviews in 1987. Harold was a "friend of the Duke of Windsor....He was to have played host to the

Duke and Duchess of Windsor during their proposed trip to the United States in 1937."[16] The vagueness of all references to Harold's employment by the British government is striking but explicable. One of his nieces told me that he "ran the code room at the embassy." They told me that both their father, Ross Sims of Montreal, and "Uncle Harold" knew Sir William Stephenson and that their father had hired girls for him in Canada.[17]

Harold Sims had, in 1926, married Emelia Mauritsen Hemmerde, the widow of Captain Eric Hemmerde, a British officer killed in France during the Great War.[18] A newspaper clipping found in Mrs. Vandenberg's diary, from January 1937, has both a picture of Mitzi and Harold and a description of her social skills. The striking thing about this description is that it fits all three of these women, not just Mitzi.

"Among the guests at the recent reception at the Norwegian Legation was Mrs. Harold Sims (center), who is always the center of an animated group at any event she attends. An exceptionally good conversationalist, she is one of the few social notables in Washington who never need to rely on the weather as a topic of repartee."

Arthur Vandenberg had indeed come a long way from the poor boy who went to work at nine years old and the impoverished student forced to drop out of college. For the next decade the women he associated with—Mitzi Sims, Cynthia, Eveline Paterson—came from a far more glamorous world than Grand Rapids. Because of their wide travels they also represented a more cosmopolitan world than Washington, D.C. They were all very handsome, and noted by even the hard-bitten for their charm.[19]

By 1940 the Vandenbergs and Simses were close friends.[20] But Harold was under great strain from overwork, and on May 6, 1940, he had a stroke and died. According to the statement issued by the first secretary of the British Embassy, F. R. Hoyer Miller, Harold "had come here early and left late every day since the war began." The *Washington Times-Herald* called Harold Sims "Great Britain's first casualty of the war to occur in this country."[21]

The *Washington Post* in its obituary succinctly states facts that have been completely weeded from the senator's own papers: "He and Mrs. Sims were close friends of Senator Vandenberg of Michigan, a Republican Presidential candidate, who was notified of his death and took charge of funeral arrangements."[22]

Mitzi and Harold Sims were unquestionably well placed to keep an eye on an important man; a December 1939 poll found a majority of 481 daily newspaper editors predicted Vandenberg would be chosen as the presidential candidate of the GOP. The exact date when Arthur Vandenberg became one of Mitzi's "beaus" is not known, but most probably it was between 1937 and 1939.

According to middle-class mores it would seem remarkable to be close friends with the husband of one's mistress, but the Simses' milieu was worldly. The recent *Life of the Party: The Biography of Pamela Digby Churchill Hayward Harriman* well illustrates the temper of the time within the British upper class. Author Christopher Ogden describes the love affair between Winston Churchill's daughter-in-law, Pamela Churchill, and President Roosevelt's Lend-Lease expediter in England, Averell Harriman. According to Ogden, Winston Churchill's intimate friend the wealthy Canadian Max Aitken, Lord Beaverbrook, "was delighted. Averell had been in Britain only a matter of days and already he was compromised." She could pass to Winston and Max what the Americans were thinking and planning. She could pass on to the Americans through Averell whatever spin Britain wanted delivered. American Ambassador Gilbert Winant was also similarly compromised. Although married, he was sleeping with Winston Churchill's daughter Sarah. This affair drove him to distraction and perhaps even to his death by suicide when she broke it off after the war.[23]

The "close" friendship of the Vandenbergs and the Simses permitted the Simses to explore the thinking of a major figure on the Senate Foreign Relations Committee during the beginning of an extremely dangerous period for the British.

Most historians consider Vandenberg's official break from isolationism to be his prominent speech in the Senate on January 10, 1945. Mrs. Vandenberg in her diary dates the break much earlier, from a radio speech he delivered on June 9, 1940. She states that the speech made Arthur the chief subject of discussion in Washington the next day.[24] Why historians have generally overlooked this speech is difficult to explain.

Walter Trohan, the reporter for the isolationist *Chicago Tribune*, tells of Vandenberg's relationship with Mitzi Sims and the senator's conversion: "One evening I attended a small dinner party in the dining room of his [Senator Vandenberg's] Wardman Park apartment.

Sen. Burton K. Wheeler (D. Mont.) and Gerald P. Nye (R. N.D.) were there along with me at a strategy huddle on keeping out of World War II. Vandenberg was known among wits in the Senate and in the press gallery as the Senator from Mitzi-gan. Mrs. Hazel Vandenberg, the Senator's second wife, had left him and returned to their Grand Rapids home because he moved Mitzi into an adjoining apartment. Mitzi acted as hostess for the dinner. When it ended and we were settled down to business, she rose and we all rose. She walked over to him and patted him on the cheek, exclaiming: 'Good night you great big statesman!'"[25]

Though there is strong testimony that Mitzi Sims was involved with Arthur Vandenberg at the time he became an internationalist, there is no definite proof that she or her husband caused this metamorphosis. But it is hard to believe that the Simses, as best social companions of the Vandenbergs, could have been without influence. Someone thought the Simses important enough to remove all references to them from Arthur Vandenberg's papers. The separate and previously unused diaries of Mrs. Vandenberg have the only mentions of Harold and Mitzi. It should be further remembered that the Sims family claimed close ties with William Stephenson.

The Simses had the most important thing a lobbyist needs—access. There is another indication that British intelligence thought Mitzi had influence over Vandenberg. This came with her sudden and unexpected return to the Vandenbergs during the great behind-the-scenes push for Lend-Lease in early 1941. When, after a week, she left the Vandenbergs again she was quickly followed by one of Britain's most famous woman spies.

In *1940: Myth and Reality*, Clive Ponting has written an interesting and useful book whose main thesis is that since 1940, Britain cultivated the myth of the "special relationship with the United States" to paper over the embarrassing fact that it was a "client state" of the United States. He is surely wrong, however, on one small statement concerning Lend-Lease: "Britain then had to wait helpless on the sidelines while Congress spent the next two months in hearings. 'Lend-Lease' finally became Law on 11 March."[26]

This feigned helplessness has long prevented historians from carefully analyzing precisely how the desperate British helped their own cause. The consequences of leaving Britain's very survival in the hands of an ignorant, capricious rabble of windbags, blown hither and thither by every gust of public opinion, was simply too much for the British to bear. Since the British had great influence with the press and few papers published news of sexual peccadilloes by public figures, the minimal chances of being exposed were trivial when weighed against the prospects of success.

One of the few public suggestions of these delicate operations has come recently from prominent British author Mary Lovell in her book *Cast No Shadow*, the biography of the famous British spy Betty Thorpe Pack—"Cynthia." Writes Lovell: "Betty's second mission for British Security Coordination was to try to convert the opinions of Senators Connally and Vandenberg into, if not support, a less heated opposition to the bill [Lend-Lease] which literally meant the difference between survival and defeat for the British. Other agents of both sexes were given similar missions with other politicians.... With Vandenberg Betty was successful; with Senator Connally, chairman of the Senate Committee on Foreign Relations (which was holding hearings on the bill), she was not."[27]

Connally seems to have seen through Cynthia's game rather quickly. Almost as soon as she had finagled an introduction at a party, Connally told her: "You're wasting your time, my dear—come over here and sit on my knee instead."[28]

Of the three women involved with Senator Vandenberg, Amy Elizabeth Thorpe Pack Brousse, known almost universally to those even mildly interested in the history of British intelligence by her *nom d'espionage*, Cynthia, is the agent we know the most about. Her death on December 1, 1963, brought not the standard cramped death notice *Time* magazine usually gives the famous but two-thirds of a page and included her debutante portrait.[29]

The secret "BSC Account" says of her: "It would be difficult to over-emphasize the importance of her work....Her security was irreproachable and her loyalty to her employers complete. She was not greedy for money but greedy only to serve a cause in which she believed. In fact she was paid a small salary which represented little more than her living expenses, although the value of her work to Britain could be assessed, if at all, in millions."[30]

Her most recent biographer, Mary S. Lovell, summarizes Cynthia's modus operandi: "She singled out top men and seduced them."[31]

Elizabeth Thorpe was born on November 22, 1910, in Minneapolis. Her father, George C. Thorpe (1875–1936) was a military man and author of several volumes on both military and legal subjects. After retiring from the Marines in 1922 with the rank of colonel, he practiced law in Washington until his death. Her socially ambitious mother, Cora Wells Thorpe, graduated cum laude from the University of Michigan and did graduate work at the Sorbonne in Paris, the University of Munich, and Columbia.[32]

Arthur Vandenberg and his future second wife, Hazel Whitaker, met at the University of Michigan during the 1900–1901 school year, Vandenberg's only year of college. Although he had Elizabeth Watson, his high school sweetheart, whom he was to marry in 1906, back in Grand Rapids, Arthur generally squired Hazel to social events at Michigan.

Elizabeth Watson Vandenberg died of a brain tumor in May 1917, leaving him with two daughters and a son. He waited only a year to marry Hazel. Hazel and Cora Thorpe, Cynthia's mother, also attended the University of Michigan in the 1901–1902 and 1902–1903 school years. They were both enrolled in the College of Literature, Science, and the Arts. They also lived within a couple of blocks of each other.[33] This may have been where they met. The tone of Hazel's diary entries indicates that they knew each other well.

On April 29, 1930, Betty Thorpe married Arthur J. Pack at the Church of the Epiphany in Washington, D.C. In the small world of British diplomacy it should not be surprising to find "H. H. Sims, attaché of the British Embassy" as a member of the wedding party.[34]

Betty was pregnant at the time of the wedding. The boy, born October 2, 1930, was raised in England by others, because Arthur feared the effects knowledge of an out-of-wedlock pregnancy would have on his diplomatic career.

The Packs were posted to Latin America in the early 1930s and in 1935 to Spain. Here Betty's lovers even included the priest who was helping her spiritual growth in her newly adopted Catholicism: "…it was more than the flame of religion that was kept alive in my breast. The priest was a good looking young man…and [there] followed a series of secret meetings once or twice a week at the apartment….as he was poor and the cost of rooms high I was always happy to help him out with the bill." Betty became involved in the Spanish Civil War and with British intelligence as well as with various lovers.[35]

The next assignment for the Packs was Poland. Betty arrived there in September 1937. In early 1938, Arthur being absent, sick in England, Betty took as lover a diplomat, Edward Kulikowski, who held a good position in the Polish Foreign Office. He casually mentioned to her that Hitler's next target was Czechoslovakia. "What is more," he told her, "Poland intends to take a bite of the cherry!" This startling bit of information she passed on to the Passport Control officer, Lieutenant-Colonel Jack Shelley. Passport Control, was, of course, the worldwide cover for SIS. By March 1938, Betty was actively working for the Secret Intelligence Service (MI-6).[36]

Betty's next conquest was Count Michael Lubienski, a handsome man with the courtly manners and charm for which the Polish aristocracy was well known. He also happened to be *chef de cabinet* to Colonel Joseph Beck, the Polish foreign minister. There is strong evidence she obtained news from Michael Lubienski of the progress the Polish were making against the German Enigma cypher machine. Until the 1970s this was one of the most closely guarded secrets of the war. Betty's role is still not entirely clear.[37] This affair with Lubienski led, in September 1938, to Beck's asking the British to get her out of Poland, which they did.

By May 1939 the Packs had been sent to Chile, where Betty whiled away her time socializing, playing polo, and writing political reports on the Nazi sympathies of prominent Chileans. This was followed in September 1939 by a series of anti-Nazi propaganda articles on the European situation. These were written under the pen name Elizabeth Thomas, and the English versions appeared in the English-language *South Pacific Mail*.

In early 1940 the German ambassador learned the true identity of "Elizabeth Thomas" and threatened to make a formal complaint to the Chilean government that Betty was abusing her diplomatic privileges. So her writing stopped. The result was that by January 1941 she was back in Washington without her husband. Betty had this time been contacted by British Security Coordination's John Pepper, "a cagey operator" according to one of his fellow BSC officers, Bill Ross-Smith. Her contacts at BSC were either Pepper or a woman named Marion de Chastellaine. It was at this time that she was given the code name Cynthia.[38]

In Washington, Betty rented a house at 3327 O Street. Betty's mother, Cora Thorpe, who lived at 2139 Wyoming Avenue, was well established in Washington society and was of great use to Betty. We have a description of this apartment and Betty from an FBI agent who interviewed her there on December 24, 1942: "It was noted during this interview that Mrs. Pack was extremely well dressed and well groomed and that she appeared to have been well educated. It was also noted that her mother's apartment was expensively furnished in good taste."[39]

Betty arrived to help with the Lend-Lease bill, passage of which was desperately needed by the British. She was not the only one who arrived unexpectedly during the Lend-Lease debates. Mitzi Sims had given up the Wardman Park apartment shortly after Harold's death and moved back to Montreal.

On Monday, February 3, 1941, Hazel Vandenberg's diary records the sudden, timely, but unexpected arrival of Mitzi. She stayed with the Vandenbergs until Tuesday, February 11, when she suddenly flew back to Montreal, never to be seen by the Vandenbergs again.

As a houseguest and one-time flame of Arthur Vandenberg's, Mitzi was during this crucial period in a good position to lobby the senator on Lend-Lease. Mrs. Vandenberg's entry of February 6, 1941, records that both she and Mitzi attended the Foreign Relations Committee hearings on Lend-Lease that day.

Mitzi certainly had time alone with Arthur: "Sat. Feb. 8, 41. Went to see 'The Male Animal' with Cora Thorpe," wrote Mrs. Vandenberg. "From there I went to the Tydings where I met Dad and Mitzi." The forces of isolationism were not to have a free time with the senator after Mitzi returned to Montreal. On February 27, 1941, Hazel Vandenberg opened her apartment door in the Wardman Park Hotel and found new company. She wrote in her diary: "Cora T[horpe] came with daughter, Betty Pack, back again from Chile for why I do not know."[40] Mrs. Vandenberg may have gotten suspicious of Betty sometime after this, because the next diary entry that mentions her reads: "Friday March 21, 1941—Lunched with the Countess Cassini at Pierre's. Mrs. Chandler, Cafritz, the Baroness von Pagenhardt, Ruth Hurley, Cora Letts, Polly Guggenheim, Betty Pack and Mrs. Fred Mitchell Gould, queer collection and one wondered why. I know why I went!"

The next Friday, Mrs. Vandenberg had been invited to tea at Betty Pack's for the Count and Countess Bouillant, but she was sick and did not go.

The record of Senator Vandenberg and Cynthia trails off here, but her career as a first-class agent was to go on to the further seductions, embassy break-ins, and code thefts that have entertained readers of four books: *The Quiet Canadian, Cynthia, A Man Called Intrepid,* and *Cast No Shadow.*

At the end of the war the British were in a difficult position. Not only was Britain destitute, the Lend-Lease debt was enormous. British Security Coordination's David Ogilvy, then working on economic matters out of the British embassy in Washington, wrote that the British government had three choices: default, pay up, or talk the Americans into canceling the debt. To default would be politically calamitous, to pay up was impossible. The third option, being the only one possible, was the one taken.[41]

Debt of $4 billion was canceled; $6 billion worth of property in Britain was sold to the king for $532 million; Britain would have to pay $118 million for orders already in transit.

Most of the debt was simply wiped away, making this a good start, but since Britain had lost one-fourth of her wealth during the war, this still left the United Kingdom destitute. Poll results indicated that the American public would be of little help. In June 1946 only 10 percent of Americans gave their unqualified approval of a loan to Britain, while 40 percent disapproved.[42]

Marquis Childs reported in the *Washington Post* that the hearing on the loan began "in an atmosphere of defeatism and pessimism" and added that "very real doubt exists whether Congress will approve the loan proposals." The *Times* of London quoted Sir Stafford Cripps, president of the Board of Trade, as saying that "it looks as if Congress may possibly turn it down."[43]

In the classic work *Sterling Dollar Diplomacy in Current Perspective,* author Richard N. Gardner gives his evaluation of Vandenberg's importance in this dark financial hour for Great Britain: "Perhaps the most powerful appeal of all was made by Senator Vandenberg. In April, before departing for the Paris meeting of the Foreign Ministers, Vandenberg announced on the floor of the Senate that he had finally decided to support the loan. He warned his colleagues: 'If we do not lead some other great and powerful nation will capitalize our failure and we shall pay the price of our default.' This was the turning point in the Senate Debate."[44]

This speech was not a reflection of the mail from home; that was running so strongly against his speech as to make it the most unpopular foreign policy speech Vandenberg had ever given.[45]

Walter Trohan has supplied a fine clue that the checkable parts prove out, but the difficulty of obtaining Office of Naval Intelligence files has prevented full confirmation: "The Office of Naval Intelligence kept a file on the activities of Sims and Paterson....In the 1948 convention at Philadelphia Vandenberg had hopes of being nominated....I played a small role in the Vandenberg stab at the nomination. Joseph Pew, head of the Sun Oil Company and a heavy party contributor, had been given the ONI file on the activities of Mitzi and Paterson. Pew was determined to take the floor and speak on the file and its disclosures. Friends of Pew asked me to persuade him not to do so because they knew I was against such mudslinging....I told Pew that Vandenberg had no chance of winning the nomination and that he would only smear himself by his proposed action, which I was certain would do so. At any length Pew did not do so."[46]

The Englishwoman involved with Senator Vandenberg during the period 1945–48 was at her recent death Eveline Mary Mardon Paterson Cotter. She was born in Naini Tal, India, on October 2, 1908. She died Lady Cotter on February 13, 1991, as the wife of Delaval James Alfred Cotter.[47] Her father had been a civil servant in India who retired to Devonshire, England, where she lived with him until she was married about 1929.

Until July 1940, she and her two children, Jeremy, ten, and Virginia, four, had divided their time between a townhouse in DeVere Gardens, Kensington, London, and a country home in Somerset. They escaped to Canada that summer on one of the last convoyed refugee vessels, the *Monarch of Bermuda*. Her husband, John, a major, had been stationed for the previous three years at Kuala Lumpur in the Malay States.

Once in North America, Eveline stayed with various relatives while speaking on behalf of Great Britain. An undated newspaper clipping from her scrapbook ends: "Mrs. Paterson has been speaking throughout the Middle west, during the past months for the benefit of relief work in Britain."

Newspaper clippings from her scrapbook give a good picture of what she was telling interviewers and audiences on her travels. In the winter and spring of 1941 she was working out of the home of her cousin Mrs. Theodore Baer in Peoria, Illinois.

In February 1941, the Peoria newspapers ran photographs and articles based on interviews with Eveline. She had clearly been well briefed and on Lend-Lease spoke the British propaganda line with exactitude. "We can win if you help us with money and munitions—we don't need your men....The English have plenty of soldiers, and if you Americans only help us by furnishing materials we are sure to win." Although not quoting her words, the reporter wrote after listening to her that the British "are certain that the conquered peoples who now are nearing famine because of the German leader will rise up against him at the first opportunity, and make a British victory possible."[48]

None of these statements was correct, but having a beautiful, charming, and well-spoken person saying them with conviction helped the British cause with the reputedly isolationist people of the Midwest. The articles and headlines—"Englishwoman Is Absorbing Speaker Here"—may to some extent have been the courtesy extended to a foreign visitor, but they are consistent in their praise of Eveline, her charm, and her ability to deliver her message.

To another Peoria reporter Eveline said: "I am quite confident that we will beat them in the end....Churchill and Bevin...are like Dynamite...."[49] Three days after publishing the interview, the *Peoria Journal and Transcript* ran a short notice for "any club or...organization which might like to get a closer understanding of some of the ordeals the courageous British are now enduring."

Those interested were given a phone number to contact "Mrs. Paterson...a charming and cultured woman." Eveline's effort apparently reaped results in Peoria. On April 20, 1941, the *Peoria Journal-Transcript* ran a photograph of the striking Mrs. Paterson, who was distinctly taller than the Rev. Edison Shepard, who was blessing the Bundles for Britain.

According to a poster and clippings in her scrapbook, Mrs. Paterson had been in Warren, New Hampshire, in November 1940: "Mrs. Eveline Paterson of London and Somerset England, and Ontario Canada, who is an authorized worker for the British War Relief heads the committee in charge" of a benefit dance. By July 1941, Eveline was in Cape Cod and was speaking before such groups as the Garden

Club of Hyannis. She must have returned to Peoria, because her daughter remembers starting school there before moving to Washington.[50]

The real question, however, is: was there a relationship between this lovely, well-briefed spokeswoman for the British cause and Senator Arthur Vandenberg? On this issue there is considerable testimony in the affirmative. One of my queries to Mrs. Paterson drew a letter from her daughter suggesting I contact her brother: "He may remember 'Uncle Arthur' (as we knew him) better than I as he is a few years older....I know there was some scandal, but M. was always adamant they were 'just friends,' and he was sympathetic listener to her pleas for the USA to join the war."[51]

When newsman Harry Costello called Drew Pearson on June 5, 1948, to tell him that Vandenberg met "Miss Paterson [sic] at Union Station in Washington and they go into the station restaurant," and that he had seen them together "recently" in New York, the timing is perfect for the Vandenberg Resolution, which cleared the way for an Atlantic alliance (NATO). It passed the Senate on June 11, 1948.[52]

In Mrs. Paterson's scrapbook are several Vandenberg items. Particularly interesting is a note on Wardman Park Hotel stationery. It bears the date "Oct. 1942" and has a photograph of the senator from *U.S. News*. Eveline appears to have known Vandenberg reasonably well by then:

> Sorry to miss you.
> Also sorry about Saturday night when I was previously engaged.
> If you are around about six we might have a drink.
> *R.*

Another piece in Mrs. Paterson's scrapbook is a cover and article from *Time* of April 30, 1945. Arthur Vandenberg is pictured on the cover, along with an article on Vandenberg as an internationalist. From 1944 to 1946 there are numerous clippings indicating that Eveline Paterson was moving in diplomatic circles. She "was a great party person," writes her daughter, "and I remember a lot of the people mentioned" in the clippings.[53]

In 1942, Eveline was involved in "improving the translation of war plans from Norwegian English to English." That year she also spent time in Canada, ostensibly auditioning for a radio show.[54]

After reading Mary S. Lovell's *Cast No Shadow* on Cynthia, Mrs. Paterson's daughter wrote of Cynthia's associates that "the only one that rang a bell…was Donald Downes [BSC/OSS man who ran Cynthia] who we knew quite well."[55]

Mrs. Paterson does remember discussing politics with Senator Vandenberg: "Particularly U.S. entry into the war and support for G[reat] B[ritain]." Is it any wonder, then, that Drew Pearson, Walter Trohan, and the FBI thought that this lovely spokeswoman for the British was a British intelligence agent?

After the war, Francis Henson, Sandy Griffith's assistant, wrote a weekly private intelligence report from Washington to Ernest Cuneo in New York. A note of June 17, 1948, attached to a newspaper clipping reads: "This is the Mrs. Paterson about whom there is so much talk.…" The clipping describes "Mrs. John Paterson…the charming…comely, statuesque blonde." The comment for insiders is the writer's feigned sorrow that Eveline cannot attend the Republican convention. The reference apparently is to the possibility that Vandenberg would be nominated as the Republican candidate.[56]

Before the FBI realized what this author was looking for, it responded to my Freedom of Information Act request with a copy of the clipping Henson sent Cuneo on Mrs. Paterson.

The clipping bore the notation "105—0122—4 ENCLOSURE." According to Ann Mari Buitrago in *Are You Now or Have You Ever Been in the FBI Files*, the prefix code 105 designates "Foreign Counterintelligence Matters…[Frequently used as a 'subversive matter' file, similar to '100;' for investigations purporting to determine whether a person or group is subject to foreign influence, control or financing—author's comment]."[57]

The last digit, the dash 4, signifies that this clipping on Eveline Paterson is the fourth item in her file. Since then, however, the FBI has denied it has a file on Mrs. Paterson. Only after several years did the FBI accept my amended FOIA request for her file without telling me no file exists. Since most of the impact of Mrs. Paterson's lobbying of Senator Vandenberg appears to have taken place outside the time period that concerns this book, a closer investigation of her influence, though merited, will have to wait.

CHAPTER 8

•••

"We Want Willkie"

When they [British intelligence] work up such an incident they apparently use the *New York Tribune* as a means of publication, much the same as they used to use the *Providence Journal* in the World War.

—Assistant Secretary of State
Adolf Berle to Sumner Welles,
September 18, 1941[1]

Indeed, no newspaper people may ever have exercised more decisive influence upon the nomination of a major party candidate than *Tribune* staff members did [in the presidential campaign of 1940]....

—Richard Kluger, *The Paper:
The Life and Death of the
New York Herald Tribune*[2]

In June 1940, the Republicans in convention in Philadelphia nominated Willkie. He was a man who had never held political office—a man who had been a bona fide registered Democrat as late as September 1939 and whose switch to the Republican Party is difficult, perhaps impossible, to document. His nomination exempted his Democratic opponent, President Franklin Roosevelt,[3] from the normal pressures of an election campaign.

This chapter does not propose a new idea; it simply explores an old idea in the light of new evidence. The stunning nature of Willkie's nomination has resulted in the recurrent theme that the nomination was the result of divine intervention. H. L. Mencken, certainly a hard-bitten journalist, and one not usually given to supernatural explanations, wrote, after watching the nomination: "I am thoroughly convinced that the nomination of Willkie was Managed by the Holy Ghost in Person." The serious literature on the convention abounds with awed titles—"Was the Nomination of Wendell Willkie a Political Miracle?"; "The Philadelphia Miracle"; "Miracle in Philadelphia."[4]

Soon after the "miracle in Philadelphia," Earl Browder and Nelson Sparks, from opposite ends of the political spectrum, proposed a more worldly explanation. They said that the nomination of Wendell Willkie had been concocted by British Ambassador Lord Lothian,[5] in connivance with Franklin Roosevelt, Thomas W. Lamont of J. P. Morgan, and columnist Walter Lippmann. Though these accusations have gone largely unnoticed by historians, two of the principles were well aware of them. Thomas W. Lamont was probably the prime mover behind the scenes in the Willkie nomination; he sent President Roosevelt a clipping of a speech by Earl Browder recorded in the Communist *Daily Worker* of September 9, 1940. This is only one of nearly forty contacts—letters, meetings, and phone calls—between FDR and Lamont during the period 1938–40.

Lamont has marked this passage for the president's attention: "...Robert Taft...was defeated in the Philadelphia Convention, and the pro-war, big business, renegade Democrat, Wendell Willkie, was nominated by a conspiratorial junta, organized by Thomas W. Lamont of the firm of J. P. Morgan, working in direct agreement with Roosevelt and engineered by Walter Lippmann. Willkie was chosen for the Republican Party by Roosevelt and Lamont, after an agreement had been reached as to fundamental policy to which all would adhere, the same policy revealed in the President's sensational coup [The Destroyers-for-Bases Deal] of September 3rd."[6]

Roosevelt wrote back to Lamont on September 13, 1940, in obvious good humor: "What is that old saying about politics and strange bedfellows? All I can say, Tom, is that if you can stand it I can." Similar charges were made in Spark's 1943 book *One Man—Wendell Willkie*.[7]

This theme was also later echoed by Harry Elmer Barnes in *Was Roosevelt Pushed into War by Popular Demand in 1941?*[8]

The two quotations that begin this chapter also suggest that Willkie's nomination should be looked at more carefully. Adolf Berle is quite correct that the *New York Herald Tribune* was a tool of British intelligence. Countless operations involved the *Herald Tribune* in one way or another. The historian of the *Herald Tribune*, Richard Kluger, is also correct in his assessment of the *Tribune*'s influence on Willkie's nomination. Now if the *Herald Tribune* was a creature of British intelligence and Willkie's nomination was a creation of the *Herald Tribune*, it follows that Willkie may well have been a creation of British intelligence, especially since Britain was in such dire need of a Republican interventionist candidate. There are now a number of facts available that support the accusations of Browder and Sparks.

First, the people who created the Willkie candidacy were working closely with Franklin Roosevelt. Second, those who created the Willkie candidacy were working closely with British intelligence and its fronts. Third, Willkie was working closely with British intelligence and its fronts, especially Fight for Freedom, on whose executive board he sat. Fourth, Willkie's close work with his ostensible opponent, Franklin Roosevelt, particularly their joint effort to eliminate members of Willkie's newly adopted Republican Party from office, is a collaboration rare, perhaps even unique, in American political history. Last, the secrecy and compartmentalization of the scheme to promote Willkie are a fundamental attribute of intelligence tradecraft; none of the individual toilers working for Willkie's nomination ever knew enough to be able to see the big picture of the operation.

Wendell Lewis Willkie was born Lewis Wendell Willkie (he disliked the original order) on February 18, 1892, in Elwood, Indiana. His mother, Henrietta, had been the first woman admitted to the Indiana bar, and she and Wendell's father, Herman, were law partners. "Wen," as family members called him, was the fourth of six children reared in an intensely intellectual, comfortable, and financially secure home. In the 1940 campaign, Willkie claimed to have grown up "the hard, not the soft way," but this assertion has little basis in fact.[9]

After graduating from Elwood High School in 1910, Willkie followed his older brothers, Robert and Fred, and sister, Julia, to Indiana University at Bloomington. He graduated in 1913. He worked two years, then returned to study law at Indiana, graduating at the top of his class and winning the award for the best thesis. He joined the army in World War I, but did not get shipped overseas until September 1918, when the war was nearly over.[10]

After the war, Willkie secured a position heading the legal department at Firestone Tire and Rubber in Akron, Ohio. He quit Firestone and in 1921 he joined the law firm of Mather and Nesbitt and quickly rose to prominence in the Akron bar; here Willkie's political career as a Democrat also blossomed. As a leader in the Akron Democratic Club, he was elected as a delegate to the 1924 national convention in New York City, where he was a floor leader for Newton D. Baker.[11]

Willkie's successful legal work for Northern Ohio Power and Light gained him the offer of a $36,000 salary to be a partner in the New York law firm representing the Morgan-dominated Commonwealth and Southern utility holding company. Willkie moved to New York in October of 1929. He became president of Commonwealth and Southern on January 24, 1933. The move did not hamper Willkie's involvement in Democratic politics. At the 1932 Democratic convention in Chicago he was a floor manager for Newton D. Baker.

Willkie had one weakness that might have been damaging to his presidential aspirations today, though in the 1930s and 1940s it caused him no public embarrassment: he was a deeply committed and practicing womanizer.

The relationship of most interest here was with Irita Van Doren, the editor of the book review section of the *New York Herald Tribune* and the ex-wife of Carl Van Doren. This was a good match intellectually. Willkie was a habitual reader and book lover. He wrote reviews for her book review section. She introduced him to her literary salon that included some of the most famous writers of the time—Carl Sandburg, Rebecca West, James Thurber, Sinclair Lewis, and Dorothy Thompson, to name a few. She taught him to pronounce the hundreds of words he had seen but never heard.

Irita was a close confidante of a woman who British intelligence said was "among those who rendered service of particular value...Helen Ogden Reid who controls *The New York Herald Tribune*."[12] Willkie met Irita in 1938 when Helen Reid, the real power at the *Herald Tribune*, had him speak at the paper's annual "forum." Despite his marriage to Edith Willkie, Wendell was by 1939 spending weekends at the farmhouse Irita and Carl Van Doren had bought in West Cornwall, Connecticut. He also accompanied her, "frequently," to dinners at the Reids'.[13]

Richard Kluger, the historian of the *Tribune*, wrote: "That summer [1939], they spent a week together at Dorothy Thompson's Vermont farm. Irita encouraged him to think more about his future in political terms and challenged him to work out his views on major issues so that he might express them more forcefully and confidently in his writings and speeches."[14]

Not only did Dorothy Thompson, as we have seen, work closely with major figures in British intelligence, but documents also strongly suggest that one of her houseguests at the time of Willkie's visit was also a British intelligence agent. One recently released document from the Soviet archives is a message from Pavel Mikhailovich Fitin, the head of the foreign intelligence directorate of the NKVD in Moscow: "Wolff's [Milton Wolf, last commander of the Abraham Lincoln Battalion in the Spanish Civil War] introduction to Colonel DONOVAN was organized by the wife of a former correspondent in Spain, VINCENT SHEEAN;...SHEEAN himself is anti-Soviet, and his wife, according to our information, is an agent of British intelligence."[15]

The long week of conversations between Willkie, the Sheeans, and Dorothy Thompson was not without its effects. Thompson emerged from this week as a great Willkie supporter, telling Helen Reid: "If the convention doesn't nominate him, I am going out into the streets and do it myself."[16]

One of Willkie's outstanding talents was his ability to appear wide-eyed and naive, a fresh innocent doing battle with reactionary forces. He used this image to gull reporters, who then passed their reports on to an equally innocent public. The often confused Kansas editor William Allen White thought Willkie was forthright and courageous. Drew Pearson has a reputation for being more hardheaded and searching, but you would never know this from his interview notes: "For sheer force of personality and character, I believe Willkie makes the greatest impact of any man I've ever talked to. He rings true in the very essence of his word."[17]

The inability of seasoned reporters to penetrate this charade is a tribute to Willkie's charisma and his apparent trustworthiness. Those behind Willkie carefully hid the well-financed organization backing him and let Willkie play the role of the energetic, innocent outsider. Taft had 102 rooms at the Benjamin Franklin Hotel, Vandenberg had forty-eight at the Adelphia, and Dewey had seventy-eight at the Hotel Walton; Willkie made a show of having only two at the Benjamin Franklin.

"Willkie's advisors," wrote biographer Donald Bruce Johnson, "did everything possible to suppress independent activities by his friends which might have altered the carefully cultivated impression among the delegates that he was 'just plain folks, just like you.' "[18]

The event that allowed the Willkie forces to take control of the mechanics of the convention was most likely a stroke of pure luck, though given the stakes, mayhem is not beyond the realm of the possible. Invariably it is in every major intelligence service's bag of tricks. When Bickham Sweet-Escott was recruited into Lawrence Grand's Section D of SIS, the man interviewing him said: "For security reasons I can't tell you what sort of job it would be. All I can say is that if you join us, you mustn't be afraid of forgery, and you mustn't be afraid of murder."[19]

Ralph E. Williams, age seventy, a "Taftite," headed the committee on arrangements of the Republican convention in Philadelphia, which was meeting at the Bellevue-Stratford Hotel. Shortly after 5:30 P.M., May 16, "Mr. Williams, leaning on a chair, started to speak. Immediately the chair slipped from his grasp, and he fell to the floor."[20]

This allowed Sam Pryor of Connecticut, a Willkie insider, to take over the convention and the allocation of essential credentials. Pryor reduced the ticket allotments to delegations committed to other candidates. Delegations committed to Willkie got their full allotment. Finally, as Pryor told it years later, he printed a duplicate set of tickets and opened up the galleries to Willkie supporters, who responded with the "We Want Willkie" chant so embossed on the memories of participants.[21]

Pryor ordered one other small job for which there is sworn testimony. Former President Herbert Hoover wanted to stay aloof from the war in Europe. He had worked on his isolationist speech for weeks, and those who read it thought it the best speech of his career. When he marched to the podium a great roar erupted from the fifteen thousand as they stood and cheered, in expectation, for seven minutes.

Sam Pryor, or someone advising him, had foreseen this embarrassing situation. An enthusiastic response from the delegates to an isolationist speech would have set entirely the wrong tone. There was no great response; in fact, the delegates could not even hear the speech. Pryor had had a faulty microphone installed for the ex-president's speech, and years later Hoover obtained a deposition to this effect.[22]

Sam Pryor's subterfuge certainly earned him the gratitude and trust of those in power, and further covert assignments.[23] Subsequently, he built the secret airports in Latin America used by the British to ferry American planes from Brazil to Africa. In later years this proven man was liaison between Pan American Airways and the CIA. "One advantage for Pryor of being an executive of an international airline," write Marylin Bender and Selig Altschul in their history of Pan Am, "was the scope it permitted him in enacting his adolescent fantasies of being a cloak-and-dagger operative."[24]

Strangely, Hoover also had difficulty making himself heard at his convention press conference at the Bellevue Hotel, because a drum corp happened to march into the lobby as he was speaking. These annoying incidents have the feel of the British intelligence political warfare game the secret "BSC Account" called "Vik."[25]

Willkie, the "dark horse," did get the nomination in June 1940. "Thank God," wrote one "key" member of FDR's cabinet of Willkie's nomination. "Now we can go on helping Great Britain during the next four months."[26]

At the Hoover Library is an interesting oral history interview with James P. Selvage, a participant in the convention. In part Mr. Selvage says: "I think it was the worst rigged convention I ever saw....I recall another funny part of it was that the...press was saying—'If you don't nominate Willkie—he is the people's choice.'...[I] went home...and the next day people up in my area in New Jersey were saying, 'Who's this guy Willkie you nominated?'...People never heard of Willkie."[27]

David Lilienthal, the first head of the TVA, had a similar experience when he and his son took a late August 1940 cab ride to Yankee Stadium; the outspoken cab driver queried: "Sa-aay, who in the hell is this guy Willkie? Who in the *hell* is he anyway?"[28]

Perhaps the experience of Selvage and Lilienthal was just a quirk. After all, there was a rising public clamor for Willkie. The Gallup poll, for example, shows an impressive and steady gain in popularity for him:[29]

	3/40	5/7	5/17	5/31	6/12	6/20
Willkie	—	3%	5%	10%	17%	29%
Dewey	53%	67%	62%	56%	52%	47%
Taft	17%	12%	14%	16%	13%	8%
Vandenberg	19%	14%	13%	12%	12%	8%
Hoover	5%	2%	2%	2%	2%	8%

What a perfect wave of rising support for the well-managed Willkie quest for the nomination. Support for all the others was reportedly sagging even more than is apparent here.

The perfect stroke came with precise timing, on Thursday morning of the Republican convention. Joseph Alsop and Robert Kintner reported in their column the results of a leaked Gallup poll. Forty-four percent of Republican voters favored Willkie, while only 29 percent chose Dewey and 13 percent wanted Taft. That night, amid the cries of "We Want Willkie" from the Sam Pryor–packed galleries, the convention stampeded for Willkie.[30]

Once the nomination was in hand, the money stopped flowing; the aura of amateurish disorganization so skillfully promoted by the well-financed campaign for the nomination gave way to full-blown chaos. The *Willkie Special* traveled almost nineteen thousand miles and emblazoned on its participants memories of wild disorder. Russell Davenport's speechwriter wife remembers the train as "a traveling equivalent of Andersonville."[31]

Pierce Butler, a senior aide, distilled the *Willkie Special* experience when he explained to a local Republican bigwig who demanded to know who was running things: "Have you ever been in a whorehouse on Saturday night, when the Madam was away and the girls were running it to suit themselves?—That's how this campaign train is run."[32]

This chaotic state of affairs reflected the real Wendell Willkie. In his memoirs, published in 1963, *New York Times* staffer Turner Catledge recorded his personal experiences with Willkie: "Willkie was a most disorganized person. If you visited his hotel room you'd likely see his clothes scattered everywhere—shirt under the bed, socks on the chandelier....In the fall of 1941, when I was about to go to work for Marshall Field's Chicago *Sun*, I had a personal experience with Willkie's lack of organization. He drew up my contractual agreement with the *Sun*....The contract he wrote was three pages long and

I couldn't understand it. I took it to another lawyer and he didn't understand it either."[33]

Who were the people who created Wendell Willkie? What was their relationship to British intelligence and FDR?

The late 1930s had been hard on President Franklin Roosevelt. Conservatives had defeated him in his attempt to pack the Supreme Court. His attempts to purge his opponents from Congress in 1938 had also been an ignominious failure. Unemployment rates, if not startling by the standards of his first two years in office, the 25 percent of 1933 or the 24 percent of 1934, were still shockingly high— 19 percent in 1938, 17.2 percent in 1939, 14.6 percent in the election year of 1940.[34]

The precarious international situation posed an opportunity for FDR to win over the very conservatives who had beaten him on the Court packing issue and exposed the failures of the New Deal. "Who, after all," asks historian Robert E. Herzstein, "needed Roosevelt in 1940, if he intended to honor the Neutrality Act in the fashion recommended by Herbert Hoover?"[35]

FDR's recent political enemies came to his rescue; they backed his vulnerable interventionist policies and supplied a cooperative candidate to oppose him in the presidential election. In the Court fight in 1937, the *New York Herald Tribune* had quickly and sharply attacked Roosevelt on the Court issue. *The New York Times* attacked the Court scheme more slowly but even more methodically.[36]

Grenville Clark, a vital force in Fight for Freedom, had, with Charles C. Burlingham, led a committee of lawyers that spearheaded the fight to block FDR's Court-packing plan and was now actively working with the president and in his administration. Clark was a formidable opponent, but just as formidable a proponent. We have also seen Burlingham as the host and friend of BSC's David Ogilvy, as a donor to the BSC attack on Congressman Fish, and as a signer of the letter to the *New York Times* endorsing the legality of the illegal Destroyer Deal.[37]

Two prominent commentators who had also launched virulent attacks on Roosevelt's Court plan were Walter Lippmann and Dorothy Thompson. Both, as we have seen, worked closely with British intelligence; both helped create the Willkie boom, even advising the candidate; both suddenly defected after Willkie had the nomination in hand: Dorothy to Franklin Roosevelt; Lippmann to an enigmatic neutrality.[38]

Without Franklin Roosevelt, or someone similarly interventionist as the president, the British could not possibly win the war. The firm commitment to fight the Germans whatever the odds was not made nearly so early as British propaganda would have had Americans believe. Only in July, after Willkie was nominated and an interventionist president assured, did the British commit themselves, after two cabinet meetings on the topic, to fighting on in the expectation that the United States would rescue them.[39] The other possible Republican nominees—Taft, Dewey, and Vandenberg—were essentially isolationists. Of these, Taft was the most isolationist of all and the most intelligent and difficult to handle—"a limited little man with ignoble values and a tough acute mind," as one British intelligence officer wrote years later.[40]

Lippmann himself wrote: "Second only to the Battle of Britain, the sudden rise and nomination of Wendell Willkie was the decisive event, perhaps providential, which made it possible to rally the free world when it was almost conquered. Under any other leadership but his, the Republican party would in 1940 have turned its back on Great Britain...."[41]

The first peacetime draft law in American history, Burke-Wadsworth, and the Destroyer Deal would not have received Roosevelt's endorsement had a genuine opposition candidate stood ready to make it a political issue in the 1940 election. Without the Burke-Wadsworth conscription law the United States would not have had the standing army that Britain would need to venture back onto the continent of Europe.

As Senator Hiram Johnson wrote his son, Willkie "had raised hell with us here by adopting the Roosevelt foreign policy, and being for conscription, etc. He really broke the back of the opposition to the conscription law." The major experts on the draft, scholars Garry Clifford and Samuel Spencer, catch the strangeness of this episode and the lack of domestic support for the draft: "...even more curious is the fact that during the early stages, both the army and the White House were at best apathetic to its passage....In its worst light, it [the passage of the draft law] might suggest that a powerful minority interest can control the democratic process for its own ends...even though the original sponsors envisaged the draft as being necessary for raising an army to participate in the European war, Congress as a whole did not consciously enact the legislation for such bellicose purpose."[42]

"We knew," wrote Francis Pickens Miller, years later, "that Roosevelt would not act [on the Destroyer Deal] until he had been reliably assured that Willkie would not attack him for giving away part of our fleet." It is clear from the testimony of the British intelligence officials that British intelligence was deeply involved in the Destroyer Deal. Colin Gubbins, the head of Special Operations Executive, cites Stephenson's work on the Destroyer Deal as the best example of important material left out of Hyde's *The Quiet Canadian*. Though Sir William Stephenson himself wrote in the 1980s that his role in the Destroyer Deal was only secondary, no insider denies he was involved.[43]

Montgomery Hyde says: "Later in the summer came the destroyer-for-bases deal in which I also played a part, along with General Donovan on the American side."[44] Several of the American participants in the dramatic effort to get Willkie's assent to the plan seem to have been greatly impressed by the drama, but they need not have worked so hard; it was a fait accompli.

In a confidential message to the British ambassador, Lord Lothian, Willkie wrote he was "in favor of doing everything possible to see that Great Britain did not get beaten in the war...[but because] of the overwhelming desire of the United States not to get involved in the war...[it would be] necessary to convince the American people about every particular step." He went on to say that he would not oppose the Destroyer Deal, but he was "most insistent that this statement of his views should not in any circumstances be allowed to leak...."[45] The Destroyer Deal was very vulnerable, not its least problem being that it was without doubt illegal.[46]

Though there is much commentary on this available, Ernest Cuneo had been helping his friend and roommate George Bowden, later a top, if unacknowledged, official of OSS, run the Destroyer Deal. Here is Cuneo: "...the Attorney General Bob Jackson had called me one morning in 1940 and asked me to come over. I found him both sad and disturbed. He said he was off to a Cabinet meeting where he had to give the President very disappointing news: the transfer of the 50 destroyers to Britain was unconstitutional. I told him not to feel too badly: that by one o'clock that day he would either reverse himself or he'd be asked for his resignation."[47]

Francis Pickens Miller, a fervent interventionist and a prime mover in Century Group/Fight for Freedom, says this: "If the Republicans had launched an all out attack on the president for doing this [giving away part of the fleet], their candidate would have attracted hundreds of thousands of America First isolationist voters who otherwise might not go to the polls. The political stakes were high and the temptation great. But there were two weighty factors in our favor. Our chairman, Lewis Douglas was one of Willkie's most ardent supporters and trusted advisors. Further, Willkie himself was a great patriot."[48]

The extremely shaky legal justification for the Destroyer Deal was a letter to the editor published in the *New York Times*, August 11, 1940, filled with disinformation and specious legal reasoning. The point at which letters to the editor, even editors of the *New York Times*, took on the force of law has never been explained. The letter had been concocted by Ben Cohen of the White House staff and John Foster, the counsel for the British embassy, and promoted by political insider and associate justice of the U.S. Supreme Court, Felix Frankfurter. Dean Acheson, a major power in Fight for Freedom, and Frankfurter's one-time student and most ardent protégé, then persuaded prestigious attorneys Charles C. Burlingham (who had been one of the prime movers against FDR's Court-packing scheme), Thomas D. Thatcher, and George Rublee to add their names to his, giving the letter in authoritative endorsements what it lacked in logic.[49]

The questionable legality of this appears to have unsettled even the usually steady FDR. David Lilienthal, the head of the Tennessee Valley Authority, wrote on September 2, 1940: "…aboard the Presidents special train, en route to Knoxville: Mr. Baruch was in my stateroom when I returned.…He said the President was deeply absorbed in something, for instead of inquiring about political prospects…he was brooding. …'I think it is something pretty serious…for he said twice on the journey something to the effect that he might get impeached for what he was about to do.' "[50]

British intelligence consistently used prominent Americans to pronounce its messages and disarm its critics. The Destroyer Deal was no exception. Hyde writes of this in *The Quiet Canadian*, the slightly shortened version of the "BSC Account": "General Pershing had been persuaded through the good offices of an intermediary, a wealthy American businessman…who was a friend of both Stephenson and the

General, to come out with a strong speech early in August supporting the destroyer deal."[51]

Pershing's eloquent speech was written for him by Walter Lippmann, who was working with British intelligence and had pressed so hard for Willkie. The Pershing speech "was the turning point in our efforts to create a public opinion favorable to the president's taking action." So three more speakers were scheduled, two of whom were working with British intelligence, William Donovan and Robert Sherwood.[52]

"Senator Taft," said Herbert Agar, a key figure in Fight for Freedom, "was the rock on which we feared that our policy [of aid to Great Britain] would founder."[53] The other prospective Republican contenders were not internationalists either. Senator Arthur H. Vandenberg had shown interest, undoubtedly under the tutelage of his neighbor at the Wardman Park Hotel, British diplomat Harold Haig Sims, with whom he lunched several times a week, or of Harold's wife, Mitzi, with whom Vandenberg was sleeping.

The central figure behind the Willkie boom was Thomas W. Lamont, the senior partner in J. P. Morgan. Lamont was a vital factor behind the scenes in most of the interventionist organizations. The French aristocrat-become-newspaperman Raoul de Roussy de Sales later worked with Sandy Griffith's BSC front France Forever. His diary entry of May 26, 1940, captures the feelings of Thomas Lamont and his friends: "Dinner last night at Jones Beach as the guest of Robert Moses....About twenty people were there, including the Tom Lamonts, the Finletters, Mrs. Pratt, Herbert Swope. The only point worth noting is that *the sole concern of all these people was how to get the United States into the war*"(emphasis added).[54]

Willkie was a media creation: those given credit for making his national image were the Luce publications—*Fortune, Time,* and *Life*—and the Cowles publications—*Look,* the *Des Moines Register and Tribune,* and the *Minneapolis Star Journal.* Luce and his wife Clare Boothe Luce were very helpful to British intelligence. The Cowles were apparently brought into this because they were cousins of Lamont, Lamont's aunt being the paternal grandmother of Gardner "Mike" and John Cowles.[55]

Though Mike Cowles was pivotal in the creation of Willkie, President Roosevelt apparently held no grudge; in fact, he was probably grateful, because he soon made Cowles domestic director of the Office of War Information. When FDR sent Willkie as his personal representative on a round-the-world flight, he sent along Mike Cowles and Joseph Barnes. Barnes, while at the *New York Herald Tribune*, had also been instrumental in promoting Willkie, but at the time of the trip he was an Office of War Information foreign propaganda supervisor.[56]

But Thomas Lamont was not Willkie's only link to the Morgan interests that so benefited his campaign. Willkie was on the board of directors of the Morgan-dominated First National Bank of New York (1940; 1943–44). His close friends included not only Lamont but Perry Hall, a vice president of Morgan Stanley & Co., and Charlton Mac-Veagh, the brother of Ambassador to Spain Lincoln MacVeagh, who had worked at J. P. Morgan. His father had been a longtime partner in the Morgan law firm of Davis, Polk, Wardwell, Gardner & Reed; his brother continued to work for that firm.

Oren Root, grandnephew of Elihu Root and also a relative of Henry Luce, creator of the Willkie Clubs, worked for Davis, Polk until he began working full-time on the Willkie campaign. Before Root took a leave of absence, Lamont had been considerate enough to intervene with one of the Davis, Polk partners who had wished to have Oren cease efforts on behalf of Willkie or be fired. "It was some ten minutes later," writes Root, "that the partner came bursting into my room with 'Well, Oren, my boy, how is the great politician feeling today? You are doing a wonderful job. Keep it up.' "[57]

Journalist Warren Moscow has described the compartmentalization (a characteristic of intelligence operations) of the advertising people operating behind the scenes for Willkie in early 1940: "Before the nomination was secured, more than twenty of them [advertising people] had been recruited for the Willkie operation, each given a specific task, but with no knowledge that he was part of a larger force embarked on a general campaign." Even Oren Root confesses that "the part I saw was only a fraction of the whole."[58]

An *Information Please* quiz show appearance and a multitude of others were, in Warren Moscow's words, "all planted by the public relations machinery at some of the meetings where the Willkie gospel, rather than Willkie, was put on exhibition."[59]

There was also a Democrats for Willkie organization led by future ambassador to Great Britain Lewis Douglas and the covert British informant John W. Hanes. Hanes had been in charge of the Treasury Department's efforts to stall German ships in American harbors so that the British could be ready for them when they tried to depart for Germany.

Hanes had then gone to work for Hearst and, as he secretly informed the British, was the one who persuaded Hearst to attack Lindbergh after his Des Moines speech in September 1941.[60] Among other accomplishments, Douglas had helped form Century Group/Fight for Freedom.[61] Douglas was also one of the interventionists who ran the William Allen White Committee. Though he was the titular head of Democrats for Willkie, Douglas took little interest in the campaign; this fed the suspicion that he was "still having *sub-rosa* contact with the opposing camp."[62]

There were others, besides Dorothy Thompson and Walter Lippmann, who promoted Willkie for the Republican nomination, but once the voters had been deprived of a real choice, went back to supporting FDR. Willkie and FDR sat down before Willkie's trip to England. "At intervals," James Roosevelt has recorded, "great bursts of laughter could be heard coming through the closed doors." FDR told Willkie, "You'll like Averell....He contributed to our campaign, you know...[FDR professed to be embarrassed by what he had just said.] Oh, that's all right, Willkie grinned. Harriman did contribute to our campaign. Harriman gave me money for my pre-convention campaign before I got the nomination, but then he contributed to your election campaign."[63]

The highlights of the preconvention campaign not already discussed are these. In January 1940, Charlton MacVeagh and Russell Davenport had secretly set up operations with a paid professional staff in the quiet Murray Hill Hotel, MacVeagh on one floor, Davenport on another, a mailroom and staff on still another. Warren Moscow was most wary of Root's claims of innocence when he noted the result of Root's little advertisement: "The day the ad appeared, the boiler factory in Murray Hill went to work. By midnight, two thousand telegrams had gone out to the mailing clubs [run by the Edison Electric Institute] suggesting a rapid response to the Root appeal. Root was snowed under."[64]

William Donovan, whom British intelligence called "our man," was also at Philadelphia. And when Allen Dulles chanced on him in his hotel lobby, Donovan had a wide grin on his face. He pointed out to

Dulles that the nomination of Willkie simplified the situation and that there was now no doubt the United States would get into the war. He also told Dulles that certain preparations would have to be made "and that's where you come in."[65]

"The most popular member of the Willkie entourage," wrote Drew Pearson, "is [Russell] Davenport whose ability to think rapidly and coherently has made a deep imprint on newsmen. He seems to be the only advisor who has Willkie's ear; most of the others seeming to be figureheads...." Davenport was an editor for Henry Luce's *Fortune* magazine and an early behind-the-scenes strategist for Willkie. In collaboration with Irita Van Doren and Willkie, Davenport turned the April 1940 issue of *Fortune* into a promotion piece for Willkie. According to Oren Root, "The *Fortune* article and the *Information Please* appearance were part of the plan, together with a number of other appearances by Willkie on public platforms and in print. The basic essential of the strategy was that it be low key. Above all, there was never, never to be any mention of the true objective, the Republican nomination."[66]

Once the publicity machine began its preconvention grind, there was another problem. The narrow, artificial base of Willkie's support, concentrated as it was around New York, was too obvious. Root consulted with Davenport, who suggested Oscaloosa, Iowa, as the site target of a Root trip. With trepidation, Root traveled west—"I was fearful that my registration at the local hotel might attract undue attention, thus spoiling the spontaneity of the result which I hoped would ensue." But everything went well. "Two days later, on May 4, there developed from Oscaloosa, Iowa—entirely spontaneously—a new one man campaign for Wendell Willkie for President."[67]

After Willkie had the nomination and was trying to rest in Colorado Springs, he was beset by a string of visitors. One was a "Mr. Franklin," a.k.a. Nelson Rockefeller. In this convoluted world Rockefeller ostensibly came "to ask permission from the Republican presidential standard-bearer, Wendell Willkie, who was on the campaign trail in a candidacy Nelson's Uncle Winthrop [Aldrich] had helped create and whose effort the Rockefeller family was heavily backing."[68]

The permission Nelson Rockefeller was requesting was to join the Roosevelt administration as Coordinator of Inter-American Affairs. Uncle Winthrop had long been a member of what Rutgers historian

Jeffery M. Dorwart called "the Roosevelt-Astor Espionage Ring." Known for most of its existence as "the Room" and code named "the Club" during World War II, this group was working with and for British intelligence and Franklin Roosevelt in February, March, and April 1940.[69]

Information from British intelligence was passed through Astor to FDR. Through Winthrop Aldrich, Astor also became informed of a wonderful opportunity to plant agents on a Chase National mission to Japan.[70] While funding the creation of Willkie and passing inside bank information on to FDR, Winthrop Aldrich also "headed the British War Relief Society in America and funded a secret pilot training program for British fliers in the United States."[71]

The complex origins of Willkie's 1941 trip to England further illustrate why historians have had such difficulty tracking events in this maze of cutouts and intermediaries. "What could be better than sending Mr. Wendell Willkie, your opponent in the recent bitter elections?" Stephenson suggested to FDR. The fact that Intrepid was the initiator of this trip is reiterated by Montgomery Hyde in *Secret Intelligence Agent*: "Shortly afterwards he [Willkie] passed through Bermuda on a visit to England, which he made at President Roosevelt's special request prompted by Stephenson."[72]

President Roosevelt liked the idea of the trip. In the next step, Justice Felix Frankfurter and publisher, Fight for Freedom activist, and British intelligence helper Harold Guinzburg cornered Willkie's mistress, Irita Van Doren, at a New Year's party. Van Doren talked to Willkie, who accepted the idea.[73]

Again the effort by British intelligence to gain credibility for its American spokesmen—Dorothy Thompson, Edgar Ansel Mowrer, William Donovan, and now Wendell Willkie—by having them visit wartime Britain met with considerable success.

Fight for Freedom used Willkie as one of its most effective speakers at its rallies. Willkie's file in the Fight for Freedom Papers is 270 pages of correspondence, telegrams, and speeches, much of it congratulatory—"Congratulations on your swell speech at San Francisco rally. Best parts were your war-mongering.—Ulric Bell."

There is also a group of interesting negative letters—some of them very caustic. The occasion of these unflattering letters was a letter, prepared by Fight for Freedom, sent by Willkie to prominent American businessmen to promote the book *You Can't Do Business with Hitler* by Douglas Miller, the one-time U.S. commercial attaché in Berlin.

For those American businessmen who were not profoundly horrified by Hitler, a reading of Miller's book would put the proper fear in them. "Mr. Miller," wrote one reviewer," devotes much of his space to the foreboding future which awaits Europe and the world in case of Hitler's victory....[Miller makes] an ardent plea for intervention of the United States in the present struggle: 'The sooner we declare war the better.' "[74] The book became an immense success, thanks to heavy promotion by the friends and fronts of British intelligence.

In March 1941, Willkie went to Canada, where he delivered a fiery speech to open the national war drive fund. By spring, Willkie "was considered the leading interventionist spokesman in America." As a member of the executive committee of Fight for Freedom, Willkie emerged as one of FFF's most popular speakers.[75]

Lindbergh's speech at Des Moines, Iowa, in early September 1941 permitted British intelligence the opportunity it sorely needed to discredit the most effective anti-interventionist speaker fighting against them. Lindbergh's charge that the British, the administration, and the Jews were trying to involve the United States in the war opened him to the charge of Fight for Freedom's Peter Cusick that he was a "barefaced" anti-Semite. Bishop Hobson of FFF prompted Willkie into action with a telegram saying that "the ugly spectacle of Nazi anti-Semitism [is] being made the plank in the platform of the America First Committee."[76]

Willkie responded on cue by calling Lindbergh's speech "the most un-American talk made in my time by any person of national reputation." Since Bill Morrell of British Security Coordination directed the work of Fight for Freedom, the Rev. Leon M. Birkhead's Friends of Democracy, and the Nonsectarian Anti-Nazi League in their efforts to discredit the anti-interventionists, the concerted attacks mentioned by historians were no coincidence. John W. Hanes, one of the leaders of Democrats for Willkie, confidentially reported to the British on how he pressured Hearst into attacking Lindbergh.

Chapter 3 suggests that the movie industry was dominated by interventionists and British intelligence agents such as the Korda brothers. The isolationist Senator Burton K. Wheeler told a radio audience that the movie companies "have been operating as war propaganda machines almost as if they were being directed from a central bureau...." Soon the Senate passed a resolution by Senator Wheeler creating a subcommittee to investigate the movies. This could have been trouble. The subcommittee was packed with isolationists—D. Worth Clark, Bone, Tobey, and Wayland Brooks.

From papers in the Fight for Freedom collection at Princeton, Mark L. Chadwin concluded that Ulric Bell "outlined the tactics" to go "fighting on the offensive...."[77] It appears that Chadwin had spotted only one of the links in the chain. Wheeler would surely have been in a dither had he known that the man coaching the movie makers, and their visible counsel, Willkie, was Sidney Bernstein, a man proud to be both a Jew and a British agent. (There were also worries about the Jewish influence in the movies.) In Willkie's Fight for Freedom file are several examples of telegrams and speeches written by FFF for others. Here is part of a telegram, with a tough speech enclosed, to Senator Carter Glass from Ulric Bell of FFF:

PERSONAL AND CONFIDENTIAL
September 15, 1941

Mr. J. W. Rixey Smith

Senator Carter Glass' Office...

Willkie is very much in need of some help from your quarter. He says it will be of infinite assistance if at this juncture...the Senator will let go with a strong blast. It may be just enough to push over the whole business and stop the inquisition....I know that you will want something as a guide and I am offering it.[78]

This heavy counterattack orchestrated by British agents threw the subcommittee into confusion; the hearings sputtered and finally died. Fight for Freedom claimed this proved the innocence of its movie allies. Today there is strong testimony that the Korda brothers were full-fledged British intelligence agents and that several of the other producers were working closely with the British.

Willkie's relationship with FDR was of special interest. At the March 1941 dinner of the White House Correspondents Association, a mock newsreel was shown titled *All We Know Is What They Let Us Write in the*

Papers or It Ain't Necessarily So. One scene, showing Roosevelt and Willkie in bed together, was titled "Bundling for Britain."[79]

Willkie and Franklin Roosevelt worked together in a way that no other "political opponents" ever have. There were, of course, the attacks Willkie made, concurrently with British intelligence, on Congressman Hamilton Fish. These were done in conjunction with President Roosevelt; they are discussed in Chapter 6, but there was more.

New York Times reporter Warren Moscow records: "Intimates of Willkie recall that there were a number of calls from the White House to Willkie in New York, after which Willkie would board a late afternoon or early evening plane for Washington. He would be met at the airport by an unmarked White House car, which left him off at the back entrance to the President's mansion. After the talk with the President, he would be taken back to the airport and be at his desk the next morning, with the same measure of secrecy used. There is no record of these trips, but the best information is that they began before Roosevelt sent his lend-lease program to Congress on 10 January 1941."[80]

Drew Pearson was to write later: "Perhaps never in American history has there been such a unique and friendly situation between two men who once engaged in a bitter cut-throat race for the White House as between Franklin Roosevelt and Wendell Willkie."[81] The depth and authenticity of this "bitterness" is much in doubt, considering their subsequent amicable relationship. Willkie later confessed of the things he had said about FDR during the 1940 presidential election that it "was campaign oratory."[82]

Willkie's record of accommodation and support after the November 1940 election is further evidence that he should be viewed as more of a stalking horse than a dark horse. Clearly he had none of the earmarks of the leader of the opposing political party. Defying almost the entire Republican Party leadership, Willkie became an outspoken advocate for Lend-Lease, which the British were extremely anxious to obtain. Willkie became an open ally of Franklin Roosevelt, a launcher of trial balloons, helping to prepare the ground for the more cautious FDR.

If British intelligence collaborator and Roosevelt speechwriter Robert Sherwood is correct, FDR was very grateful for the help. Wrote Sherwood: "Once I heard Hopkins make some slurring remark about Willkie and Roosevelt slapped him with as sharp a reproof as I ever heard him utter. He said, 'Don't ever say anything like that around here again. Don't even *think* it. You of all people ought to know that we might not have had Lend Lease or Selective Service or a lot of other things if it hadn't been for Wendell Willkie. He was a godsend to this country when we needed him most.' "[83]

During his trip to England, January 22 to February 9, 1941, Willkie enjoyed the same sort of red carpet treatment other American celebrities had received. And Willkie's assessments of the situation were just as erroneous. Willkie returned hastily to the United States on the *Dixie Clipper* with the avowed purpose of pronouncing the British propaganda message: "What the British desire from us is not men, but materials and equipment."[84] (This is the same message Senator Vandenberg's friend Mrs. Paterson was giving her audiences.)

It was patently false; there was not the faintest chance the British could have invaded the continent without American soldiers or that the goods could be transferred to England without American sailors being in danger.

Willkie's pro-administration, pro-British activity destroyed his following among Republicans in a way that no high-road, idealistic rhetoric could conceal. By midspring of 1941, Republican National Chairman John D. Hamilton wrote to a fellow Republican: "Out of the 190-odd Republican members of the House and the Senate, Willkie couldn't dig up ten friends if his life depended on it." In a March 28, 1944, letter to John Hanes, Oren Root said: "It is regrettable, but I think a conservative assumption that only a minority of all our contributors, and not much more than a majority of the Committee, are today still friendly to Willkie."[85]

All his work on behalf of the British and Franklin Roosevelt's administration had simply exhausted Willkie's credibility and fueled the suspicion—never far from the surface—that he had been a plant. If by the autumn of 1941 Willkie's credibility was diminished among rank-and-file Republicans, after the publication of Nelson Sparks's book naming the British Ambassador Lord Lothian, Thomas Lamont of Morgan, and the Reids as his political creators, it was small indeed.

Isaiah Berlin of the British embassy in Washington warned London: "A member of my staff, who has been talking to Mrs. Ogden Reid, obtained the impression that while proposing to continue her present investment in Willkie...she was well aware of the possibility of having to switch to someone else in time, and would endeavor to do so as gracefully as possible, after some formal *casus belli*, which no one could have much difficulty picking with Willkie."[86]

Isaiah Berlin's dispatches are filled with notes on personal contacts between the British Embassy and Willkie.[87] As late as December 13, 1943, Berlin was reporting to London: "Henry Luce…shows no disposition as yet to start selling his shares in Willkie, nor do the Morgan interests."

If Willkie was too severely damaged to be viable as a Republican, perhaps he could undergo yet another political transmogrification. There were emissaries from FDR—Harold Ickes, Judge Rosenman— asking if he would take the vice presidential nomination. Felix Frankfurter and Drew Pearson were also pushing hard for Willkie.[88] In Pearson's files is a 1966 letter to Matthew Rosenhaus, J. B. Williams Co., 711 Fifth Avenue, New York:

> Dear Matty:…My recollection is that you were the one who inspired me to approach Wilkie [sic] regarding the idea of running for Vice President on the Democratic ticket in 1944. As you will recall, Willkie was willing, but my efforts with FDR and with those around him failed. It was a fairly important chapter, for the most part unwritten, of that political year.[89]

Not only did this fail, but so did Willkie. He had a heart attack in August. This brought on a stay in the hospital, where he seemed to be getting better, but he caught a streptococcic throat infection and died on October 7. In referring to the death of the author of *One World*, British intelligence agent Montgomery Hyde wrote of Willkie, the habitual reader, that "by an ironic twist of fate he died from a virus contracted from another book which he had been reading."[90]

CHAPTER 9

•••

The Success
of Deception

By the late 1930s, then, it had become apparent to the British that they did not have the resources to fight a war with Germany. Only if the United States could be dragged into the war on Britain's side would there be a chance to prevent German hegemony in Europe. But the Americans were perceived as being unreliable and unpredictable. They were, in the words of the shrewd permanent undersecretary of state for foreign affairs, Sir Robert Vansittart, an "untrustworthy Race...who will always let us down."[1]

Moreover, there was ample evidence to indicate that the people of the United States were determined not to become involved in another European war; the Congress had manifestly expressed this popular desire to stay out of any conflict by passing neutrality laws. As late as the summer of 1939 the Congress—"pigheaded and self-righteous nobodies" in Neville Chamberlain's words[2] had steadfastly refused to overturn this legislation.

Because of the gravity of this situation, the British now had a desperate need to exert as much influence as possible to cause the American government to abandon its isolationist policies and enter the war on Britain's side. Given the unpredictability of Congress, it should be little wonder that the British made a major effort to influence its members and destroy the careers of those who proved resistant. It is, thus, not surprising that the British diplomat Harold Sims and his wife, Mitzi, made an effort to ingratiate themselves with Senator Arthur Vandenberg, a powerful member of the Foreign Relations Committee and potential presidential candidate in 1940; or that Mitzi suddenly reappeared during the debate on Lend-Lease; or that when Mitzi again left, one of British intelligence's most skilled operatives, "Cynthia," unexpectedly appeared at the senator's apartment.

The resources available to the British government were very limited when compared with those needed to fulfill her worldwide commitments, but among Britain's assets were its secret intelligence and propaganda agencies. These experienced tremendous growth during 1938–40. Section D is reported to have grown larger than its parent, MI-6.

British intelligence was already established in the United States before the April 1940 arrival of William Stephenson, now almost universally known as Intrepid. But operations were consolidated and greatly expanded under Stephenson; from 1940 to 1945 he represented a shifting kaleidoscope of British intelligence and propaganda agencies, most of them housed in Rockefeller Center under the name British Security Coordination (BSC). British agencies, overt and covert, worked so closely together that it is often difficult to tell precisely where black operations shade into gray and then into white. British intelligence formed one part, the most secret part, of a three-sided relationship— the Roosevelt White House and the Eastern foreign policy elite forming the other sides. President Roosevelt allowed British intelligence broad latitude in its American operations before and during World War II; this served his own purposes quite well and at the same time also served the purposes of the Anglophile foreign policy elite.

When World War II was over, those who participated in the BSC campaign to involve the United States in World War II and destroy isolationism felt that they had succeeded, that they had guided history in the desired direction, however slow and halting the process. Writing of British Security Coordination's efforts to portray the isolationists as Nazis or Nazi dupes, the "BSC Account" says: "All this [black propaganda] and much more was handed out by devious means to the great impartial newspapers of the country.... Personalities were discredited, their unsavory pasts were dug up, their utterances were printed and reprinted....Little by little, a sense of guilt crept through the cities and out across the states. The campaign took hold."[3] The very word "isolationist" became a scandalous epithet, to be hurled at one's enemies. The destruction of the isolationist opposition paved the way for the post–World War II bipartisan foreign policy that diplomatic historians have so marveled at.

Attempting to answer the question of which operations considered in this book would have been accomplished without British intelligence's expert guidance is, of course, an exercise in counterfactual history and the unknowable. This is not to say that such speculation is unnatural or that its basic assumptions are categorically without merit. Such speculation is inevitable, because secret intelligence agencies by their very nature try to keep their operations secret, to have others front for them, to stay in the background. Time after time, in his plans to unseat Congressman Hamilton Fish, SOE agent Sandy Griffith admonished his people to "remain in the background." "Events," he wrote, should appear to be "spontaneous." To fix the historical credit or blame on others, or on mere chance, is the raison d'être of covert operations.[4]

Not only did British intelligence attempt to stay in the background, its agents had circuitous contacts at so many different levels that the lineage of specific events is often difficult to trace. The manipulation of the public opinion polls is an example. Agent Sandy Griffith and his Market Analysts Inc. did spurious polls that were published by BSC fronts such as Fight for Freedom and the Committee to Defend America by Aiding the Allies. MI-6's David Ogilvy was a top man at Gallup, and David Niles, the British intelligence contact at the White House, was also the contact for informant Hadley Cantril of the Office of Public Opinion Research at Princeton. Cantril, who worked with Gallup, was also cooperating with Fight for Freedom/Century Group.

The dualistic case of Walter Lippmann is even more obscure because he was both giving and receiving advice from the British. What is clear about both the Gallup organization and Walter Lippmann is that British intelligence and its fronts were "in the loop" with them.

The counterfactual argument is legitimately based on the valid premise that the White House and the Eastern policy elite, the "Warhawks," earnestly wished for the United States to intervene in the war and assume its global responsibilities. The willingness, however, was not the deed. What British intelligence brought to the equation was sharp focus, good organization, technical expertise, and a courageous determination to do whatever was necessary—however illegal or unseemly. BSC's sharp focus and tight organization were desperately needed. Most scholars who have looked closely at the Franklin Roosevelt White House have remarked on its disorganization and confusion. After World War II, William Langer and S. Everett Gleason wrote an authoritative volume on American involvement in the war using this well-known confusion to deny that anyone in particular was to blame for the way events unfolded.

British intelligence could hardly have worked so effectively alone, however. It was, after all, a foreign intelligence service operating within the United States, but outside and often in direct contradiction to American law. Ernest Cuneo observed in a memo for his files: "So objectionable was BSC activity, and so politically dangerous was it for the American bureaucracy, that it excited strong hostility within both the Justice and State departments."[5]

For BSC to function so freely and effectively, FDR or someone similarly cooperative was needed to occupy the White House. There is now considerable evidence available affirming the charges by Earl Browder and Nelson Sparks that Wendell Willkie was a creation of Thomas Lamont of J. P. Morgan, Franklin Roosevelt, and British Ambassador Lord Lothian. Several of the principals felt that the Destroyer Deal would never have materialized without the crucial cooperation of Willkie. After the election, Willkie became spokesman for Fight for Freedom. In this capacity he performed numerous chores BSC needed done. For one he defended American moviemakers at congressional hearings when they stood accused of cooperating with the British in producing pro-interventionist propaganda movies.

Because there is little doubt that the American moviemakers had made numerous pro-Allied films before Pearl Harbor, matters could have become awkward. One propaganda historian has written of the senators' attacks on the Warner Brothers Studio: "Fortunately for Warners the Senators only saw the films and not the studio's [very incriminating] correspondence."[6] Fortunate also was the timing of the attack on Pearl Harbor. Film producer and MI-6 agent Alexander Korda was scheduled to testify before Congress on December 12, 1941.

Sir Robert Vansittart, once the permanent undersecretary of state for foreign affairs, the liaison between MI-6 and the Foreign Office, had in 1938 moved to the nebulous position of chief diplomatic adviser to the foreign secretary; from that position he worked diligently at planning for intelligence and propaganda work. In an October 1939 minute to a Foreign Office document, Vansittart wrote: "There are plenty of people in Hollywood who would be delighted to make films which work our way if they were provided with material. Many of the leading actors would give their services for nothing....So far, I repeat we have made no real use whatever of the most potent means of propaganda."[7] Vansittart here captures the essence of the situation. There were those in America who were willing to help the British, but they needed guidance and support.

Did the Louis Mumfords and their interventionist friends wish to rid their congressional district of isolationist Hamilton Fish? Yes, they certainly did. Mrs. Mumford wrote to a friend about how the work of British intelligence agent Sanford Griffith gave the campaign "direction": "Alone, I am quite sure the amateurs could not have swung it...."[8]

Was Assistant Attorney General William P. Maloney willing to chill the atmosphere of isolationism by prosecuting George Sylvester Viereck for improperly registering as a German propagandist? He definitely was willing, but where would he have been without British intelligence? It was British intelligence that supplied the key witnesses and the material evidence in the initial trial.

After that conviction was overturned, British intelligence once again lent a helping hand to prejudice the case against the defendant, supply the key witnesses, and perhaps even promote perjury by witness Sandy Griffith. Griffith may have had to commit perjury in this trial, but the Justice Department was able to get another conviction. British intelligence was such an integral part of these proceedings and the government's charges were so fragile that it is very hard to believe that it would have been pursued so relentlessly or successfully without BSC's preparation, its agents, and their testimony.

Was interventionist political columnist Drew Pearson willing to attack Congressman Fish? Yes, of course, but it was British intelligence agent Sanford Griffith who furnished Pearson with the material. When Fish responded by calling Pearson a liar, the somewhat reluctant Pearson was persuaded to sue Fish. What should he then do? asked Pearson. Griffith told him to let the suit drag on, hanging over Fish's head, and that was done. It is difficult to see how this strategic attack on Congressman Fish by Drew Pearson would have taken place without the sustained support of British intelligence.

Was President Roosevelt inhibited about telling fabricated tales to create the impression that Latin America was gravely threatened by the Nazis, thus intensifying America's fear and prodding the United States closer to war? No, numerous witnesses tell us FDR had nothing against a good fib, but the White House's ability to manufacture the documentary evidence to back him was limited. For the final coup to remove the last of the neutrality laws, British intelligence supplied the fib and the forged map of how Hitler was planning to divide up Latin America. Likewise, there was no internal impetus existing within the United States for the creation of Donovan's Coordinator of Information/Office of Strategic Services. Neither the FBI, nor navy intelligence, nor army intelligence was demanding the creation of a separate agency.[9] There is no evidence to contradict this conclusion—not in Cuneo's papers, certainly not in Tom Troy's study done twenty years ago at the CIA.

Further testimony to the success of British intelligence operations can be seen in the actions of Americans who, having learned the intelligence trade from the British, later flattered their teachers by copying their successful methods. The aggressive offensive spirit of British intelligence at war became the model for generations of American intelligence officers and government officials in the Cold War.

British Security Coordination, an activist, full-service intelligence agency, pushed into existence the Coordinator of Information, which became OSS; pushed "our man," as they called William Donovan, to its top; supplied MI-6 officer Dickie Ellis to run its daily operations and train its personnel; and supplied numerous other BSC agents and collaborators to run COI/OSS operations.[10] With the coming of the Cold War many of the key personnel trained in the front group operations—dirty tricks, black propaganda, and incessant political warfare—of British Special Operations at war moved into the CIA. Is it any wonder that the OSS developed in the image and likeness of British intelligence at war or that the CIA developed along similar lines?

Was Special Operations Executive officer Bill Morrell planting twenty items a day in the media? The CIA planted eighty.[11] Did BSC organize opposition for political candidates? The CIA did the same: the Italian election of 1948 is a known example. Did BSC introduce women and agents of influence to politicians? "The CIA maintains an extensive stable of 'agents of influence' around the world…from valets and mistresses to personal secretaries...."[12] Did BSC make Station WRUL an unwitting mouthpiece for British propaganda? The CIA ran Radio Free Europe. From Allen Dulles' operations in Guatemala and Iran to William Casey and his convoluted methods in Iran-Contra, the continuation of BSC/OSS tactics is evident.

The fronts run by British Security Coordination—Friends of Democracy, Fight for Freedom, etc.—had several distinct advantages over open attempts by the British government to affect American opinion and influence congressional action. These fronts allowed the tendentious messages of the British to come from ostensibly disinterested American mouths.

One example is the starvation of Europeans caused by the British blockade. In August 1940, former president Herbert Hoover, ignoring the possibility of Nazi diversion, presented a plan to feed the hungry civilians of Europe and thereby break the British blockade, one of Britannia's most potent weapons. Once again the anxious British were able to remain in the background; they did not have to explain why it was necessary to starve the civilians of the defeated countries; a man of God was available to give the British words the respectability. Episcopal Bishop Henry W. Hobson led Fight for Freedom in its vigorous and successful defense of the blockade. It was a necessity, explained the bishop, to starve the Europeans for their own good.[13] With good reason the British felt this argument would have been given short shift by most Americans had it been known to be an obviously self-serving pronouncement of the British government.

Perhaps one of the most remarkable achievements of the tough political warfare waged by BSC was the elimination of the prewar isolationists from the postwar foreign policy debates. The British feared that if the isolationist voices were not silenced, the United States might once again recoil into itself after the war. Note the relentless BSC campaign against Congressman Hamilton Fish, described in Chapter 6. A cursory examination of biographies of the isolationists Gerald Nye and Burton Wheeler strongly suggests they were the targets of similar campaigns. The bipartisan foreign policy of which many diplomatic historians have written was created by this elimination of strong and respected isolationist senators and congressmen.

After the war these BSC operations to involve the United States in the war and destroy isolationism were generally ignored by mainstream historians. There developed an establishment consensus that the revisionist controversy that had surrounded World War I had been a mistake and, as OSS head William Donovan explained to counterintelligence officer James Angleton, "after World War II there must be 'no rewriting of history,' as there had been after World War I."[14]

Those who had made this World War II history filled the vacuum by promulgating and financing, by writing and publishing, their very own version of it. In announcing a grant of $139,000 (later added to by the Sloan Foundation) to William Langer for a study of the origins of World War II, the 1946 annual report of the Rockefeller Foundation read: "The Committee on Studies of the Council on Foreign Relations is concerned that the debunking journalistic campaign following World War I should not be repeated and believes that the American public deserves a clear and competent statement of our basic aims and activities during the Second World War."[15] William Langer says in his autobiography, *In and Out of the Ivory Tower*, that this tendentious statement by the Rockefeller Foundation was "badly worded."[16] Perhaps, but it nonetheless catches the self-serving sense of the Rockefeller Foundation mandate.

In his history of the Council on Foreign Relations, *The Wise Men of Foreign Affairs*, Robert D. Schulzinger summarizes the messages from the council's executive director Walter Mallory: "[Mallory] railed against revisionist histories of the First World War which had undermined the public approval of an active foreign policy. [Langer's] book should counter the 'bad teaching in most schools and universities following the First World War which left the country so ill-prepared for either preventing World War II or participating in it.' "[17]

The authors of the Rockefeller-financed study *The Challenge to Isolation: The World Crisis of 1937–1940 and American Foreign Policy* were two of William Donovan's OSS men, William L. Langer and S. Everett Gleason. British Security Coordination, Intrepid, black propaganda—none of these is to be found in the Langer and Gleason study, and there is a manifestly less purposeful FDR.[18]

Historian Warren F. Kimball writes this of the Langer and Gleason work: "In fact, there are many who have denied that he [FDR] had any strategy at all. That is the thrust of arguments by early so-called 'court' historians like William Langer and S. Everett Gleason who, writing in the decade after World War II and with 'Isolationism' as the villain, sought to defend Roosevelt's actions by picturing him as one who only reacted to events, one whose foreign policy was akin to flying by the seat of the pants. After all, they imply, if Hitler and the Japanese were clearly aggressors, then why debate the issue of whether or not the President lied? The United States had done the right thing—there was no need to dig any deeper. Whether or not those deceptions were part of a clear foreign policy was never answered."[19]

The absence of a powerful and intellectually respectable revisionism after World War II also left unnoticed that Langer and Gleason were from the British intelligence-created OSS and that the Rockefellers, whose foundation financed the book, had been the rent-free provider of space in Rockefeller Center for BSC and such BSC fronts as Fight for Freedom. The activities of Nelson Rockefeller as Coordinator of Inter-American Affairs (the Rockefeller Office) might have also been revealed earlier by searching revisionist historians.[20]

Moreover, some key members of the Council on Foreign Relations also had good reason to promote an official history that would preclude any careful examination of the British efforts to involve the United States in the war. Several of its officers, directors, and prominent committee members—Francis P. Miller, Lewis W. Douglas, Whitney H. Shepardson, Stacy May, Edward Warner, and Winfield W. Riefler— had been leading members of the BSC front Century Group/Fight for Freedom.[21]

Miller, Douglas, and Shepardson had unquestionably been witting about some operations of BSC. It was Lewis Douglas who had tried to get doctoral candidate Mark Lincoln Chadwin to remove evidence of British influence on Fight for Freedom from the manuscript that became the book *The Hawks of World War II*. Whitney Shepardson was wartime head of Special Intelligence for William Donovan at OSS and worked closely with British intelligence.

Francis Miller had worked for OSS and was undeniably knowledgeable about many BSC operations. He was a close friend of BSC's Donald MacLaren, who helped run BSC's "George Office." Two decades after World War II, Miller's views were recorded by Mark Chadwin: "Right-wing 'revisionists' may have grounds to accuse the Warhawks of a 'conspiracy' to involve the United States in war but certainly not of a 'liberal conspiracy.'...The original members of the Group were predominately conservative not liberal...."[22]

Besides the deliberate attempt to promote an evasive semiofficial history, two other factors worked against a revisionist evaluation of the way the United States had become involved in the war. First, the destruction of Nazism was so universally acclaimed as a positive good that the revisionists simply found themselves on the wrong side of the political consensus. The consensus, which British black propaganda helped develop, that the Axis was not only evil but had threatened the Western Hemisphere was a major factor in the British intelligence campaign to involve the United States in the war.

Second, whereas the wide-ranging revisionism after World War I had been a wide-open debate in a time of peace, revisionism after World War II was inhibited by the emerging Cold War. The review by Samuel Flagg Bemis, the eminent Yale diplomatic historian, of George Morgenstern's *Pearl Harbor: The Story of the Secret War* in the March 1947 edition of *Modern History* is the classic illustration of the way in which the Cold War constrained responsible historians. While agreeing with Morgenstern that much of the blame for Pearl Harbor rested in Washington and "that the majority of the congressional committee...[investigating the Pearl Harbor disaster] was biased and trying to protect its party leaders," Bemis nonetheless wrote that "this revisionist attempt...in this year 1947 is serious, unfortunate,...deplorable. Unfriendly critics will pick sentences...to hurt Morgenstern's own country, our still free Republic."[23] The Soviet menace and World War III seemed to loom just over the horizon as Bemis summed up the revisionist threat: "After winning the second World War will the new revision help to lose the second peace as the first revision helped to lose the first peace?"[24]

The peace was kept, but so were many secrets. This work has attempted to uncover and piece together the known facts. We will never know the full story, of course: most of its principals have carried their secrets to the grave. Our knowledge of the British operations will always remain incomplete.

One thing is clear, however. Britain's World War II influence-shaping campaign in the United States was one of the most important and successful covert operations of history. As such, it deserves careful examination at a time when intelligence organizations are under fire for conducting covert operations at all. Rarely informed of anything but the failures of covert operations, their opponents seem off on a cloud—a morally defensible cloud, perhaps, but still a cloud. In a time of great national crises and dwindling resources, covert operations were the tool that ultimately was responsible for saving England. As history knows now, England's saving was the world's.

...

Glossary of
Individuals and
Organizations

Agar, Herbert Sebastian (1897–1980). London correspondent and later editor for the *Louisville Courier-Journal*; speaker and policy-maker for Fight for Freedom; special assistant to U.S. ambassador in London, Gil Winant; stayed in England after the war.

Agar, William (1894–1972). Educator; older brother of Herbert Agar; Princeton Ph.D.; full-time employee of Fight for Freedom; also ran the Rockefeller Center office of another BSC front, the American Irish Defense Association.

Aglion, Also Aghion, Raoul. Said to have been legal attaché in the French legation at Cairo before the fall of France in June 1940; then moved to the United States, where he worked for SOE Political and Minorities Section of British Security Coordination with the cover symbol G.411; wrote pro-British articles for *The Nation*; general secretary of the Free French delegation to the United States; wrote book *Fighting French* telling of de Gaulle's greatness and great support among the French people.

AIPO. American Institute of Public Opinion; polling organization run by George Gallup and penetrated by BSC.

Aitken, Max (Lord Beaverbrook) (1879–1964). Newspaper owner; close friend and adviser to Prime Minister Winston Churchill; close friend of fellow Canadian and BSC intelligence chief Sir William Stephenson.

189

America First. Anti-interventionist organization which sought to keep the United States out of the war. BSC declared and fought a covert political war on America First.

American Irish Defense Association (also Irish-American Defense Association). BSC front organized by agent Sandy Griffith in an unsuccessful attempt to persuade Irish-Americans to endorse aid for Britain.

American Labor Committee to Aid British Labor (ALCABL). Branch of the American Federation of Labor; used as a front by BSC.

American Youth Congress. Youth organization under strong Communist influence and thus strongly against United States involvement in European affairs during the period of the Hitler Stalin Pact (August 1939 to June 1941).

Ascoli, Max (1898–1978). Head of the Italian-American Mazzini Society. BSC claimed a close working relationship with Ascoli and IAMS.

Astor, Vincent (1891–1959). Ran a private intelligence service, called "the Room" or "the Club," for his friend and kinsman President Franklin Roosevelt.

Ayer, Alfred Jules (1910–89). Philosopher; SOE agent posted to BSC from October 1941 to March 1943 with cover symbol G.426, thus part of Political and Minorities Section; worked on intelligence on Latin America, with particular reference to Argentina and Chile, political, and S.O. planning.

Backer, George (1903–74). Author; publisher of the *New York Post*; also served as propaganda policy director for the U.S. Office of War Information. The "BSC Account" mentions him as having "rendered service of particular value."

Balderston, John (1889–1954). London correspondent of the *New York World*, 1923–31; Hollywood screenwriter; headed the William Allen White News Service, an offspring of the British puppet Inter-Allied Information Committee; major figure in Fight for Freedom.

Bell, Ulric (1891–1960). Washington correspondent of *Louisville Courier-Journal*, 1921–41; chairman of executive committee of Fight for Freedom; deputy to BSC collaborator Robert Sherwood at overseas branch of Office of War Information.

Belmonte Letter. Fake letter created by BSC and leaked to Bolivian government; implicated Bolivia's military attaché to Germany in a plot to overthrow Bolivian government. Consequence: arrests in Bolivia, German minister to Bolivia thrown out, reinforced British propaganda theme that Hitler threatened Latin America.

Berle, Adolf (1895–1971). Lawyer; State Department official; Pan Americanist; wished to stay out of European war and thus was early seen as an enemy by BSC; held unwelcome idea that only American intelligence services should operate in the United States.

Birkhead, the Rev. Leon M. (1885–1954). Unitarian minister who ran the Friends of Democracy; specialized in tough attacks on isolationists.

BIS. British Information Service; British Ministry of Information's administrative offices in Rockefeller Center, New York City; worked with BSC, also housed in Rockefeller Center.

Bruce, David K. E. (1898–1977). Headed the Secret Intelligence (SI) branch of COI/OSS until 1943; later headed Marshall Plan in France and served as U.S. ambassador to Britain.

Bryce, John F. C. "Ivar." SOE agent; code number G.140; brother-in-law of columnist Walter Lippmann; took credit for idea of phony map showing how Nazis planned to divide Latin America. The map was used by FDR in his Navy Day speech of 1941 to call for an end to all neutrality laws.

BSC. British Security Coordination; umbrella agency in charge of all British covert operations in the Western Hemisphere. Run by Sir William Stephenson (Intrepid) 1940–46.

"BSC Account." "British Security Coordination (BSC). An Account of Secret Activities in the Western Hemisphere, 1940–45" called the "Bible" by insiders; a selective after-action report on the work of BSC in the Western Hemisphere. About 35 percent of this very secret account is contained in Montgomery Hyde's *The Quiet Canadian.*

CDAAA. Committee to Defend America by Aiding the Allies (White Committee, after its nominal leader, Kansas journalist William Allen White). Its directors interlocked with those of Fight for Freedom. Several BSC agents worked for CDAAA.

Century Group. See Fight for Freedom.

CIAA. Coordinator of Inter-American Affairs (first called the Office of Coordinator of Commercial and Cultural Relations). The Coordinator 1940–44 was Nelson Aldrich Rockefeller; this U.S. government organization used BSC-supplied information to carry out the British agenda in Latin America.

COI. Coordinator of Information; American counterpart of BSC. Planned by and created at the behest of British intelligence by FDR's presidential order of July 1941; run by BSC officer Dick Ellis.

Coit, Richard Julius Maurice Carl Wetzler (b. 1887). Born surname: Wetzlar; banker; chief of staff to William Stephenson; cover symbol G.100; brought into BSC in summer 1940 because of knowledge of Brazil and German banking; sent by BSC to Brazil in late 1940, 1941, and early 1942.

Committee for Inter-American Cooperation. BSC front; used for black-propaganda work and cover for agents in Latin America.

Committee on Public Information. American propaganda agency during World War I. Headed by George Creel, this organization generated strong public feelings against all things German.

Coudert Group. Interventionist organization called together in October 1939 at the Down Town Association in New York by prominent lawyer Frederick R. Coudert to support lifting the embargo on supplies to Britain and France; at April 1940 CG meeting all present pledged to see that the Republicans and Democrats did not cater to the public's antiwar feelings.

Council for Democracy. Interventionist organization tied to Fight for Freedom; produced lofty moral statements and scholarly studies; useful, but not militant enough and had little grass-roots support.

Council on Foreign Relations. Formed in 1921 by an assortment of Anglophile Americans, many of them veterans of the Versailles Peace Conference; based in New York City; from 1922 published influential journal *Foreign Affairs*; voice of the American foreign policy establishment.

Cowles, Gardner Jr. "Mike" (1903–85). Publisher of the *Des Moines Register* and *Look* magazine; U.S. director of OWI, 1942–43; cousin of Morgan banker Thomas W. Lamont; promoter of Wendell Willkie; accompanied Willkie on 1942 round-the-world trip.

Cuneo, Ernest (1905–88). Code name Crusader; lawyer, journalist, author, intelligence officer; Roosevelt administration insider; attorney for columnists Drew Pearson and Walter Winchell and wrote much of Winchell's material; liaison between BSC, the White House, OSS, the State Department, the Treasury, and the Justice Department.

Cynthia. Code name for Amy Elizabeth Thorpe Pack Brousse (1910–63), wife of British diplomat Arthur Pack; MI-6 agent who worked in Spain, Poland, Chile, and the United States. Her classic tactic: "She singled out important men and seduced them." Isolationist Arthur Vandenberg was one of her targets.

Deakin, Major Frederick William Dampier "Bill" (b. 1913). Literary secretary to Winston Churchill from 1936 to December 1939; posted to BSC August 1941 to June 1942; worked in SOE's Political and Minorities Section (South American affairs) at BSC with cover symbol G.401; returned to UK and in May 1943 led first British military mission to Tito.

Department E.H. Stands for Electra House; this was a black propaganda agency run by Sir Campbell Stuart that came under the British Foreign Office; one of three agencies (the others being Section D of MI-6 and MI R of the War Office) brought together in July 1940 to form Special Operations Executive (SOE).

De Wohl, Louis (1903–61). Hungarian-born astrologer employed by British intelligence. His bogus anti-Hitler predictions were planted in American newspapers.

Dies Committee. U.S. House of Representatives Select Committee on Un-American Activities, 1938–44; this committee's investigators stumbled on BSC agent Sandy Griffith (G.112); obtained copies of Griffith's phone calls, telegrams, and bank records; Clerk of the House of Representatives kept these records closed until 1996.

Donovan, William Joseph "Wild Bill" (1883–1959). Congressional Medal of Honor in World War I. BSC called him "our man" and pushed him into position as head of COI/OSS, which had been created at request of BSC and according to British plans.

Douglas, Lewis (1894–1974). President of Mutual Life Insurance Co., 1940–47; ran meetings of Century Group/Fight for Freedom; leader of CDAAA; leading figure in nomination of Wendell Willkie and British-instigated Destroyer Deal; U.S. ambassador to England, 1947 to 1950.

Ellis, Colonel Charles Howard "Dick" (1895–1975). Professional member of MI-6; assistant to Sir William Stephenson ("Intrepid"); actually ran Donovan's COI office and produced the blueprint for the American OSS; also suspected of working for German and Soviet intelligence services.

Emmet, Christopher Temple, Jr. (1900–74). Journalist; cousin of BSC collaborator Robert Emmet Sherwood; worked closely with BSC agent Sandy Griffith; vice president of BSC front France Forever.

Field, Marshall III (1893–1956). Publisher; born in Chicago, reared and educated in England; close to his cousin British MOI propagandist Ronald Tree; member of executive committee of Fight for Freedom; funded interventionist papers *PM* and *Chicago Sun*.

Fight for Freedom (FFF). BSC front; militant interventionist group which called for an American declaration of war on Germany; started as Miller Group/Century Group in late spring 1940; used by BSC for vigorous attacks on isolationists.

Fish, Hamilton (1888–1991). Vocal anti-interventionist Republican congressman from President Franklin Roosevelt's home district in New York. The successful BSC campaign to destroy his reputation and remove him from office was run by BSC agent Sandy Griffith.

FO. British Foreign Office; nominally in control of SIS; contact between SIS and the FO was through the permanent undersecretary of state, who from 1938 to 1946 was Sir Alexander Cadogan.

France Forever. BSC front organized by BSC agent Sandy Griffith; supported British declaration that obscure French tank general Charles de Gaulle was the true voice of France.

Friends of Democracy. BSC front ostensibly run by Unitarian minister Leon M. Birkhead; specialized in vitriolic, name-calling attacks labeling isolationists as Nazis.

George Office. Cover name for organization that managed part of BSC's economic warfare campaign; named for its director, George Merten, a German economist. The George operation was given to OSS to protect it from the FBI.

Griffith, Sanford (1893–1974). Journalist, stockbroker, BSC intelligence agent with SOE cover symbol G.112; ran BSC fronts such as France Forever, American Irish Defense Association; ran campaign to drive Hamilton Fish from Congress; rigged polls suggesting that various groups favored aiding Britain; oversaw writing of scripts for shortwave radio station WRUL.

Guinzburg, Harold (1899–1961). President of Viking Press; involved in intelligence; made daily decisions at Fight for Freedom; official of OWI.

Halpern, Alexander J. (ca. 1879–1956). Russian lawyer; in 1917 he had been secretary to the cabinet in the Kerensky government in Russia; at BSC, symbolized first as G.111; under this symbol he was responsible for controlling Arabic, Senegalese, French, Persian, Italian, and Turkish broadcasts by the supposedly independent Boston shortwave station WRUL; later G.400 and thus the leader of SOE's Political and Minorities Section at BSC.

Henson, Francis (1906–63). Journalist; assistant to British intelligence agent Sandy Griffith at polling firm Market Analysts Inc.; worked on BSC political warfare and poll-rigging projects with Griffith.

Hoke, Henry (1894–1970). Editor and publisher of the *Reporter of Direct Mail Advertising*; Intrepid's "friend in advertising" who helped stop free mailing of Nazi and isolationist propaganda under the congressional frank.

Hyde, H. Montgomery (1907–89). BSC agent who edited the "BSC Account" for publication as *The Quiet Canadian* or, in the United States, *Room 3603*. Despite successful sales, few in journalism or academia realized this book's importance. Hyde also wrote two other books on BSC operations, *Cynthia* and *Secret Intelligence Agent*.

IAIC. Inter-Allied Information Committee. Covertly formed in 1940; funded by British to see that the lesser Allies spoke the British propaganda line; later became UNIO, the United Nations Information Organization.

Ingersoll, Ralph (1900–85). Editor of interventionist newspaper *PM* (which was owned by Marshall Field III). The "BSC Account" lists Ingersoll as among "those who rendered service of particular value."

INTREPID. New York cable address of BSC head Sir William Stephenson (48000), which became synonymous with him on the publication of the 1976 book *A Man Called Intrepid* by William Stevenson (no relation).

Korda, Alexander (1893–1956). Filmmaker; British intelligence agent. Made wartime U.S. films sympathetic to Britain; allowed BSC to use his offices; was frequent visitor to Intrepid in Rockefeller Center.

Korda, Vincent (1896–1979). British intelligence agent; brother of Alexander Korda; Oscar award-winning art director of *The Thief of Baghdad*.

Lamont, Thomas William (1870–1948). Director and chairman of board of J. P Morgan banking firm; behind-the-scenes power in interventionist movement. Was in close contact with President Roosevelt; was instrumental in Republican nomination of Wendell Willkie for president in 1940.

Langley, Noel (b. 1911). Worked in Hollywood 1936–42 as screenwriter; engaged by BSC to work in the Political and Minorities Section by September 1942 with the symbol G.433.

L.A.T.I. Operation. Fraudulent letter produced by BSC containing negative comments about the president of Brazil and purporting to have been written by the head of the Italian airline L.A.T.I. L.A.T.I. was fined and its officials were jailed; it lost its landing rights and no longer broke the British blockade of Europe.

League for Human Rights. BSC front attached to the American Federation of Labor.

Levy, Benn W. (1900–73). Playwright; SOE cover symbol at BSC was G.145.

Lippmann, Walter (1889–1974). Newspaper columnist; brother-in-law of SOE agent Ivar Bryce; major influence in nomination of Willkie for president. The "BSC Account" lists him as "among those who rendered service of particular value."

Lothian, Lord (1882–1940). British ambassador to U.S.; worked very closely with BSC head, Sir William Stephenson.

Maschwitz, Eric (1901–69). Officer of Special Operations Executive (SOE); cover symbol G.106; ran Station M, the producer of bogus documents BSC used to attack its enemies and further interventionism.

Menzies, Brigadier General (later Sir) Stewart Graham (1899–1974). Head of MI-6, 1939–52; called "C."

MEW. British Ministry of Economic Warfare. Cover for Special Operations Executive (SOE).

MI-5. The British domestic security service. Had responsibilities similar to those of the American FBI.

MI-6. World War II designation of the British overseas SIS. Had responsibilities similar to those of today's American CIA.

Miller, Francis Pickens (1895–1978). Rhodes scholar; founding member of Fight for Freedom; OSS officer.

Miller Group. See Fight for Freedom.

Mokarzel, Salloum (1881–1952). Editor of *Al Shoda*, the Arabic daily newspaper of New York City; president of the Lebanese League of Progress. BSC claims to have worked closely with him.

Morrell, Sydney "Bill" (1912–85). Journalist; advertising man; SOE black propagandist with cover symbol G.101. Worked for BSC; coordinated the work of agent Sandy Griffith.

Mowrer, Edgar Ansel (1892–1977). Journalist; correspondent for Secretary of the Navy Frank Knox's *Chicago News*; deputy director to Robert Sherwood at OWI. Accompanied Donovan on his 1940 trip to London and coauthored nationally distributed series of exaggerated articles on the threat of the Nazi fifth column.

New York Herald Tribune. Favorite outlet for stories BSC wished to see published in mainstream American press.

Niles, David (1882–1952). White House official and the usual contact for BSC and BSC fronts such as Fight for Freedom.

NKVD. People's Commissariat of Internal Affairs; Soviet security service. Predecessor to the KGB (Committee for State Security); thoroughly penetrated BSC and OSS.

Non-Sectarian Anti-Nazi League. BSC front. According to BSC documents this front was "used for vehement exposure of enemy agents and isolationists."

Nye Committee (1934–36). Special Senate Committee on Investigation of the Munitions Industry led by Senator Gerald P. Nye (R-N.D.); sensational revelations of this committee provided background for the passage of a series of American neutrality laws.

Office of Civilian Defense. Agency of the U.S. Government that promoted interventionist propaganda before Pearl Harbor.

Ogilvy, David (1911–99). British intelligence officer; worked simultaneously for George Gallup's American Institute of Public Opinion and for BSC; later a prominent advertising man. His brother Francis had been one of the earliest recruits to Section D of MI-6.

ONI. Office of Naval Intelligence, either British or American.

OSS. Office of Strategic Services. On June 12, 1942, COI was separated into two parts, OSS and OWI. OSS was placed under the U.S. military and its operations excluded from the Western Hemisphere.

Overseas News Agency (ONA). Branch of the Jewish Telegraph Agency. British intelligence subsidized ONA in return for cooperation.

OWI. Office of War Information. Created in June 1942 with Robert Emmet Sherwood as head; responsible for overseas U.S. propaganda other than black.

Parry, Alfred (1901–92). Born in Russia as Abraham Paretsky; BSC agent Sandy Griffith's man in the Chicago Committee to Defend America/Fight for Freedom office; later worked for the OSS and still later for the CIA.

Passport Control. Between the world wars this was the worldwide cover for Britain's SIS.

Patterson, Paul Chenery (1878–1952). Publisher of *Baltimore Sun*; listed in the "BSC Account" as one of "those who rendered service of particular value."

Pearson, Drew (Andrew Russell) (1897–1969). Wrote "Washington Merry-Go-Round" newspaper column, 1931–65. His column and radio broadcast were vehicles for British black propaganda and character assassination. His former student and attorney Ernest Cuneo was White House liaison with BSC.

PID. Political Intelligence Department of the Foreign Office. At first a genuine department of the FO which was used as cover for covert propaganda. The covert operations continued under this name even after the real department was abolished.

PWE. Political Warfare Executive; the British Foreign Office psychological warfare and black propaganda unit. Until July 1940 much of this unit had been part of MI-6, Section D; then, until the summer of 1941, it was SO.1 of SOE.

The Quiet Canadian. Unknown to historians or journalists of the time, this stunning book leaked roughly 35 percent of the very secret after-action report "BSA Account." Passages deemed too sensitive were changed or removed from the American version, *Room 3603*.

Reid, Helen Rogers (1882–1970). Wife of Ogden Mills Reid, owner of the *New York Herald Tribune*. Mrs. Reid really ran the paper; the "BSC Account" lists her as "among those who rendered service of particular value." Was a major force in promoting Willkie for the Republican nomination in 1940.

Rockefeller Office. See CIAA.

The Room; the Club. President Roosevelt's personal intelligence service of upper-class anglophile New Yorkers, led by FDR's friend and kinsman Vincent Astor. Astor was a conduit for information from British intelligence to FDR.

Room 3603. See *The Quiet Canadian*.

Ross-Smith, A. M. "Bill" (d. 1993). British intelligence officer who worked for BSC; code number 48907. Conceived and ran the "ships watch scheme," which developed agents on neutral ships to watch for anti-British activity.

Section D. Special sabotage and black-propaganda section of MI-6. Created on April Fools' day 1938, it grew very rapidly and by 1940 was larger than the rest of MI-6. Became part of SOE July 1940.

Security Executive. Worldwide responsibilities for supervision of British internal security during World War II; little is known of the details of the Security Executive; once headed by Duff Cooper.

Shepardson, Whitney Hart (1890–1966). Rhodes scholar; assistant to President Wilson's confidant Colonel House at Paris peace talks, 1919; wrote June 1940 demand that U.S. declare war on Germany for group that became Fight for Freedom; friend and failed biographer of Bill Stephenson and Bill Donovan; first OSS Secret Intelligence (SI) chief in London; special assistant to Ambassador Winant in London in 1942.

Sherwood, Robert Emmet (1896–1955). Pulitzer Prize–winning playwright and author; member of Canadian Black Watch in World War I; FDR speechwriter. Allowed British intelligence to review FDR speeches; promoted British intelligence agenda with FDR. Lived half of each year in England.

SIS. Secret Intelligence Service; also known by its World War II designation MI-6, or Broadway after its address, near the St. James Park underground station.

SO.1. Covert propaganda department of Section D of MI-6. It was moved to the new Special Operations Executive (SOE) on the creation of that unit in July 1940; moved to the Political Warfare Executive (PWE) in summer 1941.

SO.2. Sabotage department of MI-6 Section D. It became part of the new Special Operations Executive (SOE) in July 1940.

SOE. Special Operations Executive; also known as Baker Street after the location of its offices near the fictional address of Sherlock Holmes. Formed by Churchill, July 19, 1940, as amalgamation of Section D of MI-6; MI R, the War Office's guerrilla warfare research group; and Department EH, Sir Campbell Stewart's secret propaganda unit.

Station M. Phony-document factory located in Toronto, run by Eric Maschwitz, G.106 of SOE. Ink, paper, and typewriter specialists worked together to produce authentic-looking documents to back BSC's various covert action programs.

Stephenson, Sir William Samuel (1896–1989). Canadian-born industrialist better known today as Intrepid, from the cable address of his office; head of BSC, which ran British intelligence operations in the Western Hemisphere. Knighted in 1945; code number 48000.

Stout, Rex (1886–1975). Mystery writer; worked for BSC on such projects as the attack on Standard Oil of New Jersey.

Swope, Herbert Bayard (1882–1958). Active in Fight for Freedom; guiding hand behind Overseas News Agency, which was subsidized by and worked closely with BSC.

Tunney, Gene (1897–1978). One time world heavyweight champion boxer; close friend of Sir William Stephenson. Introduced Stephenson to J. Edgar Hoover, head of the FBI; ostensibly funded anti-Communist youth group the National Foundation for American Youth, headquartered in Rockefeller Center.

Union Now Movement. Plan put forth by one-time *New York Times* League of Nations correspondent Clarence K. Streit (1896–1986); proposed that the United States amalgamate with Britain in two books: *Union Now: The Proposal for Inter-Democracy Federal Union* (1940) and *Union Now with Britain* (1941).

Viereck, George Sylvester (1884–1962). Registered German propagandist. BSC worked very closely with the Justice Department to supply the evidence to convict Viereck of improperly registering. BSC persevered when the first conviction was overturned by the U.S. Supreme Court; got conviction on the second try.

Wellington House. Headquarters of British World War I propaganda operations aimed at winning American sympathy for the British cause.

Wheeler-Bennett, John (1902–75). Covert British propagandist; worked closely with Intrepid.

White Committee. The Committee to Defend America by Aiding the Allies (CDAAA); known by name of its nominal chairman, Kansas journalist William Allen White. Used by BSC.

Williams, Valentine (1883–1946). Arrived in United States in July 1941 as representative of SO.1 with BSC head William Stephenson to advise and guide him on all matters of propaganda; to lecture, broadcast, and write as much as possible; and to further the cause of General de Gaulle in America; his SOE cover symbol was G.131.

Williams, Wythe (1881–1956). Journalist; faded reporter from World War I; used surprising appointment as editor of *Greenwich* (Connecticut) *Time* to make national reputation for scoops on Hitler's actions; became prominent radio news analyst in 1940–41 for Mutual Broadcast System; BSC black propagandist Bill Morrell was feeding him these inside scoops; wrote, with BSC agent Sandy Griffith's man Albert Parry, propaganda book *Riddle of the Reich*.

Willkie, Wendell (1892–1944). Lifelong Democrat and interventionist; never elected to public office. In 1940, in the most bizarre convention of the century, the Republicans nominated Willkie for president; this enabled FDR to consummate the Destroyer Deal and to continue to press forward with his interventionist policies. Willkie worked with FDR to eliminate isolationist Republicans such as Fish from office and was an activist in Fight for Freedom.

Winant, John Gilbert (1889–1947). Republican governor of New Hampshire; director of the International Labor Office in Geneva, 1938–39; ambassador to Great Britain, 1941–46. Worked closely with Sir William Stephenson in creation of Donovan's COI.

Winchell, Walter (1897–1972). Strongly anti-Nazi newspaper and radio columnist. Worked closely with BSC; his column was largely written by Ernest Cuneo, the White House liaison with BSC.

Wiseman, Sir William (1885–1962). SIS officer in charge of U.S. operations during World War I; close confidant of Colonel House, adviser to President Woodrow Wilson; interwar partner in investment banking firm of Kuhn, Loeb; active in BSC work in early days of World War II.

WRUL. Boston shortwave radio station whose foreign-language broadcasts were covertly written and subsidized by BSC.

...

Notes

Abbreviations

AHVP   Arthur Hendrick Vandenberg Papers. Bentley Historical Library, University of Michigan, Ann Arbor, Mich.
CDAAAP   Committee to Defend America by Aiding the Allies (William Allen White Committee) Papers. Seeley Mudd Library, Princeton University, Princeton, N.J.
CIAFI   CIA documents obtained through the Freedom of Information Act.
CTEP   Christopher T. Emmet Papers. Hoover Institution on War, Revolution and Peace, Stanford, Calif.
DH   *Diplomatic History* (journal).
DPP   Drew Pearson Papers. Lyndon B. Johnson Library and Museum, Austin, Tex.
EBP   Ellsworth Barnard Papers. Manuscripts Department, Lilly Library, Indiana University, Bloomington, Ind.
ECP   Ernest Cuneo Papers. Franklin D. Roosevelt Library, Hyde Park, N.Y.
EPCP   Lady Cotter (Eveline Mary Paterson) Papers. Privately held by her daughter Virginia Owen, London, England
FBIF   Federal Bureau of Investigation Files obtained through Freedom of Information Act requests.
FDRL   Franklin D. Roosevelt Library, Hyde Park, N.Y.
FDRP   Franklin D. Roosevelt Papers. Franklin D. Roosevelt Library, Hyde Park, N.Y.
FFFP   Fight for Freedom Papers. Seeley Mudd Library, Princeton University, Princeton, N.J.
FHP   Francis Henson Papers. Held by Henson/Farrow family in Maryland.
FO   Foreign Office Records. Public Records Office (Kew), London, England.
GCP   Grenville Clark Papers. Dartmouth College Library, Hanover, N.H.
HHP   Herbert Hoover Papers. Herbert Hoover Presidential Library, West Branch, Iowa.
HHVP   Hazel Harper Vandenberg Papers. Bentley Historical Library, University of Michigan, Ann Arbor, Mich.

HMHP   H. Montgomery Hyde Papers. Churchill College Library, Cambridge, England.

IANS   *Intelligence and National Security* (journal published in London by Frank Cass).

JBP   John Buchan (Lord Tweedsmuir) Papers. Douglas Library, Queen's University, Kingston, Ont., Canada.

JCH   *Journal of Contemporary History.*

KRP   Kermit Roosevelt Papers. Library of Congress, Washington, D.C.

LDP   Lewis W. Douglas Papers. Special Collections, University of Arizona Library, Tucson, Ariz.

MLP   Mary S. Lovell Papers. Privately held. Stroat, Nr Chepstow Gwent, England.

MMP   Marie Meloney Papers. Rare Book and Manuscript Library, Butler Library, Columbia University, New York, N.Y.

SII   *Studies in Intelligence* (the CIA's scholarly in-house journal; many of the articles are classified).

TWLP   Thomas W. Lamont Papers. Historical Collections, Soldier's Field Baker Library, Harvard University, Boston, Mass.

WJDP   William J. Donovan Papers. U.S. Army Military History Institute, Carlisle Barracks, Carlisle, Pa.

WLP   Walter Lippmann Papers. Sterling Memorial Library, Yale University, New Haven, Conn.

WTP   Walter Trohan Papers. Herbert Hoover Presidential Library, West Branch, Iowa.

WWP   Wendell Willkie Papers. Manuscripts Department, Lilly Library, Indiana University, Bloomington, Ind.

PREFACE

1. Robin W. Winks, *Cloak and Gown: Scholars in the Secret War, 1939–1961* (New York: William Morrow, 1987), 476; Christopher Andrew and David Dilks, eds., *The Missing Dimension: Government and Intelligence Communities in the Twentieth Century* (Urbana, Ill.: University of Illinois Press, 1984), 1.

2. Ronald Lewin, "A Signal-Intelligence War," in *The Second World War: Essays in Military and Political History*, ed. Walter Laqueur (London: Sage Publications, 1982), 185–86. This shortcoming in the official histories has been lessened by the publication of the official series *British Intelligence in the Second World War*, written under the direction of F. H. Hinsley.

3. ECP, Box 51, Unidentified file.

4. Fishel, review of Fargo, *The Broken Seal*, in *SII* 59, no. 1 (Winter 1968), 81.

5. James Bamford, *The Puzzle Palace: A Report on America's Most Secret Agency* (Boston: Houghton Mifflin, 1982), 309.

6. David Hackett Fischer, *Historians' Fallacies: Toward a Logic of Historical Thought* (New York: Harper Torchbooks, 1970), 76.

7. L. B. Kirkpatrick, review of Hyde, *The Quiet Canadian*, in *SII* 7, no. 3 (Summer 1963): 122–25.

8. Bill Ross-Smith to author, 14 June and 16 April 1993.

INTRODUCTION

1. Randolph Churchill recollections in Martin Gilbert, *Winston S. Churchill*, vol. 6, *Finest Hour 1939–41*, 358.
2. Justice D. Doenecke, "Historiography: U.S. Policy and the European War, 1939–1941," *DH* 19 (Fall 1995): 690.
3. W. K. Hancock and M. M. Gowing, *British War Economy* (London: His Majesty's Stationery Office, 1949), 101–2, 71, 69.
4. *Ibid.*, 65.
5. *Ibid.*, 107.
6. JBP, Reel 6, John Buchan to Stair A. Gillon, 11 October 1937. The letter continued: "I think there is just a chance of America now coming back into the fold and working along with the European democracies....I feel the most useful work I can do is in connection with the U.S.A. I have Cordell Hull coming up to stay with me in a fortnight for some serious talks." Buchan reported his talks to the prime minister and received a letter dated 19 November 1937 in reply: "I was delighted to receive your letter of the 25th October and to have your very interesting account of your conversations with Roosevelt and Cordell Hull. You will doubtless have noticed that in recent speeches I have gone out of my way to encourage those sections of American opinion that seem to have welcomed the President's Chicago speech." Chamberlain to Buchan, JBP, Reel 6, Box 9.
7. King, Diary, 10 and 11 June 1939, pp. 675–784, MG26, J13 Public Archives of Canada, quoted in Benjamin D. Rhodes, "The British Royal Visit of 1939 and the Psychological Approach to the United States," *DP* 2 (Spring 1978): 210.
8. Rhodes, "British Royal Visit," 211.
9. JBP, Box II Correspondence, a) General May 1939–Feb. 1940, Reel 7, Chamberlain to Buchan, 7 July 1939.
10. G. William Domhoff, "The Power Elite and Its Critics," in *C. Wright Mills and the Power Elite*, ed. G. William Domhoff and Hoit B. Ballard (Boston: Beacon Press, 1968), 251–78.
11. Douglas Little, "Crackpot Realists and Other Heroes: The Rise and Fall of the Postwar American Diplomatic Elite," *DH* 13 (Winter 1989): 99–111.
12. Lord Robert Cecil, memo, 18 September 1917, CAB 24/26, GT 2074, quoted in David Reynolds, "Rethinking Anglo-American Relations," *International Affairs* 65 (Winter 1988/89), 95.
13. U.S. Department of Commerce, *Historical Statistics of the United States: Colonial Times to 1970*, 380.
14. ECP, Box 51, Unidentified File, "Dear Montgomery" letter, 29 January 1988, 2.

CHAPTER 1: ORGANIZATION, METHODS, AND OFFSPRING

1. Created by President Roosevelt's executive order on August 16, 1940, this organization was called the Office of the Coordinator of Commercial and Cultural Relations Between the American Republics. Later this was changed to the Coordinator of Inter American Affairs. It became known as the Rockefeller Office because of its head, thirty-two-year-old Nelson Rockefeller.
2. Thomas F. Troy, "The Coordinator of Information and British Intelligence," *SII* 18, no. 1-S (Spring 1974): 15.
3. Clive Ponting, *1940: Myth and Reality* (Chicago: Ivan R. Dee, 1990), 60.

4. Troy, "Coordinator of Information," 48.

5. Anthony Cave-Brown, *"C": The Secret Life of Sir Stewart Menzies, Spymaster to Winston Churchill* (New York: Macmillan, 1987), 195.

6. Troy, "Coordinator of Information," 17; H. Montgomery Hyde, *The Quiet Canadian* (London: Hamish Hamilton, 1962), 28. This quote is illustrative of the substantial differences between the British version of Hyde's book, titled *The Quiet Canadian*, and the American version, titled *Room 3603* (New York: Farrar, Straus, 1962). What appears to be the quotation in question reads differently on page 28 of *Room 3603*: "…to counter the enemy's subversive plans throughout the Western Hemisphere, and to promote sympathy for the British cause in the United States. This included counter-espionage, political warfare and special operations." This is one of many changes suggested by David Ogilvy in a nine-page letter (1 Janurary 1963) of potential changes he sent to Sir William Stephenson to be passed on to Montgomery Hyde. Sir William, by this time very nervous about the project, wrote across the top of the letter "David's points indicate why I have been against an American edition. WS, Jan. 17/63." The letter is in the Hyde Papers, Churchill College, Cambridge. For commentary on this see Timothy J. Naftali, "Intrepid's Last Deception: Documenting the Career of Sir William Stephenson," *IANS* 8, no. 3 (July 1993): 81 and nn. 62, 63.

7. Troy, "Coordinator of Information," 18–19.

8. During the period of the German-Russian nonaggression pact, August 23, 1939, to June 22, 1941, the American Youth Congress (AYC) was strongly under the influence of Communists and was strongly against intervention in the European war. The opposition to this youthful peace lobby was organized and led by the National Foundation for American Youth and its leader Murray Plavner. Gene Tunney apparently financed this organization, with offices in, once again, Rockefeller Center. Joseph Jaffe, Jr., "Isolationism and Neutrality in Academe, 1938–1941" (Ph.D. diss., Case Western Reserve University, 1979), 289.

9. Letters from Gene Tunney to Thomas F. Troy, 6 and 18 August and 18 September 1969, cited in Troy, "Coordinator of Information," 22–23.

10. Hyde, *Room 3603*, 31–32. Laurance Rockefeller contributed more than $10,000 (about $100,000 in 1996 dollars) to Fight for Freedom and also made an "arrangement" for the rent and for the expenses of the committee at the Rockefeller Center Club. Mark Lincoln Chadwin, *The Hawks of World War II: The Interventionist Movement in the U.S. Prior to Pearl Harbor* (Chapel Hill, N.C.: University of North Carolina Press, 1968), 177.

11. The new name BSC was apparently suggested by J. Edgar Hoover. Hyde, *Room 3603*, 52.

12. Occasionally a reference to Menzies is found in Cadogan's printed diaries: "Thursday, 7 December 1944….'C' at 4:30 for gossip. He off to Belgium and he not so pessimistic as P.M. regarding present situation on western front." *The Diaries of Sir Alexander Cadogan O.M., 1938–1945*, edited by David Dilks (New York: G.P. Putnam's Sons, 1972), 685.

13. Christopher Andrew, *Her Majesty's Secret Service: The Making of the British Intelligence Community* (New York: Viking, 1986), 467.

14. John Wheeler-Bennett, *Special Relationship* (London: Macmillan, 1975), 153–54.

15. Sweet-Escott, *Baker Street Irregular* (London: Methuen, 1965), 21–24. Quoted in Andrew, *Secret Service*, 472.
16. For the SOE code-name system I am thankful to the SOE Adviser, Gervase Cowell. Letters to author dated 9 March, 5 April, and 25 October 1995.
17. Valentine Williams Personal File (SOE Archives), Duncan Stuart, CMG, The SOE Adviser, to author November 25, 1996.
18. This is from a list in ECP, Box 107, CIA file.
19. Maschwitz, *No Chip on My Shoulder*, 144–45, quoted in Hyde, *Quiet Canadian*, 135.
20. Public Records Office (PRO) HS 1/333. Professor Nick Cull supplied me with this document, and Gervase Cowell, the SOE Adviser, identified G.106 as Maschwitz.
21. ECP, Box 107, CIA file, eighteen unnumbered pages.
22. Nathan Miller, *Spying for America: The Hidden History of U.S. Intelligence* (New York: Paragon House, 1989), 42.
23. Paul Kramer, "Nelson Rockefeller and British Security Coordination," *JCH* 16 (January 1981): 76.
24. *Ibid.*, 77.
25. *Ibid.*, 78.
26. *Ibid.*, 79.
27. *Ibid.*, 83.
28. *Ibid.* For a contrary view on the effectiveness of these operations, see the admittedly cantankerous Spruille Braden, *Diplomats and Demagogues* (New Rochelle, N.Y.: Arlington House, 1971), 263.
29. Kramer, "Rockefeller and British Security," 83–84.
30. *Ibid.*, 84.
31. ECP, Box 107, Intrepid file. Cuneo reasons in this article that Ellis could not have been a Soviet mole because he and Intrepid "were as close as a picture to its frame." Cuneo goes on to say that Stephenson told him the Soviet Union would explode its first atom bomb "on or about Sept. 27, 1949." (It went off four weeks early.) "When Sir William gave me this staggering information on Feb. 18, 1948—a year and a half in advance of the event—I asked him how good the source was. He answered, 'Triple A, Triple 1.' I asked the question which never should be asked: Exactly how do you know?

    " 'We have a little window,' Sir William said. Moles were then called 'little windows.'

    "Except to transmit this to U.S. authorities, I have never before disclosed this. I do so now as some evidence in defense of the honor of Col. Ellis.

    "What Sir William knew, Dickie Ellis knew. Hence, If Dickie Ellis had been a KGB mole, he would have reported the British mole in the Kremlin to his true masters. He had not."
32. Troy, "Coordinator of Information," 109.
33. *Ibid.*, 108.
34. Memorandum from Desmond Morton to Colonel E. I. Jacob, 18 September 1941, Churchill Papers, Box 145, Folder 463, Item 2, quoted in Troy, "Coordinator of Information," 109.
35. FDRL, Berle, Box 213, Berle to Wells, September 18, 1941. Diary Vol. VII, 2, 122–23.

36. Sir William S. Stephenson, "Early Days of OSS (COI)," 7–8. OSS Records, ca 1960. Typescript, quoted in Troy, "Coordinator of Information," 100.

37. *Ibid.*

38. *Ibid.*, 101.

39. *Ibid.*, 103.

40. Edmond Taylor, *Awakening from History* (Boston: Gambit, 1969), 308.

41. Troy, "Coordinator of Information," 104.

42. ECP, Box 107, CIA file.

43. The CIA is not unique. This legacy, particularly of Special Operations Executive, has been very evident in France. For the French experience, see Douglas Porch, "French Intelligence Culture," *IANS* 10 (July 1995): 486–511. For a suggestion that the example of Eric Maschwitz's fakery at "Station M" may have influenced more recent Canadian covert operations, see Nick Cull, "Did the Mounties and the NFB fake Nazi atrocity pictures?" *Globe and Mail* June 3, 1995 *FOCUS* (Birmingham, England), Section D.

44. ECP, Box 107, CIA file.

45. *Ibid.*

CHAPTER 2: THE FRONTS

1. ECP, Box 51, Unidentified file, "Dear Montgomery" letter, 29 January 1988, 2.

2. PRO OF 898/103 Political Warfare Executive, Morrell, "SO.1," 10 July 1941.

3. David Ignatius, "Britain's War in America: How Churchill's Agents Secretly Manipulated the U.S. before Pearl Harbor," *Washington Post*, 17 September 1989, C-2.

4. Morrell, "SO.1," 10 July 1941.

5. Richard F. Cleveland was the son of former president Grover Cleveland.

6. Francis Pickens Miller, *Man from the Valley: Memories of a 20th Century Virginian,* (Chapel Hill, N.C.: University of North Carolina Press, 1971), 89–90.

7. Whitney Shepardson (1890–1960) also worked very closely with British intelligence. BSC officer Bill Ross-Smith wrote that like Robert Sherwood, [Whitney] Shepardson was not BSC but only a "collaborator." Bill Ross-Smith to author, 16 April 1993. Shepardson joined OSS and was sent to London as Secret Intelligence Service chief. The London positions of OSS were reserved for the most unreserved of Anglophiles. See also Chapter 3.

8. Morrell, "SO.1," 10 July 1941.

9. LDP, Box 82, Folder 20.

10. Chadwin, *Hawks*, 139.

11. Wheeler-Bennett, *Special Relationship*, 151.

12. *Ibid.*, 154.

13. Cull, "British Campaign," 448; Wheeler-Bennett, *Special Relationship*, 155.

14. Wheeler-Bennett, *Special Relationship*, 58.

15. Chadwin, *Hawks*, 201.

16. FFFP, Cusick to Bell and Agar, 6 March 1941, Cusick file.

17. Chadwin, *Hawks*, 204.

18. *Ibid.*, 201–2.

19. *Ibid.*, 205.

20. *Ibid.*, 177.
21. Ignatius, "Britain's War," C-2.
22. ECP, Box 51, Unidentified file, "Dear Montgomery" letter, 29 January 1988, 2.
23. FFFP, David Niles file.
24. FFFP, *Labor News Service* 1, 13 June 1941.
25. *Ibid.*, 25 July 1941.
26. *Ibid.*, 6 December 1941, 8.
27. FDRL, President's Personal File (PPF) 7426, Woll to FDR, 23 April 1941.
28. *Ibid.*, 23 April 1941 and 7 March 1941.
29. Timothy R. Dzierba, "Organized Labor and the Coming of World War II, 1937–1941" (Ph.D diss., State University of New York at Buffalo, 1983), 32–33.
30. FFFP, Abe Rosenfield to Mr. Bluestone, 24 May 1941.
31. See FDRL, PPF 7426, letters of 12 July 1941 and 5 May 1941.
32. FFFP, *Labor News Service* 1, 11 July 1941, 2.
33. FFFP, Birkhead file, Francis P. Miller to G. Bernard Noble, 23 October 1940.
34. Wayne S. Cole, *Charles A. Lindbergh and the Battle against American Intervention in World War II* (New York: Harcourt Brace Jovanovich, 1974), 139.
35. The original says: "It is a complete attack upon Henry Ford for his anti-Nazi [*sic*] leanings." This report by Morrell was apparently written off the top of his head under great deadline pressure, and never proofread. This is only one of numerous minor slips.
36. FFFP.
37. Cole, *Lindbergh*, 140. For Stout's work for British intelligence, see John McAleer, *Rex Stout: A Biography* (Boston: Little, Brown, 1977), 295–96. For Stout as an officer of Friends of Democracy, see Cole, *Lindbergh*, 139–40. For Stout as a sponsor of Fight for Freedom, see Chadwin, *Hawks*, 168.
38. FFFP, L. M. Birkhead to Ulric Bell, dated 4 February 1940 [should be 1941]. The 1940 date on the letter is certainly an error, as the letter is about events of 1941. The Fight for Freedom Committee did not exist in February 1940, and the letter is addressed to the RKO Building in Rockefeller Center. FFF did not occupy that space in February 1940.
39. *Ibid.*
40. Cole, *Lindbergh*, 147–48.
41. Hyde, *Quiet Canadian*, 73–74.
42. François Kersaudy, *Churchill and de Gaulle* (New York: Atheneum, 1982), 76–103.
43. ECP, Box 25, Henson files.
44. *New York Times*, 29 September 1940, 12.
45. *Ibid.*, 9 March 1941, 22.
46. ECP, Box 25, Henson files.
47. Cull, Nicholas John, "The British Campaign Against American 'Neutrality' Publicity and Propaganda" (Ph.D. diss., University of Leeds, 1991), 552.
48. *New York Times*, 21 December 1940, 4.
49. *Ibid.*, 28 May 1941, 9.
50. FFFP, WMCA file.
51. *New York Times*, 15 July 1941, 13. For other material on this episode, see Cole, *Lindbergh*, 129–35.

52. *New York Times*, 12 November 1941, 3. For Rex Benson's relationship to Menzies and SIS, see Cave-Brown, "*C*," *passim*.

53. John Colville, *The Fringes of Power: 10 Downing Street Diaries, 1939–1955* (New York: W.W. Norton, 1985), 306.

54. H. Montgomery Hyde, *Secret Intelligence Agent: British Espionage in America and the Creation of the OSS* (New York: St. Martin's Press, 1982), 91; Harold Nicolson, *The War Years, 1939–1945*, ed. Nigel Nicolson (New York: Atheneum, 1967); *Volume II of the Diaries & Letters*, 142–43; and Steve Neal, *Dark Horse: A Biography of Wendell Willkie* (Garden City, N.Y.: Doubleday, 1989), 199–200.

55. Obituary of James Byrne, *New York Times*, 5 November 1942.

56. Duncan Stuart, CMG, The SOE Adviser at the Foreign and Commonwealth Office, to author December 20, 1996.

57. ECP, Box 25, Henson files. In CTEP, Box 13, American Irish Defense Association file, there is a "Draft of Irish Declaration" dated 25 August 1941.

58. Another mentioned was Father Vincent Donovan, National Director of Catholic Thought Association. Father Donovan was the brother of William Donovan, whom Intrepid maneuvered into becoming the head of COI/OSS.

59. Ignatius, "Britain's War," C-2.

60. ECP, Box 13, American Irish Defense Association file.

61. Chadwin, *Hawks*, 148.

62. CTEP, Box 13, American Irish Defense Association file, paper titled "Material for Mr. Berney Hershey's Broadcast over WMCA on Committee for American Irish Defense."

63. Jane Harriet Schwar, "Interventionist Propaganda and Pressure Groups in the United States, 1937–1941" (Ph.D. diss., Ohio State University, 1973), 116.

64. *Ibid.*, 152.

65. *Ibid.*, 194.

66. *Ibid.*, 209.

67. Cull, "British Campaign," 380.

68. Leslie Halliwell, *Halliwell's Film Guide* (New York: Harper and Row, 1989) comments on *Lives of a Bengal Lancer*, 608; comments on *Prisoner of Zenda*, 829.

69. Cull, "British Campaign," 250.

70. *Ibid.*, 365.

71. William R. Keylor, "How They Advertised France," *DH* 17 (Summer 1993), 364.

72. Schwar, "Interventionist Propaganda," 170–71.

73. *Ibid.*, 153.

74. *Ibid.*, 202, 208.

75. Eichelberger, *Organizing for Peace*, 145, 146.

76. *Ibid.*, 146, 147.

77. Hyde, *Quiet Canadian*, 157–60; Ignatius, "Britain's War," C-2; Schwar, "Interventionist Propaganda, 216 n. 75.

78. PRO FO 898/103 Sydney Morrell, SO.1 Organisation, 10 July 1941; also Morrell of 19 June 1941 (SOE Archives), Duncan Stuart, CMG, The SOE Adviser at FCO, to author, November 25, 1997.

CHAPTER 3: THOSE WHO RENDERED SERVICE OF PARTICULAR
VALUE

1. FBIF, Ernest Cuneo file, 94-4-4411-63 (item 63), letter of 14 March 1969. The crux of Cuneo's argument is that since every major power knows it is being tapped, the Supreme Court ruling "raises a most delicate problem...the few untapped foreign ambassadors will deeply resent the dire insult that what they have to say isn't even worth bugging."

2. Ignatius, "Britain's War," C-2.

3. ECP, Box 51, Unidentified file, "Dear Dick" letter.

4. Ignatius, "Britain's War," C-2.

5. *Ibid.*

6. E. J. Kahn, Jr., *The World of Swope* (New York: Simon & Schuster, 1965), 433–37.

7. National Security Agency, VENONA Messages, No. 389–390.

8. ECP, Box 107, Crusader to Intrepid file.

9. McAleer, *Rex Stout*, 295–97.

10. Troy, COIBI, 103.

11. Taylor to author, 29 June 1991.

12. Tom Troy, "George," in Hayden Peake and Samuel Halpern, eds., *In the Name of Intelligence* (Washington, D.C.: NIBC Press, 1995), 479–498.

13. ECP, Box 51, Unidentified file, Cuneo to Montgomery [Hyde], 29 January 1988, 3.

14. WJDP, Box 120 B, Folder 78, Sir William Stephenson. The paper goes on to say: "On a long-range basis the British method is to take a person who is young and newly engaged upon a career useful to British intelligence and so to pay him and otherwise assist him as increasingly to develop his usefulness over an extended period of years." This is the very method the Soviets used to insinuate Philby, Burgess, Maclean, Blunt, and John Cairncross into British intelligence.

15. FFFP, Bell to Backer, 30 September 1941, thanking Backer for $2,000 donation.

16. Gleeson, *They Feared No Evil*, 54.

17. Wheeler-Bennett, *Special Relationship*, 154.

18. Harrison Evans Salisbury, *Without Fear or Favor* (New York: Times Books, 1980), 453–54.

19. Susan Ann Brewer, "Creating the 'Special Relationship': British Propaganda in the United States During the Second World" (Ph.D. diss., Cornell University, 1991), 384.

20. FFFP, Robert Spivak file.

21. Williams to Dalton, September 15, 1941, Valentine Williams Personal File (SOE Archives, FCO), Duncan Stuart, CMG, The SOE Adviser to author, November 25, 1996.

22. ECP, Box 51, Unidentified file.

23. Although no wartime thank-you notes from British Intelligence have been found, here are two from J. Edgar Hoover in a later period testifying to Cuneo's influence on the column: "...I have not had the opportunity until now to drop you this confidential note of appreciation for what I know was a very constructive influence in connection with one broadcast and one column by our friend. In fact, I could see your fine hand particularly in the column" (J. E. Hoover to Cuneo, 15 February

1950). "I wanted to drop you this personal note to tell you how effective Walter was last night and that I could see your fine hand in the background. Thanks a million" (J. E. Hoover to Cuneo, January 29, 1951). Both these letters are in FBIF, Ernest Cuneo file, 94-4-4411.

24. ECP, Box 107. Secretary of the Treasury Morgenthau's assistant John W. Hanes (of the knitwear family) was in charge of the Treasury Department's part in this 1939 attempt to make German ships easy targets for the British. Hanes soon quit the Treasury over some vague complaint and went to work on the Willkie campaign. He later helped the British campaign against Lindbergh by getting William Randolph Hearst to attack the flier. For Hanes's part in holding the German ships, see Donald Cameron Watt, *How War Came: The Immediate Origins of the Second World War, 1938–1939* (New York: Pantheon, 1989), 556.

25. Obituary of Helen Reid, *New York Times*, 28 July 1970, 1.

26. Cave-Brown, *"C,"* 35, 46. Except for Joseph Kennedy, the ambassadorship to England seems to have been a special preserve for those and their families who worked closely with British intelligence. Barry Bingham, owner of the *Louisville Courier-Journal*, the son of FDR's first ambassador to England, was closely involved with British intelligence. He paid the salaries of Herbert Agar and Ulric Bell while they devoted their time to running Fight for Freedom. During the war he was an intelligence officer in England, and after the war he worked on the Marshall Plan intelligence cover in France with such as E. Howard Hunt. He also allowed the CIA to use his newspaper as a cover. Gilbert Winant, who took the post of ambassador in February 1941, helped Intrepid promote an American intelligence service with Donovan at the helm (Troy, "Coordinator of Information," 103–4). Lewis Douglas, as we will see, was closely embroiled in the work of British intelligence, not only with such agents as Rex Benson and John Wheeler-Bennett and fronts such as Fight for Freedom and the William Allen White Committee but in fulfilling such needs as the Destroyer Deal and the nomination of Wendell Willkie. Later ambassador David Bruce was acceptable enough to be named head of Donovan's organization in London. Bruce had been a member of Vincent Astor's "Room" intelligence group. The strong Anglophile Winthrop Aldrich of Chase Bank also served as ambassador to Great Britain.

27. Dorothy Thompson's FBI file numbers: 62–74478, 65–16748 sub A, 65–16748, 9–7646, 9–8306, 9–7990, 9–9588.

28. Quoted in Marion K. Sanders, *Dorothy Thompson: A Legend in Her Time* (Boston: Houghton Mifflin, 1973), 289–91.

29. Ignatius, "Britain's War," C-1, C-2.

30. PRO FO 371/2422B, A/2299/26/45, Reith to Halifax, 27 March 1940; PRO FO 371/26186, A5348/118/45, Halifax to FO, No. 127, 2 July 1941, and Minute by North Whitehead, 11 July 1941; in Cull, "British Campaign," 471.

31. Walter Lippmann, *Public Philosopher: Selected Letters of Walter Lippmann*, edited by John Morton Blum (New York: Ticknor & Fields, 1985), 433; WLP, Box 59, Folder 314.

32. Roosevelt, *Public Papers of Franklin Roosevelt*, ed. Rosenman 10:438–44.

33. Documents on German Foreign Policy (DGFP) Series D, Vol. 13, Ribbentrop to Thomsen, 10 December 1941; Cull, "British Campaign," 540.

34. Ivar Bryce, *You Only Live Once: Memories of Ian Fleming* (Frederick, Md.: University Publications of America, 1984), 62–63.

35. *Ibid.*, 63; Cull, "British Campaign," 529–40. Also see John F. Bratzel and Leslie Rout, "FDR and the 'Secret Map,' " *Wilson Quarterly*, 1 January 1985, 167–73. A better journal article than Rout and Bratzel is Francis MacDonnell, "The Search for a Second Zimmerman Telegram: FDR, BSC, and the Latin American Front," *IANS* 4, no. 4: 496–99.

36. For Bryce's OSS number, see his picture OSS identification card among the illustrations in *You Only Live Once*. His SOE number was G-140. *You Only Live Once*, 63, 50. Ivar divorced Mrs. Lippmann's sister and in 1950 married Josephine Hartford, granddaughter of the founder of the Great Atlantic and Pacific Tea Company, and thus became the stepfather-in-law of Senator Claiborne Pell of Rhode Island. After the war he went to work for Ernest Cuneo at the North American Newspapers Alliance (NANA). Cuneo, Ian Fleming, and Bryce became good friends after the war. Bryce died in 1985. See obituary of Josephine Hartford Bryce, *New York Times*, June 10, 1992, D20.

37. WLP, Box 59, Folder 314, Bryce to Lippman, 23 March [1942].

38. *Ibid.*

39. Cull, "British Campaign," 552.

40. Ignatius, "Britain's War," C-2; Hyde, *Quiet Canadian*, 189–91.

41. Ellic Howe, *The Black Game* (London: Queen Anne Press, 1982), 213–15; Peter Buitenhuis, *The Great War of Words* (Vancouver: University of British Columbia Press, 1987), Cull, "British Campaign," 129–31; David Lloyd Jones, "Marketing the Allies to America," *Midwest Quarterly* 29 (Spring 1988): 378.

42. Charles Cruickshank, *SOE in Scandinavia* (Oxford, England: Oxford University Press, 1986), 28.

43. Stuart H. Loory, "The CIA's Use of the Press: A 'Mighty Wurlitzer,' " *Columbia Journalism Review* 13, no. 3 (September/October 1974): 9–18, mentions CIA "contracts with some 30 journalists," "efforts to plant false or misleading stories," "cash payments...for information," "access to information in the home offices," "secret ownership of 40 percent of...the Rome *Daily American*."

44. *Book Review Digest 1942*, 251.

45. Martha J. Hoppin, *The Emmets: A Family of Women Painters* (Pittsfield, Mass., 1982), 7; Tara L. Tappert, *The Emmets: A Generation of Gifted Women* (New York: Borghi, c. 1993).

46. John Mason Brown, *The Worlds of Robert E. Sherwood* (New York, 1962), 258, 259.

47. Ignatius, "Britain's War," C-2. I am grateful to Dr. Tim Naftali, who had an opportunity to read and take notes on the secret "BSC Account" for confirming that this claim is found in the "BSC Account," on page 15; Stephenson, *Early Days...*, 7–8, in Troy, "Coordinator of Information," 100.

48. Schwar, "Interventionist Propaganda," 185, 184.

49. H.L. Mencken, *The Diary of H. L. Mencken*, edited by Charles A. Fecher (New York: Alfred A. Knopf, 1989), 388.

50. *Ibid.*, 309.

51. For the story of the Countess of Athlone and FANY, see Irene Ward, *F.A.N.Y. Invicta* (London: Hutchinson, n.d.). The FANYs performed a myriad of tasks for

SOE. They were largely upper-class and highly cultured. Some performed duties as drivers for visiting VIPs; others were infiltrated into Europe to help "set Europe ablaze"; others were hostesses, radio operators, and code workers.

52. Athlone (1874–1957) had been Prince Alexander of Teck until World War I, when like the rest of the royal family he discarded his German-sounding name.

53. Cave-Brown, "*C*," 52–54, 110.

54. *Time*, 28 October 1940, 11, 12. For Athlone's appointment, see *Time*, 15 April 1940, 36–37; for correspondence, FDRL, President's Personal File (6957).

55. Chadwin, *Hawks*, 170.

56. In February 1942, Francis Pickens Miller was recruited, by Robert Sherwood, to Donovan's Coordinator of Information as chairman of the board of the Foreign Information Service. There he worked with Edmond Taylor. Miller, *Man from the Valley*, 105–14; obituary of Ulric Bell, *New York Times*, 18 January 1960, 27.

57. For the judge's pro-Britishness, see the book by his granddaughter Sallie Bingham, *Passion and Prejudice* (New York: Alfred A. Knopf, 1989), 204–5.

58. Chadwin, *Hawks*, 201.

59. FFFP, letter from Robert Bingham, 28 October 1940.

60. FFFP, Bingham file.

61. For MacLaren as BSC agent who became a member of Donovan's COI/OSS, see Miller, *Man from the Valley*, 109.

62. Chadwin, *Hawks*, 114.

63. Stephen Becker, *Marshall Field III: A Biography* (New York: Simon & Schuster, 1964), 63; Christopher Hitchens, *Blood, Class, and Nostalgia: Anglo-American Ironies* (New York: Farrar, Straus & Giroux, 1990), 311–16.

64. Turner Catledge, *My Life and the Times* (New York: Harper & Row, 1971), 126.

65. Becker, *Marshall Field III*, 279.

66. FFFP, Courteney Barber file, telephone interviews with Louise Parry, March 12, 1997, and April 8, 1997.

67. Walter Trohan, *Political Animals: Memoirs of a Sentimental Cynic* (Garden City, N.Y.: Doubleday, 1975), 169; Becker, *Marshall Field III*, 202–7, 216; Ignatius, "Britain's War," C-2.

68. Chadwin, *Hawks*, 64.

69. FBIF, Harold Guinzburg file, 77-19605.

70. Hyde, *Quiet Canadian*, 199, says: "Stephenson himself was attracted by two [American writers]…Walter Lippmann…and Leonard Lyons [who wrote] 'In the Lyons Den.' "

71. Maugham was a veteran of the Secret Intelligence Service. In 1917 he had been hired by Sir William Wiseman, head of SIS in the United States, and sent to Russia. His Ashenden stories reflected his SIS experience.

After being chased out of Europe by the Germans in 1940, Maugham was sent to the United States by the BIS to do propaganda. It was during this period that he became a luncheon companion of Jerome Weidman. "The Ministry of Information," writes Weidman, "promptly assigned him to the Untied States.…Nelson Doubleday, Maugham's American publisher, arranged to build a modest house for him on the Doubleday family plantation.…while work went forward…Maugham spent his time working on a novel called *The Hour Before the Dawn*, which the

British Ministry of Information had asked him to write." Jerome Weidman, *Praying for Rain* (New York: Harper & Row, 1986), 208, 222–224.

72. Dates are from James M. Salem, *A Guide to Critical Reviews: Part I, American Drama, 1909–1982*, 3rd ed., 487.

73. Oren Root, *Persons and Persuasions* (New York: W. W. Norton, 1974), 53.

74. Cull, "British Campaign," 52.

75. Raimund von Hofmannsthal (d. 1974), son of librettist Hugo von Hofmannsthal, was connected to the world of intelligence and propaganda in other ways. He married Vincent Astor's sister Alice and had two daughters by her. At the New Year 1939, Raimund divorced Alice Astor and married Elizabeth Paget, the niece of Diana Cooper, the wife of Churchill's friend Duff Cooper. Duff ran Britain's propaganda arm, the Ministry of Information, from May 11, 1940. He was succeeded in that job by Brendon Bracken in 1941. By late 1941 or early 1942 he started a period of what his granddaughter calls "secret work"; he was head of the Security Executive. Duff knew and liked Raimund, but to judge by Duff's letters, Raimond did have his drawbacks. Duff wrote in a letter on September 12, 1938: "What is amusing is that his advances in courtship are identical with Raimund's...but my new lover has it all over Raimund every time, for one reason his hand is not like a hippopotamus's tongue." Duff and Diana Cooper, *A Durable Fire*, 292; A. J. Ayer, *Part of My Life* (New York: Harcourt Brace Jovanovich, 1977), 259.

76. Cull, "British Campaign," 436.

77. The enemies were "Professional Isolationist Anglophobes"—Hearst, McCormick, and Patterson newspapers, Senators Burton Wheeler and Gerald Nye, and Representative Hamilton Fish; "Professional Liberals and Left Wing"—*The Nation, The New Republic*, the pro-Indian nationalist journalist Louis Fischer, the New School for Social Research, and Communists; "New Internationalist-Imperialists"—presidential candidate Wendell Willkie and Henry and Clare Booth Luce. "Breakdown of Anti-British Groups and Individuals in U.S.A.," 17 April 1943, Graham Spray Papers, MG30, D297, Vol. 46-13, Public Archives of Canada, in Brewer, "Creating the 'Special Relationship,' " 253–54.

78. Chadwin, *Hawks*, 48.

79. PRO FO 371/26187, A/6013/118/45, Campbell to Martin, 28 July 1941, in Cull, "British Campaign," 502–3.

80. Anthony Read and David Fischer, *Colonel Z: The Secret Life of a Master of Spies* (New York: Viking, 1985), 176–80.

81. ECP, Box 107, "Clips from Claridges" file, 4 [my pagination].

82. Michael Korda, *Charmed Lives*, 146.

83. Hyde, *Secret Intelligence Agent*, 163, 162; Korda, *Charmed Lives*, 146; telephone interview with Elinore Little Nascarella, 15 January 1996.

84. Claude Edward Marjoribanks Dansey was born in 1876 in London to a father in the First Life Guards. In *"C,"* 127, Cave Brown writes: "...Dansey became (as Menzies was to discover) a man who could commit murder easily...in short a man capable of anything, and therefore exactly the sort who could rise to great heights in the secret service...." Read and Fischer, *Colonel Z*, 176–87; Korda, *Charmed Lives*, 138–39.

85. Korda, *Charmed Lives*, 155; Hyde, *Secret Intelligence Agent*, 245. Korda family tradition says that Churchill wrote a propaganda speech for Korda's famous movie *That*

Hamilton Woman, about the hero of Trafalgar, Lord Nelson. In a footnote, Michael Korda says of the speech: "It reads in part: 'Napoleon can never be master of the world until he has smashed us up—and believe me, gentleman, he means to be master of the world. You cannot make peace with dictators, you have to destroy them....' The entire tone of the speech is faintly Churchillian, and it is difficult to believe that Alex would have included a scene quite as unsuitable as this if he had not felt obliged to do so because of its authorship." *Charmed Lives*, 154.

86. Chadwin, *Hawks*, 64–65.
87. Hitchens, *Blood, Class, and Nostalgia*, 85.
88. FFFP, F. H. Peter Cusick file, telegrams of 8 May 1941. One of them, addressed to Kenneth Thomson in Hollywood, says: "Spyros Skouras will call you tomorrow about a luncheon we are arranging with Walter Wanger and others in Hollywood Tuesday....There are five of us coming from here [New York] to discuss our needs and plans for the immediate future." Chadwin, *Hawks*, 64–65; Hitchins, *Blood, Class, and Nostalgia*, 85; Halliwell, *Halliwell's Film Guide*, 1989, 367.

CHAPTER 4: THE VOICE OF THE PEOPLE

1. James G. Schneider, *Should America Go to War? The Debate over Foreign Policy in Chicago, 1939–1941* (Chapel Hill, N.C.: University of North Carolina Press, 1989), xvii.
2. Irving Crespi, *Public Opinion Polls and Democracy* (Boulder, Colo.: Westview Press, 1989), 40–42.
3. Letter to the author from Dr. Timothy Naftali of the University of Hawaii at Manoa, 18 October 1993. Dr. Naftali was allowed to read the secret history and take extensive notes, a number of which he has generously shared with me. The information on Cantril and the penetration of Gallup are found on pages 170–72 of the "BSC Account" which in other respects is much like pages 192–94 of Hyde, *Quiet Canadian*. The material on dissuading Gallup from publishing some poll results harmful to the British is from page 176 of the "BSC Account," which is essentially "identical" to page 198 of *Quiet Canadian*.
4. Richard W. Steele, "The Pulse of the People: Franklin D. Roosevelt and the Gauging of American Public Opinion," *JCH* 9, no. 4 (October 1974): 195.
5. CTEP, Box 46, "Nonpartisan Committee to Defeat Hamilton Fish."
6. America First Committee papers, Box 9, "Hamilton Fish file," Hoover Institution, Stanford, in Richard Kay Hanks, "Hamilton Fish and American Isolationism, 1929–1944" (Ph.D. diss., University of California at Riverside, 1971), 286–87.
7. For a few of the many references to Franklin Roosevelt's sensitivity to public opinion and his determination not to get too far ahead of the public, see Robert Herzstein, *Roosevelt and Hitler: Prelude to War* (New York: Paragon House, 1989), 236, 237, 239, 291; Steele, "Pulse of the People," 195–216.
8. Although the Warhawks may have been the tools of British intelligence, they were already by June 1940 conversant in manipulating the president with a coordinated blitz of planted stories and letters. In May 1940, Whitney Shepardson, Francis Miller, and Henry Wriston of Brown had wished to secure the position of minister to Canada for J. Pierrepont Moffat. According to Chadwin: "This trio had quietly contacted a few of their friends whose judgement they knew President Roosevelt valued, among them editorial writers for the *New York Times* and the *New York*

Herald Tribune." Their campaign was rewarded with success. Chadwin, *Hawks,* 33–34.

9. Roger Stagner, "An Analysis of American Institute of Public Opinion Polls Relating to Intervention in the European War," *Congressional Record,* 9 May 1941, 3840.

10. Steele, "Pulse of the People," 197.

11. *Ibid.,* 198.

12. Ignatius, "Britain's War," C-2.

13. Steele, "Pulse of the People," 199.

14. Warren I. Cohen, *The Chinese Connection: Roger S. Greene, Thomas W. Lamont, George E. Sokolsky and American–East Asian Relations* (New York: Columbia University Press, 1978), 238.

15. Steele, "Pulse of the People," 200. FBIF, John Franklin Carter file, 62-47509, says that Carter graduated from Yale in 1919 and worked for the State Department at various foreign embassies until 1932. During the New Deal he had been an assistant to Rexford Guy Tugwell. The FBI believed him to be hostile. The FBI, resenting rivals, was very irritated; this irritation was shared by Vincent Astor, "Area Controller" and New York contact with British intelligence.

16. Steele, "Pulse of the People," 201; Ignatius, "Britain's War," C-2. Swing and Shirer are also frequently mentioned in British propaganda reports as friends of the British.

17. FDRL, President's Secretary's File (PSF) "Rowe," James Rowe to FDR, 3 October 1940. "[Concerning rumor that the Gallup poll was rigged] I have of course grave doubts about the accuracy of the story. However, Gallup is known to be very strong for Willkie." Steele, "Pulse of the People," 208 n. 24.

18. One must remember the Rockefeller/Aldrich connection. The Rockefellers picked up the rent for BSC's office space in Rockefeller Center and did the same for Fight for Freedom (they also subsidized some of FFF's expenses). Nelson Aldrich Rockefeller also created the Coordinator of Inter-American Affairs office to aid British intelligence in Latin America. Numerous other British intelligence fronts and propaganda organizations called Rockefeller Center home; *New York Times,* 30 May 1969, 27. This unit became the Foreign Broadcast Monitoring Service when it was absorbed by the Federal Communications Commission in 1941. More recently it has been operated by the CIA as the Foreign Broadcast Information Service. G. J. A. O'Toole, *The Encyclopedia of American Intelligence and Espionage, from the Revolutionary War to the Present* (New York: Facts on File, 1988), 196.

19. MLP Ogilvy to Stephenson, 13 November 1962.

20. Michael Leigh, *Mobilizing Consent* (Westport, Conn.: Greenwood Press, 1976), 74.

21. Cantril to Niles, 23 March 1943, "Cantril Notebooks," vol. 2, in Leigh, *Mobilizing Consent,* 82, 15.

22. Naftali to author, 18 October 1993.

23. Schwar, "Interventionist Propaganda," 299.

24. Michael Wheeler, *Lies, Damn Lies and Statistics* (New York: Liveright, 1976), 115–16.

25. David Ogilvy, *Blood, Brains and Beer: The Autobiography of David Ogilvy* (New York: Atheneum, 1978), 82; Hyde, *Secret Intelligence Agent,* 17–23.

26. Charles Burlingham, Dean Acheson, and Thomas Thatcher signed the letter to the *New York Times* that had been concocted by Ben Cohen and counsel to the

British embassy John Foster. This specious piece of legal reasoning was the justification for the Destroyer Deal. Acheson had his Yale classmate Charles Merz, editor of the *Times* editorial page, run the letter. Ogilvy, *Blood, Brains and Beer*, 70–72.

27. MLP Ogilvy to Stephenson, 13 November 1962; Ogilvy, *Blood, Brains and Beer*, 86; Bill Ross-Smith to Montgomery Hyde, November 1962. Ogilvy suggested that reference to himself in *The Quiet Canadian* should read: "W.[illiam] S. S.[tephenson] made Ogilvy his representative at the Washington embassy, where he worked in liaison with Noel Hall and OSS, largely in the field of economic warfare. At one period Ogilvy was giving OSS (Col. Francis Pickens Miller) an average of fifty secret reports a day." Ogilvy to Stephenson, 13 November 1962. Ogilvy's OSS contact was the same Francis Pickens Miller who had directed the Century Group. He was one of the original Warhawks, who had published the letter in June 1940 demanding the United States declare war on Germany immediately. In a letter of January 1, 1963, from Barbados, Ogilvy sent nine pages of changes he thought necessary to make *The Quiet Canadian* more accurate and less offensive to Americans. Ogilvy's economic warfare work was one cause of the strained relations between BSC and the FBI. Hyde had written: "For some months Hoover was convinced that Stephenson was deliberately withholding information from his agents and passing it on to Donovan instead. This was not true." *Quiet Canadian*, 166. Ogilvy counters: "Yes it *was* true. B.S.C. agents in Latin America passed their economic stuff to OSS (via myself); also their political stuff—I think."

28. Crespi, *Public Opinion Polls and Democracy*, 15; *New York Times*, 1 May 1971, 36.

29. O'Toole, *Encyclopedia of American Intelligence and Espionage*, 395; obituary of Elmer Burns Roper, Jr., *New York Times*, 1 May 1971, 36.

30. Chadwin, *Hawks*, 212; Ronald Tree, *When the Moon Was High: Memoirs of War and Peace, 1897–1942* (London: Macmillan, 1975), 94.

31. Obituary of Harry Hubert Field, *New York Times*, 5 September 1946, 4. Field was killed in an airplane crash in Paris as he returned from attempting to establish public opinion polls "for all of Europe."

32. Hackett, *America by Number: NORC Report 1991* (Chicago: National Opinion Research Center, 1992), 1, 2, 8, 10, 79.

33. *Ibid.*, 7, 33.

34. William Stevenson, *A Man Called Intrepid: The Secret War* (New York: Ballantine, 1976), 324–325.

35. FFFP, *Labor News Service*, 21 November 1941.

36. FFFP, "Notes Taken by Mr William Agar at Executive Committee Meeting of the Fight for Freedom Committee," 8 May 1941.

37. FFFP, Box 103, telegram from Abe Rosenfield, "Fight For Freedom, Inc.," to the Statler Hotel, Detroit, 10 November 1941.

38. FFFP, Robert Spivak file. Merle Miller (1919–86) later made a wide reputation for his biographies: *Plain Speaking: An Oral Biography of Harry S. Truman* and *Lyndon: An Oral Biography*. He was quite open about his homosexuality, writing *On Being Different: What It Means to Be a Homosexual*. He was much less forthcoming about his extensive work for Fight for Freedom. During the time he was a major force in FFF's press operations he listed himself in his *Who's Who* biography as "Washington corr. *Phila. Record* 1940–41; editor *Yank Mag.* 1941–45." *Who's Who*, 43rd ed., 1984–85, vol. 2 For his Fight for Freedom work, see his thick file in FFFP.

39. FHP.
40. FFFP, *Labor News Service*, 1 (6 December 1941), 3; David Reynolds, *The Creation of the Anglo-American Alliance, 1937–1941: A Study in Competitive Cooperation* (Chapel Hill, N.C.: University of North Carolina Press, 1981), 330 n. 18. Reynolds cites Ickes Papers 371/5 as his authority.
41. Philip Goodhart, *Fifty Ships That Saved the World: The Foundation of the Anglo-American Alliance* (Garden City, N.Y.: Doubleday, 1965), 113.
42. Leonard Doob, *Public Opinion and Propaganda* (New York: Henry Holt, 1948), 140.
43. Benjamin Ginsberg, *The Captive Public* (New York: Basic Books, 1986), 60.
44. Hadley Cantril, *Gauging Public Opinion* (Princeton, N.J.: Princeton University Press, 1944), 108–10.
45. *Ibid.*, 114.
46. Justice D. Doenecke, ed., *In Danger Undaunted: The Anti-Interventionist Movement of 1940–41 as Revealed in the Papers of the America First Committee* (Stanford, Calif.: Hoover Institution Press, 1990), 29–30, 66; Harry S. Ashmore, *Unseasonable Truths* (Boston: Little, Brown, 1989), 218–19.
47. Rowena Wyant, "Voting Via the Senate Mailbag," *Public Opinion Quarterly* 5 (Fall 1941), 373–74.
48. WJDP, Box 81 B.
49. WJDP, Volume 34, William J. Donovan Personal, Box 81B.
50. ECP, Box 25, Henson file.
51. "There are no limits to...my willingness to be of help," Frankfurter had told British Ambassador Lord Lothian. J. Garry Clifford and Samuel Spencer, *The First Peacetime Draft* (Lawrence, Kan.: University Press of Kansas, 1986), 63. Gerald T. Dunne, *Grenville Clark: Public Citizen* (New York: Farrar, Straus & Giroux, 1982), 127. Also, J. Garry Clifford, "Grenville Clark and the Origins of Selective Service," *Review of Politics* 35 (January 1973), 23–24.
52. Clifford, "Grenville Clark," 32.
53. Clifford, *First Peacetime Draft*, 139; Clifford, "Grenville Clark," 33, 53.
54. "Washington Letter," 14 August 1940, British Library of Information no. 362, FO 371/2421/131, RBFO, in Clifford, *First Peacetime Draft*, 284 n. 113.
55. Stimson Diary, 22 August 1940, quoted in Clifford, "Grenville Clark," 33.
56. Professor Beale lost the battle against the draft bill, but he did get in a telling blow against the bandwagon effect Pearley Boone was building in conjunction with Harvard professors in the Harvard Defense Group. In the late summer the Harvard Defense Group issued a press release claiming that there was "practically unanimous support" for conscription at the University of North Carolina. Since he did not believe the UNC faculty could reach unanimous agreement on anything, Beale called the Harvard professors on this, and they beat an indelicate retreat with an apology. Clifford, *First Peacetime Draft*, 144.
57. Ross Stagner, "An Analysis of American Institute of Public Opinion Polls Relating to Intervention in the European War," *Congressional Record*, 9 May 1941, 3840–42. Although Stagner was commissioned to make this study by the America First Committee, it remains an excellent, careful analysis of the polls for this period.
58. *Ibid.*, 3841.
59. FFFP, *Labor News Service* 1, no. 28 (6 December 1941): 3.

60. Louis D. Rubin, Jr., "Did Churchill Ruin 'The Great Work of Time'? Thought on the New British Revisionism," *Virginia Quarterly Review* 70 (Winter 1994): 75.

61. FFFP, Box 169, clipping, "Congress Inquiry Sought for Polls." According to Ernest Cuneo, after the president intervened to make Alben Barkley the Senate leader he "was in an immensely strong position in his continuing fight with the Hill, because he had both majority leaders and they could prevent plays from forming against him." Interview with Ernest Cuneo, 23 April 1970, at Mr. Cuneo's office, Washington, D.C., LBJ Library Oral History Collection, Austin, Tex.

62. *Congressional Record*, 6 May 1941, 3606.

CHAPTER 5: G.112 LT. COMMANDER GRIFFITH

1. Duncan Stuart, CMG, The SOE Adviser at the FCO, to author, March 11, 1997.

2. Thomas M. Johnson, "They Told All," *American Legion Magazine* 26 (February 1939): 16.

3. Sandy Griffith's *Who's Who* entries of 1938–39 and 1958–59.

4. Telephone interview with Peter Griffith, 1 December 1993.

5. Letter to author, from A. M. "Bill" Ross-Smith, 6 April 1992.

6. Telephone interview with Peter Griffith, 7 July 1993. For Ellis as recruiter for British intelligence, see Winks, *Cloak and Gown*, 166–67.

7. Letter to author from A. M. "Bill" Ross-Smith, 27 March 1992. Ross-Smith's agent number was 48907.

8. Shirer, *Berlin Diary*, 126. For other references to Bill Morrell and his pregnant wife, see pp. 127 and 130. In a letter to me, 24 November 1992, William L. Shirer wrote: "Yes, I knew Bill Morrell, an old colleague of mine in Europe, who worked for British Intelligence during the war. He was intelligent; a good writer. As I remember, he worked mostly in America."

9. David Stafford, *Camp X* (Toronto: Lester & Orpen Dennys Ltd., 1986), 209; ECP, Box 25, Henson files, Henson to Cuneo, 2 October 1941.

10. Mary Elizabeth Allison, "America's 'Grandes Dames' " *Life* 64 (January 26, 1968): 44–45.

11. Tappert, *The Emmets: A Generation of Gifted Women*, 4–5.

12. Nelson W. Aldrich, Jr., *Old Money: The Mythology of America's Upper Class* (New York: Vintage, 1988), 63.

13. Obituary of Christopher T. Emmet, *New York Times*, 14 February 1974; CTEP, Box 33, France Forever file.

14. CTEP, Box 13, American Irish Defense Association; FFFP, Bell File, Emmet to Ulric Bell, 31 July 1941, and Emmet to Bell, 25 November 1941; Emmet obituary.

15. Christopher Simpson, *Blowback* (New York: Weidenfield & Nicolson, 1988), 222–23.

16. Much of the biographical information is from the Francis Henson Papers, held by the Henson/Farrow family in Maryland. The Hensons were aviation pioneers; Henson Airlines is now part of U.S. Air. In a letter of 9 July 1944 from "Camp Hq. Camp Lee Va." addressed "Dear Hingham," Henson summarized his political philosophy and the events of his life that had brought him to his ideas.

17. FHP, résumé (of which there are several versions). Other versions of this résumé can be found in ECP, Henson files.

18. Goodhart, *Fifty Ships*, 113.
19. ECP, Box 25, Henson files, "Opinion Poll at the Republican National Convention," 19–25 June 1940, Market Analysts Inc., New York World's Fair, Flushing, N.Y.
20. ECP, Box 25, Henson files, Griffith to Cuneo, 22 July 1940.
21. ECP, Box 25, Henson files.
22. *Ibid.*, letter of 9 August 1940.
23. *Ibid.*, Griffith to Cuneo, 9 August 1940.
24. *Ibid.*, Griffith to Cuneo, 1 October and 3 August 1940.
25. Doenecke, ed., *In Danger Undaunted*, 11, 15, 23, 36, 37, 45, 47, 48, 50, 57, 64n, 72n, 95, 99, 103, 152, 159, 180, 227, 453–54, 465–66.
26. ECP, Box 25, Henson files, "Report on Interview with William R. Castle—19 November 1940."
27. Brewer, "Creating the 'Special Relationships,'" 237.
28. "Breakdown of Anti-British Groups and Individuals in U.S.A.," April 1943, Spry papers, Vol. 46-18, Public Archives of Canada; Law Committee, January 1944, FO 381/38522, PRO; MacDugal Report, March 12, 1943, CO875/18/12, PRO; in Brewer, "Creating the 'Special Relationship,'" 313–14.
29. ECP, Box 25, Henson files, memo, Henson to Cuneo, undated. Probably from 1942 or 1943, because this series of textbooks was reviewed in *Social Education* 7 (1943), 183.
30. FFFP, Market Analysts Inc. File contains all of this newspaper commentary.
31. CTEP, Box 76, Sanford Griffith file, Emmet to Griffith (at 5146 Plankinton Arcade, Milwaukee, Wisconsin), 12 September 1941.
32. FFFP, Box 66, Spivak to David Stern et al., 21 November 1941.
33. FFFP, *Labor News Service* 1 (6 December 1941), 3.
34. Hyde, *Quiet Canadian*, 124.
35. Troy, "'George': OSS's FBI Secret," 480, 483.
36. *Ibid.*, 483.
37. Miller, *Man from the Valley*, 109.
38. McAleer, *Rex Stout*, 295–96, McAleer's notes for this episode include correspondence with George M. Merton of 15 September 1972 and with Sylvia Porter of 3 October 1972. Porter (born Feldman) professionally used the name of her first husband, whom she divorced in 1931. She married G. Summer Collins in 1943. Her biography in *Contemporary Authors* 81–84:451 lists a volume titled *The Nazi Chemical Trust in the United States*, published by the National Policy Committee, 1942.
39. Anthony Sampson, *The Seven Sisters* (New York: Viking Press, 1975), 79.
40. ECP, Box 25, Henson files, Henson to Cuneo, undated. Probably July 1942, because William Floyd II wrote a follow-up letter dated 24 July 1942.
41. *Ibid.*, Floyd to Cuneo, 24 July 1942.
42. I. F. Stone, "Esso Family Reunion," *Nation*, 12 July 1943, 826–27.
43. *Ibid.*; *Who's Who in America* 1940–41, 1106.
44. Sampson, *Seven Sisters*, 80.
45. Ignatius, "Britain's War," C-2; Troy, "'George': OSS's FBI Secret," 485.

46. ECP, Box 25, Henson files.
47. Jack Anderson, *Washington Post*, 30 November 1975, in McAleer, *Rex Stout*, 558–59 n. 9.
48. FHP, Henson to Griffith, 3 August 1943, from Camp Special Service Office, Camp Hq., Camp Lee, Va.
49. Neal Gabler, *Winchell: Gossip, Power, and the Culture of Celebrity* (New York: Alfred A. Knopf, 1994), 613.
50. Robert E. Stripling to The Honorable Martin Dies, November 12, 1942, Box 76, Market Analysts: Sanford Griffith, Frederick McKee, Francis Henson, Records Group 233, House of Representatives, Records of the Select Committee on Un-American Activities, 1938–44 (The Dies Committee), National Archives and Records Administration (hereafter, Dies Committee, NARA).
51. Memo to Mr. Dies, attached to Sanford Griffith's bank account, Box 76, Record Group 233, Dies Committee, NARA.
52. Niel M. Johnson, *George Sylvester Viereck: German American Propagandist* (Urbana, Ill.: University of Illinois Press, 1972), 198–200.
53. *Ibid.*, 224, 227; *Washington Post*, 11 October 1941, 1.
54. Hyde, *Secret Intelligence Agent*, 198.
55. Johnson, *George Sylvester Viereck*, 231–33.
56. Quoted in Wesley McCune, *The Nine Young Men* (New York: Greenwood Publishers, 1947), 154–55.
57. *Ibid.*, 154.
58. Johnson, *George Sylvester Viereck*, 242–43.
59. Hyde, *Secret Intelligence Agent*, 200.
60. Johnson, *George Sylvester Viereck*, 250–51.
61. FHP, Henson to Griffith, 3 August 1943.
62. CTEP, Box 76, Griffith file, Emmet to Griffith, 19 January 1946.

CHAPTER 6: DESTROYING CONGRESSMAN FISH

1. CTEP, Box 65, Burlingham file, Emmet to Burlingham, 4 November 1940.
2. Ignatius, "Britain's War," C-2.
3. Wheeler, *Yankee from the West*, 404, 408–9. The book attacking Wheeler was *The Plot Against America; Senator Wheeler and the Forces Behind Him*, by David George Kin, real name Plotkin. The book attacking Senator Nye was *Under Cover* by John Roy Carlson, real name Avedis Derounian (New York: E. P. Dutton, 1943).
4. Wayne S. Cole, *Senator Gerald P. Nye and American Foreign Relations* (Westport, Conn.: Greenwood Press, 1962), 216.
5. Brewer, "Creating the 'Special Relationship,' " 436.
6. J. G. Donnelly, August 1945, FO371/44557 AN2560/22/45, PRO.
7. Obituary of Hamilton Fish, *New York Times*, 20 January 1991, 26.
8. Hanks, "Hamilton Fish," 189, 191.
9. CTEP, Box 46, Nonpartisan Committee to Defeat Hamilton Fish file, List of Donors.
10. CTEP, Box 46, NPCDHF file. Other members of the committee: Mr. and Mrs. Lewis Mumford, Amenia, New York; Mr. and Mrs. Lee Woodward Ziegler, Newburgh, New York; Mr. John Wing, Millbrook, New York; Mr. Guy S. Bailey,

Amenia, New York; George Field, New York City; Mr. Arthur Goldsmith, New York City.

11. DPP, Container 150, 3 of 3, Hamilton Fish, #1.

12. Hamilton Fish, *Memoirs of an American Patriot* (Washington, D.C.: Regnery/Gateway, 1991), 145–46.

13. ECP, Box 25, Henson files, Henson to Cuneo (The Moorings, 1909 Que St. N.W., Washington, D.C.), 18 October 1940.

14. CTEP, Box 46, NPCDHF file, "Receipts."

15. *New York Times*, 4 October 1940, 22.

16. *New York Times*, 19, 11, 30, and 16 October 1940, in Hanks, "Hamilton Fish," 260.

17. *New York Times*, 9 November 1938, 3.

18. ECP, Box 25, Henson files, Griffith to Cuneo, 13 November 1940.

19. CTEP, Box 46, NPCDHF file, "Recommendations by Sanford Griffith for Hamilton Fish Campaign and Continuation."

20. *Ibid.*

21. *Ibid.*

22. FFFP, Box 9, James Causey file. Causey spoke of himself as a constituent of Hamilton Fish, but his address on the poll is Room 803, 63 Wall Street, New York City.

23. Hanks, "Hamilton Fish," 286–88.

24. *Congressional Record*, 26 June 1941, 5552.

25. Hanks, "Hamilton Fish," 298–300.

26. CTEP, Box 46, NPCDHF file, "Recommendations," 2–3.

27. *Ibid.*, 3–4.

28. CTEP, Box 46. For Mumford on the NPCDHF, see Financial Report of Receipts and Expenditures of Nonpartisan Committee to Defeat Hamilton Fish. For Mumford as sponsor of Fight for Freedom, see Chadwin, *Hawks*, 168.

29. Chadwin, *Hawks*, 53.

30. Hanks, "Hamilton Fish," 302–3.

31. *Ibid.*, 321.

32. Ignatius, "Britain's War," C-2.

33. Hyde, *Quiet Canadian*, 87.

34. Naftali to author, 18 October 1993; obituaries of Henry Hoke in *New York Times*, 23 November 1970, 40, and *Howard County Times* [Columbia, Md.], 26 November 1970; FHP, Henson to Griffith, 3 August 1943.

35. *New York Times*, 13 June 1940, 5.

36. ECP, Box 25, Henson files. For the closeness of Henson and Hoke see letter from Hoke, 11 January 1946.

37. Hyde, *Quiet Canadian*, 88.

38. FFFP, Hamilton Fish file, press release marked "For A.M. Release."

39. FFFP, Hamilton Fish file.

40. Hanks, "Hamilton Fish," 328.

41. *Ibid.*, 329–36.

42. DPP, Box F 33, 1 of 3, Viereck Trial Clippings.

43. Hanks, "Hamilton Fish," 370–72.

44. *New York Times*, October 15, 1942, 19.

45. Davenport, "Hot Seats," *Collier's*, 5 September 1942, 18–19; Jordy and Chasen, "Keep Them Out!" *Nation*, 24 October 1942, 415–17.

46. DPP, Container F 150, 3 of 3, Fish #1, Scheiber to Pearson, 7, 19, 20 October and 20, 23 November 1942.

47. DPP, Container F 150, 3 of 3, Hoke to Pearson, 29 October 1942.

48. DPP, F 150, 3 of 3, Fish #2, Hoke to Pearson, 29 October 1942.

49. *Ibid.*

50. Hyde, *Quiet Canadian*, 70–71; Ignatius, "Britain's War," C-2, reports the same incident is found in the "BSC Account," in nearly identical language. Ignatius adds the name Torkild Reiber of Texaco as one of Westrick's chief contacts in the oil business. Hyde in *Quiet Canadian* calls him "the president of a certain oil company."

51. DPP, Container F 150, 3 of 3, Fish, #2; *New York Mirror*, 29 October 1942, and *New York World Telegram*, 29 October 1942.

52. DPP, Container F 150, 3 of 3, Fish, *Beacon News* (Beacon, N.Y.), 2 November 1942.

53. Robert Divine, *Second Chance: The Triumph of Internationalism in America During World War II* (New York: Atheneum, 1967), 73.

54. *New York Times*, 5 November 1942, 30.

55. DPP, Container F 150, 3 of 3, Fish, Hansen-Sturm to Pearson, 7 November 1942, and Pearson reply, 24 November 1942.

56. DPP, Container F 150, 3 of 3, Fish, #1, Pearson to Griffith, 12 November 1942.

57. DPP, Container F 150, 3 of 3, Fish, #1, Pearson to Hoke, 12 November 1942; Griffith to Pearson, 19 November 1942.

58. DPP, Container F 150, 3 of 3, Fish, #1, Pearson to Griffith, 23 November 1942.

59. EBP, "Relations with Roosevelt," 7.

60. EBP, quotes from "Correspondence," 34.

61. Hassett, *Off the Record with F.D.R. 1942–1945* (New Brunswick, N.J.: Rutgers University Press, 1958), 87.

62. E.g., material in Prime Ministers Office Files (PREM) 4, 26/6 and 27/1; FO 371, files 30715, 31723, 34162, in Christopher Thorne, *Allies of a Kind: The United States, Britain and the War Against Japan, 1941–1945* (New York: Oxford University Press, 1978), 221.

63. Ignatius, "Britain's War," C-2.

64. EBP, "Correspondence," 18.

65. Sir Isaiah Berlin, *Washington Despatches, 1941–1945: Weekly Political Reports from the British Embassy* (Chicago: University of Chicago Press, 1981), entries for 1 August 1942, 21 November 1942, 3 July 1943, 25 July 1942, 8 August 1942, 27 December 1942, 24 January 1943, 13 February 1943, 22 October 1943, 22 November 1943, 6 December 1943, 11 December 1943.

66. *Washington Evening Star*, 3 May 1944, A-4.

67. Chadwin, *Hawks*, 228.

68. For Anderson's poem see *New Yorker*, 28 May 1944, 28. See also *New York Times*, 27 July 1944, 7; 29 July 1944, 15; 30 July 1944, 1; 31 July 1944, 8; 26 August 1944, 13. For Stout, see *New York Times*, 3 November 1944, 14, in Hanks, "Hamilton Fish," 397.

69. Hanks, "Hamilton Fish," 405.
70. CTEP, Box 65, Burlingham file, Emmet to Burlingham, 4 November 1940.

CHAPTER 7: UNCLE AUTHOR

1. Anderson, "Britain's Fetching Lobbyists," *Washington Post–Times Herald*, 14 September 1969, B-7.
2. ECP, Box 108, Michael Straight file.
3. Rovere, "New Man in the Pantheon," *New Yorker*, 24 March 1962, 150–66. Rovere, like many, dates Vandenberg's conversion from his famous Senate speech of 10 January 1945. I place his conversion much earlier, as early as mid-1940.
4. R. W. Apple, Jr., *New York Times*, 6 May 1987.
5. Drew Pearson, *Drew Pearson Diaries,1949–1959*, edited Tyler Abel (New York: Holt, Rinehart & Winston, 1974), 158.
6. C. David Tompkins, *Senator Arthur H. Vandenberg: The Evolution of a Modern Republican, 1884–1945* (Lansing, Mich.: Michigan State University Press, 1970), 2.
7. *Ibid.*, 6, 7, 15–25, 28, 42–43.
8. Walter Trohan to author, 6 July 1987.
9. Virginia Owen to author, 9 December 1989. Lady Cotter was too infirm to write me; Virginia Owen, her daughter, wrote down her answers to a series of questions.
10. Tompkins, *Vandenberg*, 94–95.
11. *Ibid.*, 126–227.
12. *Ibid.*, 167.
13. Arthur Krock, *The Consent of the Governed and Other Deceits* (Boston: Little, Brown, 1971), 163–64.
14. HHVP, Diary entry of 6 May 1937.
15. *Montreal Daily Star*, 7 May 1940, 18; *Washington Star*, 7 May 1940, A-2; *Washington Post*, 7 May 1940, 11; *Washington Times Herald*, 7 May 1940.
16. *Washington Post*, 7 May 1940, 11.
17. Telephone interviews with Mrs. Bogart and Mrs. Carsley, May and June 1987.
18. *Washington Star*, 7 May 1940, p. A-2.
19. Pearson, *Diaries*, entry of 20 April 1951, 157–59.
20. HHVD, entries for the first four months of 1940. In particular see entries of 18 April, 5 May, and 6 May 1940.
21. Obituary of Harold Sims, *Washington Times-Herald*, 7 May 1940.
22. *Washington Post*, 7 May 1940, 11.
23. Chris Ogden, *The Life of the Party: The Biography of Pamela Digby Churchill Hayward Harriman* (Boston: Little, Brown, 1994), 122–124, 120.
24. HHVD, June 9, 1940.
25. Trohan to author, 6 July 1987.
26. Clive Ponting, *1940: Myth and Reality* (Chicago: Ivan R. Dee, 1990), 212.
27. Mary S. Lovell, *Cast No Shadow: The Life of Betty Pack, the American Spy Who Changed the Course of World War II* (New York: Pantheon Books, 1992), 146.
28. *Ibid.*
29. *Time*, 20 December 1963.
30. "BSC Account," 153, in Lovell, *Cast No Shadow*, page preceding contents, titled "Betty."

31. Lovell, *Cast No Shadow*, xiii.

32. Obituary of George Thorpe, *New York Times*, 29 July 1936, 19. Cora Wells Thorpe died at age seventy-three, 9 August 1954. *Washington Post*, 10 August 1954, 22.

33. Karen L. Jana, reference librarian at the Bentley Historical Library at the University of Michigan, kindly answered my questions on the University of Michigan connection between Hazel Vandenberg and Cora Thorpe.

34. *New York Times*, 30 April 1930, 17. Other members of the party were matron of honor the bride's cousin Mrs. Christian L. Christensen, daughter of Federal Trade Commissioner C. H. March; Miss Gertrude Lamont, daughter of the secretary of commerce; best man was Captain J. T. Godfrey, assistant military attaché of the British embassy; Ronald Ian Campbell, counselor at the British embassy; British Ambassador and Lady Lindsey also attended.

35. Lovell, *Cast No Shadow*, 37, 57.

36. *Ibid.*, 85–87.

37. *Ibid.*, 88–97.

38. *Ibid.*, 142.

39. FBIF Special Agent in Charge S. K. McKee to Director FBI (GED: MG 65-3575), 22 January 1943, RE: MRS. ARTHUR PACK, with aliases ESPIONAGE (F).

40. HHVD. "Cora T," Cora Thorpe, was sometimes called "Lil Thorpe" in Mrs. Vandenberg's diaries.

41. David Ogilvy, Notes on American Public Opinion in Relation to U.K., 25 September 1945, Canceling/44608 AN3037/109/45, PRO, in Brewer, "Creating the 'Special Relationship,' " 412.

42. Leonard S. Cottrell and Sylvia Eberhart, *American Opinion on World Affairs in the Atomic Age* (Princeton, N.J.: Princeton University Press, 1948), 130, in Richard N. Gardner, *Sterling Dollar Diplomacy in Current Perspective: The Origins and Prospects of Our International Economic Order* (New York: Columbia University Press, 1980), 236.

43. Gardner, *Sterling Dollar Diplomacy*, 237.

44. *Ibid.*, 250.

45. Vandenberg, *Private Papers*, 231.

46. Trohan to author, 6 July 1987.

47. Virginia Owen (Mrs. Paterson's daughter) to author, 3 January 1993. Also her death certificate from North Dorset, entry Number 53.

48. *Peoria Journal-Transcript*, 11 February 1941.

49. *Peoria Star*, February 11, 1941. The story is illustrated with a photograph of Eveline, her daughter, Virginia, and her cousin Mrs. Theodore Baer, with whom she was staying in Peoria. My thanks to Virginia Owen for sending this and other items from her mother's scrapbook.

50. The scrapbook of Eveline Paterson; also Virginia Owen to author, 25 March 1992.

51. Owen to author, 11 January 1992.

52. DPP, Container F 32, 3 of 3, Vandenberg File, Memo to DP from JD of June 5, 1948.

53. Owen to author, 25 March 1992.

54. *Ibid.*

55. Owen to author, 3 January 1993.

56. ECP, Henson files.
57. Mari Ann Buitrago, *Are You Now or Have You Ever Been in the FBI Files?* (New York: Grove Press, 1981), Appendix C.

CHAPTER 8: WE WANT WILLKIE

1. FDRL, Berle, Box 213, also FDRL Berle Diary Vol. VII, 2 122–123.
2. Richard Kluger, *The Paper: The Life and Death of the New York Herald Tribune* (New York: Alfred A. Knopf, 1986), 322.
3. ECP, Box 107, "For the Record: Crusader to Intrepid," File, 86. The generally reliable Ernest Cuneo repeats several times in his papers that the movement for a third term started in July 1938: "...the historians and the record to the contrary, F.D.R. gave the green light to a Third Term. I wrote the first 'Draft F.D.R.' speech, delivered by Governor Frank Murphy at Traverse City on 25 July 1938. I had Walter Winchell pick it up and he trumpeted it to 40 million people daily for the next two years, plus driving it into 8 out of 9 American adults every Sunday night."
4. H. L. Mencken to *New York Daily News* reporter Doris Fleeson, 3 July 1940, quoted in *The New Mencken Letters*, edited by Carl Bode (New York: Dial Press, 1977), 463. Other examples: Hugh Ross, "Was the Nomination of Wendell Willkie a Political Miracle?" *Indiana Magazine of History* 58 (June 1962): 79–100. Ross lists Chapter 9, "Miracle in Philadelphia," of Joseph Barnes, *Willkie* (New York, 1952). Eugene H. Rosenbloom, *A History of Presidential Elections* (New York: Macmillan, 1957), has a chapter on the nomination, 460–65, subtitled "The Philadelphia Miracle."
5. The British ambassador from mid-1939 until his unexpected death in December 1940, Lord Lothian worked very closely with British intelligence. Hyde writes of "Lothian, who had always been *en rapport* with Stephenson" (*Secret Intelligence Agent*, 22). In September 1939, Sir William Wiseman, the World War I head of British intelligence in the United States, visited Assistant Secretary of State Adolf Berle. Wiseman was, in 1939, an aide to the new Ambassador Lothian. Startled, Berle wrote a memorandum: "Well, I thought, under the cover of some courteous remarks, this approaches the fantastic. For Lothian, in an earlier incarnation, was Sir Phillip Kerr, Lloyd George's secretary. As young men, he and Wiseman were the brain trusters; Wiseman arranged many of the meetings between Colonel House, Lloyd George's private emissaries and the British Ambassador....The history of our past English 'interpretations' was a history of half truths, broken faith, intrigue behind the back of the State Department, and even the President, and everything that goes with it." FDRL, Berle Diary, 13 September 1939, 2–3.
6. Presidents Personal File (PPF), FDRL, File 70. The address from which this was taken was delivered at Olympic Auditorium in Los Angeles by the strange expedient of a phonograph record. According to the speech, Browder was unable to attend in person because the Roosevelt administration had gone to federal court and obtained an order preventing him from leaving New York.
7. FDRL, PPF 70, Lamont, Thomas W. 1938–40, Roosevelt to Lamont, 13 September 1940; C. Nelson Sparks, *One Man—Wendell Willkie* (New York: Raynor, 1943).
8. Neal, *Dark Horse*, 3.
9. *Ibid.*, 16.
10. *Ibid.*, 19.

11. Ignatius, "Britain's War," C-2.
12. The organizer of these three-day "forums" was Marie (Missy) Meloney, for some years the editor of the *New York Herald Tribune Sunday Magazine*. Kluger, *Paper*, 286. Her only child, William Brown Meloney, had been a member of William Donovan's law firm. One intelligence author writes: "...Meloney and her son enjoyed a close relationship with the President and his wife, particularly Eleanor Roosevelt. Since Meloney's country home lay near the Roosevelt's in Hyde Park, she met them frequently." Brian R. Sullivan, " 'A Highly Commendable Action': William J. Donovan's Intelligence Mission and Roosevelt," *INS* 6 (April 1991): 339, 343. From the fragmentary correspondence in the Marie M. Meloney Papers at Columbia University's Rare Book and Manuscript Library it appears that Donovan and Mrs. Meloney had a very close relationship. Kluger, *Paper*, 327.
13. Kluger, *Paper*, 327.
14. Harvey Klehr, John Earl Haynes, and Fridrikh Firsov, *The Secret World of American Communism* (New Haven, Conn.: Yale University Press, 1995), 262, 265.
15. Sanders, *Dorothy Thompson*, 254.
16. Walter Johnson, *William Allen White's America* (New York: Henry Holt, 1947), 530; DPP, Container No. F 33, Willkie, Wendell L. File.
17. Donald Bruce Johnson, *The Republican Party and Wendell Willkie* (Urbana, Ill.: University of Illinois Press, 1960), 74–75.
18. In Howe, *Black Game*, 32.
19. My request for Mr. Williams's autopsy report was returned from the Thomas Jefferson University Hospital in Philadelphia with a form letter. The block checked said: "Patient records dated prior to 1975 are no longer available." Letter from Ms. Belinda Benson, Correspondence Secretary Medical Records Department, 4 April 1990. If it still exists, this autopsy report deserves a thorough review by a forensic specialist knowledgeable in the intelligence techniques of the time.
20. D. B. Johnson, *Republican Party*, 92.
21. HHP, Post Presidential Subject files, Gahagan/HH Campaign Deposition by Dorothy Emerson, 3 July 1947, Gahagan/HH 1940.
22. HHP. See also the letter by Herbert Hoover's son Allan and the oral history by James P. Selvage in "Campaign 1940, Post Pres. Subjects." Pryor's work at the convention caused a rift between himself and Herbert Hoover that Pryor was never able to heal.
23. Marylin Bender and Selig Altschul, *The Chosen Instrument: Juan Trippe, Pan Am: The Rise and Fall of an American Entrepreneur* (New York: Simon & Schuster, 1982), 480.
24. Neal, *Dark Horse*, 102; Ignatius, "Britain's War," C-2.
25. Goodhart, *Fifty Ships*, 108.
26. HHP, Oral History, James P. Selvage, 25, 26.
27. David E. Lilienthal, *Volume I* (New York: Harper & Row), 205–6.
28. *Public Opinion Quarterly* 4 (September 1940), 537.
29. Stevenson, *Intrepid*, 507, mentions the involvement of the Alsop brothers in BSC operations. The brothers were relatives of FDR. Neal, *Dark Horse*, 186.
30. Davenport, *Too Strong for Fantasy*, 277.
31. Neal, *Dark Horse*, 148.

32. Catledge, *My Life and the Times*, 120.

33. Richard J. Jensen, "The Causes and Cures of Unemployment in the Great Depression," *Journal of Interdisciplinary History* 19 (Spring 1989): 557.

34. Herzstein, *Roosevelt and Hitler*, 406.

35. Alfred Haines Cope and Fred Krinsky, "Introduction" in *Franklin D. Roosevelt and the Supreme Court* (Lexington, Mass.: Heath, 1969), vi, 27–30.

36. Clifford and Spencer, *The First Peacetime Draft*, 23.

37. Ronald Steel, *Walter Lippmann and the American Century* (Boston: Little, Brown, 1980), 387–89; Lerner, "The Supreme Court and American Capitalism," in Cope and Krinsky, *Franklin D. Roosevelt and the Supreme Court*, 58–59; Neal, *Dark Horse*, 158; D. B. Johnson, *Republican Party*, 142.

38. Ponting, *1940*, 75.

39. Malcolm Muggeridge, *Like It Was: The Diaries of Malcolm Muggeridge* (New York: William Morrow, 1982), 218.

40. Quoted in Neal, *Dark Horse*, viii.

41. Hiram Johnson to Hiram W. Johnson, Jr., 30 August 1940, Johnson Papers, Bancroft Library, University of California, Berkeley, California, in Cole, *Roosevelt and the Isolationists, 1932–45* (Lincoln: University of Nebraska Press), 395; J. Garry Clifford and Samuel R. Spencer, *First Peacetime Draft* (Lawrence: University of Kansas Press, 1986), 5.

42. Miller, *Man from the Valley*, 102; Naftali, "Intrepid's Last Deception," 82, 96, n. 69.

43. Hyde, *Secret Intelligence Agent*, xvii.

44. Lothian to Halifax, 29 August 1940, FO 800/324, Halifax Papers, Public Records Office London, in Cole, *Roosevelt and the Isolationists*, 395.

45. Robert Shogan, *Hard Bargain: How FDR Twisted Churchill's Arm, Evaded the Law, and Changed the Role of the American Presidency* (New York: Scribner, 1995), 259–60.

46. ECP, Box 111, Crusader to Intrepid file.

47. Miller, *Man from the Valley*, 102. Douglas was an ardent Anglophile and later United States ambassador to Great Britain whose father (the father had renounced his United States citizenship and become a British citizen) had financially supported him his whole life under the apparent understanding that Lewis would help the British whenever he had the opportunity.

48. A group of journalists purchased full-page advertisements in papers across the nation to promote the Destroyer Deal. Donald B. Johnson writes of those who placed the advertisements: "The group included Barry Bingham, publisher of the *Louisville Courier-Journal*; Herbert Agar, the editor of the paper; Walter Lippmann; Joseph Alsop; Robert S. Allen; Frank Kent of the *Baltimore Sun*; Geoffrey Parsons, chief editorial writer of the *New York Herald Tribune*; Russell Davenport, and a number of others." D. B. Johnson, *Republican Party*, 126n.

49. Lilienthal, *Volume I, the TVA Years 1939–1945*, 209.

50. Hyde, *Quiet Canadian*, 41, gives the intermediary the name Albert Younglove Gowen. Francis Pickens Miller, one of the founders of Fight for Freedom, was involved with this event. In his autobiography, *Man from the Valley*, 98–101, he gives the intermediary's name as George A. C. Christiancy. Why Hyde disguised the name is not clear. He also did this with one of Cynthia's targets, Captain Charles Brousse, whom he called Captain Bestrand. Hyde, *Quiet Canadian*, 109.

Miller says George Christiancy's name was passed to him from Walter Mallory of the Council on Foreign Relations, at the suggestion of Frank Altschul.

51. Miller, *Man from the Valley*, 100–101.

52. Goodhart, *Fifty Ships*, 106.

53. Raoul de Sales, *The Making of Yesterday: The Diaries of Raoul de Roussy de Sales* (New York: Reynal & Hitchcock, 1947), 124.

54. Corliss Lamont, *The Thomas Lamont Family in America* (1962).

55. Obituary of Gardner Cowles, *Des Moines Register*, 9 July 1985, 1A; D. B. Johnson, *Republican Party*, 215n.

56. Philip Burch, Jr., *Elites in American History* (New York: Holmes & Meier, 1980), 366. Oren Root says: "Through his mother he [Henry Luce] and I were distantly related...." Root also writes that he was an occasional dinner and house guest of the Luces and that is where he was on December 7, 1941, when Pearl Harbor was attacked. Root, *Persons and Persuasions*, 53, 31.

57. Warren Moscow, *Roosevelt and Willkie* (Englewood Cliffs, N.J.: Prentice-Hall, 1968), 54; Root, *Persons and Persuasions*, 37.

58. Moscow, *Roosevelt and Willkie*, 54.

59. Watt, *How War Came*, 556.

60. For Lewis Douglas's connection with Fight for Freedom, see Chadwin, *Hawks*, 43, 50–51, 75, 78–80, 89, 96, 105, 110.

61. Jaffe, "Isolationism and Neutrality," 139–40.

62. Quoted in Neal, *Dark Horse*, 191.

63. Moscow, *Roosevelt and Willkie*, 56, 61.

64. Leonard Mosley, *Dulles: A Biography of Eleanor, Allen, and John Foster Dulles and Their Family Network* (New York: Dial, 1978), 107–8, 504n, cites a note in the Dulles papers. Several things in Mosley's account, however, seem out of sequence. In particular, Mosley seems to put Donovan's trip to England before the convention.

65. DPP, Container G 247 Willkie, #1; Neal, *Dark Horse*, 67; Root, *Persons and Persuasions*, 27.

66. Root, *Persons and Persuasions*, 34–35.

67. Neal, *Dark Horse*, 130; Peter Collier and David Horwitz, *The Rockefellers: An American Dynasty* (New York: Holt Rinehart and Winston, 1976), 214.

68. Winthrop W. Aldrich (1885–1974) was the son of Nelson Aldrich, senator from Rhode Island from 1881 to 1911 and one of the founders of the Federal Reserve System. Aldrich was a 1907 graduate of Harvard College and a 1910 graduate of the Harvard Law School. Winthrop's sister Abby G. Aldrich had married John D. Rockefeller, Jr., thus making him uncle to the five Rockefeller brothers, John D. III, Nelson, Laurance, David, and Winthrop. Aldrich was associated with Rockefeller interests from the 1920s. Aldrich took over the chairmanship of the Chase National Bank in early 1933 and held that position until January 1953, when President Eisenhower appointed him ambassador to Great Britain. Like Lewis Douglas, David Bruce, and Gil Winant, Aldrich was a known quantity to the British long before he arrived at the Court of St. James's.

69. Jeffrey M. Dorwart, "The Roosevelt-Astor Espionage Ring," *New York History* 62 (July 1981): 315.

70. Dorwart writes: "Everyone of the old ROOM members held deep family, educational and emotional bonds to England and to English society and institutions." Dorwart, "Roosevelt-Astor," 315–16.

71. Stevenson, *A Man Called Intrepid*, 169; "BSC Account," 16; Hyde, *Secret Intelligence Agent*, 91.

72. Neal, *Dark Horse*, 188. Chadwin, *Hawks*, 133, gives a less complete and more garbled version of the same event involving officials of Fight for Freedom.

73. Michael T. Florinsky, review of Douglas Miller, *You Can't Do Business with Hitler*, in *Political Science Quarterly* 56 (December 1941): 639.

74. Neal, *Dark Horse*, 211; Chadwin, *Hawks*, 179.

75. FFFP, Hobson to Willkie, telegram, 23 September 1941.

76. Chawin, *Hawks*, 216–18.

77. FFFP, Willkie File.

78. *Christian Science Monitor*, 17 March 1941, in Sargent, *Getting U.S. into War*, 503.

79. Moscow, *Roosevelt and Willkie*, 204–5.

80. DDP, G-247, 1 of 2.

81. *Congressional Record*, 12 November 1941, 8801.

82. Robert E. Sherwood, *Roosevelt and Hopkins: An Intimate History* (New York: Harper, 1948), 635.

83. Neal, *Dark Horse*, 202.

84. *Ibid.*, 189; EBP, Summaries of Willkie Correspondence, 36.

85. Berlin, *Washington Despatches*, 291.

86. *Ibid.*, entries for 1 August 1942, 21 November 1942, 3 July 1943, 25 July 1942, 8 August 1942, 27 December 1942, 24 January 1943; 13 February 1943, 22 October 1943, 22 November 1943, 6 December 1943, 11 December 1943, 13 December 1943.

87. Neal, *Dark Horse*, 313, 317; Hyde, *Quiet Canadian*, 204–8. Pearson's inside contacts in the administration have been excised from page 205 of *Room 3603*, the U.S. edition of *Quiet Canadian*. According to *Quiet Canadian* they were Ickes, Morgenthau, and Biddle. Ignatius, "Britain's War," C-2.

88. DPP, Container F 33, 2 of 3.

89. Hyde, *Secret Intelligence Agent*, 91.

CHAPTER 9: THE SUCCESS OF DECEPTION

1. David Dimbleby and David Reynolds, *An Ocean Apart: The Relationship Between Britian and America in the Twentieth Century* (New York: Random House, 1988), 102–3.

2. JBP, Neville Chamberlain to Buchan (Lord Tweedsmuir), dated July 1939.

3. Ignatius, "Britain's War," C-2.

4. For comment on this, see U.S. Congress, Senate, Select Committee to Study Governmental Operations with Respect to Intelligence Activities, *Alleged Assassination Plots Involving Foreign Leaders*, Senate Report No. 94-465, 94th Cong., 1st sess., 1975, 3, 6, 7.

5. ECP, Box 107, CIA file.

6. Cull, "British Campaign," 126.

7. PRO FO 371/22839, A/7053/7052/45, minute by Vansittart, 21 October 1939, in Cull, "British Campaign," 115. Vansittart was quite familiar with the film business.

8. CTEP, Box 46, Nonpartisan Committee to Defeat Hamilton Fish file, Sophie Mumford to Betty Maclean, 7 November 1940.

9. In a memo for his files, Cuneo wrote: "To sum it up, outside the COI/OSS there was no significant person, organization, or group that wanted a new agency or an independent coordinator. There were no discernable attitudes or forces working in that direction....No, there never was the possibility...without the impetus...from outside." ECP, Box 107, CIA file.

10. Robert Sherwood, Bill Morrell, Donald Downes, Edmond Taylor, Donald Mac-Laren, George Merton, Elizabeth Thorpe Pack (Cynthia), George Bowden, and Ivar Bryce are examples. This area merits closer study.

11. Loch K. Johnson, *America's Secret Power: The CIA in a Democratic Society* (New York: Oxford University Press, 1989), 25.

12. *Ibid.* Loch K. Johnson was associated with the CIA. This book may be a planned leak.

13. Chadwin, *Hawks*, 138–41.

14. Anthony Cave-Brown, *The Last Hero: Wild Bill Donovan* (New York: Times Books, 1982), 651.

15. Rockefeller Foundation, *Annual Report, 1946*, 188–89, 33.

16. William Leonard Langer, *In and Out of the Ivory Tower* (New York: Neale Watson Academic Publications, 1977), 210.

17. Robert D. Schulzinger, *The Wise Men of Foreign Affairs:The History of the Council on Foreign Relations* (New York: Columbia University Press, 1984), 130.

18. See William L. Langer and S. Everett Gleason, *The Challenge to Isolation: The World Crises of 1937–1940 and American Foreign Policy*, 2 vols. (New York: Harper Torchbooks, 1952), 716, n.18, listing Donovan's letters to England of August 27, 1940. These letters were addressed to: Brenden Bracken, Colonel S. G. Menzies, Admiral Godfrey, Sir Cyril Newal and Sir Ronald Tree. None are identified or elaborated on, and none of these can be located in the index. The most important individuals mentioned are Colonel S. G. Menzies—"C," the head of the Secret Intelligence Service (MI-6)—and Admiral Godfrey, the head of the Office of Naval Intelligence, whose facile aide Ian Fleming worked for Stephenson for a time. Ronald Tree, of British Information Services (propaganda), who was Marshall Field's first cousin, had been in charge of Donovan in England.

19. Warren F. Kimball, *The Juggler: Franklin Roosevelt as Wartime Statesman* (Princeton, N.J.: Princeton University Press, 1991), 13–14.

20. Kramer, "Nelson Rockefeller and British Security Coordination," *JCH* 16 (January 1981): 76.

21. Laurence H. Shoup and William Mintner, *Imperial Brain Trust* (New York: Monthly Review Press, 1977), 123.

22. Chadwin, *Hawks*, 71.

23. Samuel Flagg Bemis, "First Gun of a Revisionist Historiography for the Second World War," *Modern History* 19 (March 1947): 56–59.

24. *Ibid.*, 59.

•••

Bibliography

PRINTED MEMOIRS, DIARIES, AND DOCUMENTS

Ayer, A. J. *Part of My Life*. New York: Harcourt Brace Jovanovich, 1977.

Beevor, J. G. *S.O.E. Recollections and Reflections, 1940–1945*. London: Bodley Head, 1981.

Berle, Adolf. *Navigating the Rapids, 1918–1971: From the Diaries of Adolf Berle*. Edited by Beatrice Bishop Berle and Travis Beal Jacobs. New York: Harcourt Brace Jovanovich, 1973.

Berlin, Sir Isaiah. *Personal Impressions*. New York: Viking Press, 1980.

———. *Washington Despatches, 1941–1945: Weekly Political Reports from the British Embassy*. Chicago: University of Chicago Press, 1981.

Bingham, Sallie. *Passion and Prejudice*. New York: Alfred A. Knopf, 1989.

Blum, John M. *From the Morganthau Diaries: Years of War, 1941–1945*. Boston: Houghton Mifflin, 1975.

Bryce, Ivar. *You Only Live Once: Memories of Ian Fleming*. Frederick, Md.: University Publications of America, 1984.

Cadogan, Sir Alexander. *The Diaries of Sir Alexander Cadogan O.M., 1938–1945*. Edited by David Dilks. New York: G. P. Putnam's Sons, 1972.

Catledge, Turner. *My Life and the Times*. New York: Harper & Row, 1971.

Cavendish, Anthony. *Inside Intelligence*. London: Collins, 1990.

Channon, Sir Henry. *Chips: The Diaries of Sir Henry Channon*. Edited by Robert Rhodes James. London: Weidenfeld & Nicolson, 1967.

Churchill, Winston. *The Second World War: The Gathering Storm*. Boston: Houghton Mifflin, 1948.

Churchill, Winston, and Franklin D. Roosevelt. *Churchill and Roosevelt: The Complete Correspondence*. Edited with Commentary by Warren F. Kimball. Princeton, N.J.: Princeton University Press, 1984.

Colville, John. *The Fringes of Power: 10 Downing Street Diaries, 1939-1955*. New York: W. W. Norton, 1985.

Cooper, Duff. *A Durable Fire: The Letters of Duff and Diana Cooper, 1913–1950*, ed. Artemis Cooper. London: Collins, 1983.

Cope, Alfred H. *Franklin D. Roosevelt and the Supreme Court.* Rev. ed. Edited with an introduction by Alfred Haines Cope and Fred Krinsky. Lexington, Mass.: Heath, 1969.

Davenport, Marcia. *Too Strong for Fantasy.* New York: Scribner, 1967.

de Sales, Raoul de Roussy. *The Making of Yesterday: The Diaries of Raoul de Roussy de Sales.* New York: Reynal and Hitchcock, 1947.

Delmer, Sefton. *Black Boomerang.* New York: Viking, 1962.

Doenecke, Justice D., ed. *In Danger Undaunted: The Anti-Interventionist Movement of 1940–41 as Revealed in the Papers of the America First Committee.* Stanford, Calif.: Hoover Institution Press, 1990.

Downes, Donald. *The Scarlet Thread.* New York: British Book Centre, 1953.

Eichelberger, Clark M. *Organizing for Peace: A Personal History of the Founding of the United Nations.* New York: Harper and Row, 1977.

Fish, Hamilton. *Memoirs of an American Patriot.* Washington, D.C.: Regnery, Gateway, 1991.

Frankfurter, Felix. *From the Diaries of Felix Frankfurter.* With a biographical essay and notes by Joseph Lash. New York: W. W. Norton, 1975.

Gleeson, James Joseph. *Now It Can Be Told.* New York: Philosophical Library, c. 1952.

Hyde, H. Montgomery. *Secret Intelligence Agent: British Espionage in America and the Creation of the OSS.* Foreword by Sir William Stephenson ("Intrepid"). New York: St. Martin's Press, 1982.

Johns, Philip. *Within Two Cloaks.* Letchworth, Herfordshire: Garden City Press, 1979.

Klehr, Harvey, John Earl Haynes, and Fridrikh Firsov. *The Secret World of American Communism.* Russian documents translated by Timothy D. Sergay. New Haven, Conn.: Yale University Press, 1995.

Krock, Arthur. *The Consent of the Governed and Other Deceits.* Boston: Little, Brown, 1971.

Lamont, Corliss. *The Thomas Lamonts in America.* South Brunswick: A. S. Barnes, 1971. First published in 1962 as *The Thomas Lamont Family in America.*

Langer, William Leonard. *In and Out of the Ivory Tower.* New York: Neale Watson Academic Publications, 1977.

Lilienthal, David E. *The Journals of David E. Lilienthal*, Volume I, *The TVA Years 1939–1945.* New York: Harper and Row, 1964.

Lippmann, Walter. *Public Philosopher: Selected Letters of Walter Lippmann.* Edited by John Morton Blum. New York: Ticknor & Fields, 1985.

Maschwitz, Eric. *No Chip on My Shoulder.* London: Herbert Jenkins, 1957.

McBaine, Turner H. *A Career in the Law at Home and Abroad.* With an Introduction by Charles B. Renfrew. Interview conducted by Carole Hicke. Berkeley, Calif.: University of California, 1989.

Mencken, H. L. *The Diary of H. L. Mencken.* Edited by Charles A. Fecher. New York: Alfred A. Knopf, 1989.

———. *The New Mencken Letters.* Edited by Carl Bode. New York: Dial, 1977.

Miller, Francis Pickens. *Man from the Valley: Memoirs of a 20th Century Virginian.* Chapel Hill, N.C.: University of North Carolina Press, 1971.

Morgan, Kay Summersby. *Past Forgetting: My Love Affair with Dwight D. Eisenhower.* New York: Simon & Schuster, 1975.

Muggeridge, Malcolm. *Like It Was: The Diaries of Malcolm Muggeridge.* Selected and edited by John Bright-Holmes. New York: William Morrow, 1982.

Nicolson, Harold. *The War Years, 1939–1945: Volume II of Diaries and Letters,* ed. Nigel Nicolson. New York: Atheneum, 1967.

Ogilvy, David. *Blood, Brains and Beer: The Autobiography of David Ogilvy.* New York: Atheneum, 1978.

Pearson, Drew. *Drew Pearson Diaries, 1949–1959.* Edited by Tyler Abel. New York: Holt, Rinehart & Winston, 1974.

Rogers, James Grafton. *Wartime Washington: The Secret OSS Journal of James Grafton Rogers, 1942–1943.* Edited by Tom Troy. Frederick, Md.: University Publications of America, 1987.

Roosevelt, Franklin, and Felix Frankfurter. *Roosevelt and Frankfurter: Their Correspondence, 1928-1945.* Annotated by Max Freedman. London: Bodley Head, 1968.

Root, Oren. *Persons and Persuasions.* New York: W. W. Norton, 1974.

Stuart, Sir Campbell. *Secrets of Crew House: The Story of a Famous Campaign.* London: Hodder & Stoughton, 1920.

Taylor, Edmond. *Awakening from History.* Boston: Gambit, 1969.

Tree, Ronald. *When the Moon Was High: Memoirs of War and Peace, 1897–1942.* London: Macmillan, 1975.

Trohan, Walter. *Political Animals: Memoirs of a Sentimental Cynic.* Garden City, N.Y.: Doubleday, 1975.

Vandenberg, Arthur H. *The Private Papers of Senator Vandenberg.* Boston: Houghton Mifflin, 1952.

Weidman, Jerome. *Praying for Rain.* New York: Harper & Row, 1986.

Wheeler, Burton K., with Paul F. Healy. *Yankee from the West.* Garden City, N.Y.: Doubleday, 1962.

Wheeler-Bennett, John. *Special Relationship.* London: Macmillan, 1975.

Wright, Peter, with Paul Greengrass. *Spycatcher: The Candid Autobiography of a Senior Intelligence Officer.* New York: Viking, 1987.

SECONDARY SOURCES

Books

Aldrich, Nelson W., Jr. *Old Money: The Mythology of America's Upper Class.* New York: Vintage, 1988.

Alsop, Joseph. *FDR, 1882–1945: A Centenary Remembrance.* Picture sections compiled and written by Roland Gelatt, photo research by Laurie Platt Winfrey. New York: Viking, 1982.

Andrew, Christopher. *Her Majesty's Secret Service: The Making of the British Intelligence Community.* New York: Viking, 1986.

Andrew, Christopher, and David Dilks. *The Missing Dimension: Government and Intelligence Communities in the Twentieth Century.* Urbana, Ill.: University of Illinois Press, 1984.

Andrew, Christopher, and Jeremy Noakes, eds. *Intelligence and International Relations, 1940–1945.* Exeter, England: Exeter University Publications, 1987.

Ashmore, Harry S. *Unseasonable Truths: The Life of Robert Maynard Hutchins.* Little, Brown, 1989.

Bamford, James. *The Puzzle Palace: A Report on America's Most Secret Agency.* Boston: Houghton Mifflin, 1982.

Barnes, Harry Elmer, ed. *Perpetual War for Perpetual Peace: A Critical Examination of the Foreign Policy of Franklin Delano Roosevelt and Its Aftermath.* Caldwell, Idaho, 1953.

Beard, Charles A. *President Roosevelt and the Coming of the War, 1941.* New Haven, Conn.: Yale University Press, 1948.

Becker, Stephen. *Marshall Field III: A Biography.* New York: Simon & Schuster, 1964.

Belden, Thomas Graham, and Marva Robins Belden. *The Lengthening Shadow: The Life of Thomas J. Watson.* Boston: Little, Brown, 1962.

Bender, Marylin, and Selig Altschul. *The Chosen Instrument: Juan Trippe, Pan Am: The Rise and Fall of an American Entrepreneur.* New York: Simon & Schuster, 1982.

Bird, Kai. *The Chairman: John J. McCloy, the Making of the American Establishment.* New York: Simon & Schuster, 1992.

Blum, John Morton. *From the Morgenthau Diaries: Years of Urgency, 1938–1941.* Boston: Houghton Mifflin, 1965.

Browder, Robert Paul. *Independent: A Biography of Lewis Douglas.* New York: Alfred A. Knopf, 1986.

Brown, John Mason. *The Ordeal of a Playwright: Robert E. Sherwood and the Challenge of War.* Introduction by Norman Cousins. New York: Harper & Row, 1970.

Bruner, Jerome S. *Mandate from the People.* New York: Duell, Sloan & Pearce, 1944.

Buitenhuis, Peter. *The Great War of Words: British, American and Canadian Propaganda and Fiction, 1914–1933.* Vancouver: University of British Columbia Press, 1987.

Buitrago, Ann Mari. *Are You Now or Have You Ever Been in the FBI Files?* New York: Grove Press, 1981.

Burch, Philip, Jr. *Elites in American History.* New York: Holmes & Meier, 1980.

Byrnes, Garrett D. *The Providence Journal, 150 Years.* Providence, R.I.: Providence Journal Company, 1980.

Cantril, Hadley. *Gauging Public Opinion.* Princeton, N.J.: Princeton University Press, 1944.

Carlson, John Roy (Avedis Derounian). *Under Cover.* New York: E. P. Dutton, 1943.

Cave-Brown, Anthony. *Bodyguard of Lies.* New York: Bantam Books, 1975.

———. *"C": The Secret Life of Sir Stewart Menzies, Spymaster to Winston Churchill.* New York: Macmillan, 1987.

———. *The Last Hero: Wild Bill Donovan.* New York: Times Books, 1982.

Chadwin, Mark Lincoln. *The Hawks of World War II: The Interventionist Movement in the U.S. Prior to Pearl Harbor.* Chapel Hill, N.C.: University of North Carolina Press, 1968.

Chernow, Ron. *The House of Morgan: An American Banking Dynasty and the Rise of Modern Finance.* New York: Atlantic Monthly Press, 1990.

Clifford, J. Garry, and Samuel Spencer. *The First Peacetime Draft.* Lawrence, Kan.: University Press of Kansas, 1986.

Cohen, Warren I. *The Chinese Connection: Roger S. Greene, Thomas W. Lamont, George E. Sokolsky and American–East Asian Relations.* New York: Columbia University Press, 1978.

Cole, Robert. *Britain and the War of Words in Neutral Europe, 1939–45: The Art of the Possible.* New York: St. Martin's Press, 1990.

———. *Roosevelt and the Isolationists, 1932–45*. Lincoln, Neb.: University of Nebraska Press, 1983.

Cole, Wayne S. *Charles A. Lindbergh and the Battle Against American Intervention in World War II*. New York: Harcourt Brace Jovanovich, 1974.

———. *Senator Gerald P. Nye and American Foreign Relations*. Westport, Conn.: Greenwood Press, 1962.

Collier, Peter, and David Horowitz. *The Rockefellers: An American Dynasty*. New York: Holt Rinehart and Winston, 1976.

Copeland, Miles. *Without Cloak or Dagger: The Truth About the New Espionage*. New York: Simon & Schuster, 1974.

Costello, John. *Mask of Treachery*. New York: William Morrow, 1988.

Cottrell, Leonard S., and Sylvia Eberhart. *American Opinion on World Affairs in the Atomic Age*. Princeton, N.J.: Princeton University Press, 1948.

Crespi, Irving. *Public Opinion Polls and Democracy*. Foreword by Albert H. Cantril. Boulder, Colo.: Westview Press, 1989.

Cruickshank, Charles. *Deception in World War II*. Oxford, England: Oxford University Press, 1979.

———. *SOE in Scandinavia*. Oxford, England: Oxford University Press, 1986.

Deacon, Richard. *Spyclopedia: The Comprehensive Handbook of Espionage*. New York: William Morrow, 1987.

Dimbleby, David, and David Reynolds. *An Ocean Apart: The Relationship Between Britain and America in the Twentieth Century*. New York: Random House, 1988.

Divine, Robert A. *Second Chance: The Triumph of Internationalism in America During World War II*. New York: Atheneum, 1967.

Dobson, Alan P. *U.S. Wartime Aid to Britain, 1940–1946*. New York: St. Martin's Press, 1986.

Doenecke, Justice D. *Not to the Swift*. Cranbury, N.J.: Associated University Presses, 1979.

Doherty, Thomas. *Projections of War: Hollywood, American Culture and World War II*. New York: Columbia University Press, 1993.

Donner, Frank J. *The Age of Surveillance: The Aims and Methods of America's Political Intelligence System*. New York: Alfred A. Knopf, 1980.

Doob, Leonard. *Public Opinion and Propaganda*. New York: Henry Holt, 1948.

Dorwart, Jeffery M. *Conflict of Duty: The U.S. Navy's Intelligence Dilemma, 1919–1945*. Annapolis, Md.: Naval Institute Press, 1983.

Drawbell, James Wedgwood. *Dorothy Thompson's English Journey: The Record of an Anglo-American Partnership*. London: Collins, 1942.

Dunlop, Richard. *Donovan, America's Master Spy*. Skokie, Ill.: Rand McNally, 1982.

Dunne, Gerald T. *Grenville Clark: Public Citizen*. New York: Farrar, Straus & Giroux, 1982.

Fischer, David Hackett. *Historians' Fallacies: Toward a Logic of Historical Thought*. New York: Harper Torchbooks, 1970.

Fish, Hamilton. *FDR: The Other Side of the Coin: How We Were Tricked into World War II*. New York: Vantage Press, 1976.

———. *Tragic Deception: FDR and America's Involvement in World War II*. Old Greenwich, Conn.: Devin-Adair, 1983.

Foot, M. R. D. *SOE: An Outline History of the Special Operations Executive, 1940–46.* Frederick, Md.: University Publications of America, 1984.

Fowler, W. B. *British-American Relations, 1917–1918: The Role of Sir William Wiseman.* Princeton, N.J.: Princeton University Press, 1969.

Gabler, Neal. *Winchell: Gossip, Power, and the Culture of Celebrity.* New York: Alfred A. Knopf, 1994.

Gardner, Richard N. *Sterling Dollar Diplomacy in Current Perspective: The Origins and the Prospects of Our International Economic Order.* New York: Columbia University Press, 1980.

Gates, John D. *The Astor Family.* Garden City, N.Y.: Doubleday, 1981.

Gilbert, Martin. *Finest Hour: Winston S. Churchill, 1939–1941.* New York: Houghton Mifflin, 1983.

Ginsberg, Benjamin. *The Captive Public.* New York: Basic Books, 1986.

Gleeson, James. *They Feared No Evil: The Woman Agents of Britain's Secret Armies, 1939–45.* London: Robert Hale, 1976.

Goodhart, Philip. *Fifty Ships That Saved the World: The Foundation of the Anglo-American Alliance.* Garden City, N.Y.: Doubleday, 1965.

Hackett, Jeff. *America by Number: NORC Report 1991.* Chicago: National Opinion Research Center, 1992.

Hagland, David G. *Latin America and the Transformation of U.S. Strategic Thought, 1936–1940.* Albuquerque, N.M.: University of New Mexico Press, 1984.

Halliwell, Leslie. *Halliwell's Film Guide.* New York: Harper and Row, 1989.

Hancock, W. K., and M. M. Gowing. *British War Economy.* London: His Majesty's Stationery Office, 1949.

Hassett, William D. *Off the Record with FDR, 1942–1945.* New Brunswick, N.J.: Rutgers University Press, 1958.

Herzstein, Robert E. *Roosevelt and Hitler: Prelude to War.* New York: Paragon House, 1989.

Hinsley, F.H., et al. *British Intelligence in the Second World War: Its Influence on Strategy and Operations.* Vol. 1, New York: Cambridge University Press, 1979.

Hitchens, Christopher. *Blood, Class, and Nostalgia: Anglo-American Ironies.* New York: Farrar, Straus & Giroux, 1990.

Howe, Ellic. *The Black Game.* London: Queen Anne Press, 1982.

Hyde, H. Montgomery. *Cynthia.* New York: Farrar, Straus & Giroux, 1965.

———. *Room 3603.* New York: Farrar, Straus, 1962.

Isaacson, Walter, and Evan Thomas. *The Wise Men: Six Friends and the World They Made: Acheson, Bohlen, Harriman, Kennan, Lovett, McCloy.* New York: Simon & Schuster, 1986.

Johns, Philip. *Within Two Cloaks.* Letchworth, Hertfordshire: Garden City Press, 1979.

Johnson, Donald Bruce. *The Republican Party and Wendell Willkie.* Urbana, Ill.: The University of Illinois Press, 1960.

Johnson, Loch K. *America's Secret Power: The CIA in a Democratic Society.* New York: Oxford University Press, 1989.

Johnson, Niel M. *George Sylvester Viereck: German American Propagandist.* Urbana, Ill.: University of Illinois Press, 1972.

Johnson, Walter. *William Allen White's America.* New York: Henry Holt, 1947.

Kahn, E. J. *The World of Swope.* New York: Simon and Schuster, 1965.

Kersaudy, François. *Churchill and De Gaulle.* New York: Atheneum, 1982.

Kimball, Warren F. *The Juggler: Franklin Roosevelt as Wartime Statesman.* Princeton, N.J.: Princeton University Press, 1991.

Kluger, Richard. *The Paper: The Life and Death of the New York Herald Tribune.* New York: Knopf, 1986.

Koppes, Clayton R. *Hollywood Goes to War: How Politics, Profits, and Propaganda Shaped World War II Movies.* New York: Free Press, 1987.

Korda, Michael. *Charmed Lives: A Family Romance.* New York: Random House, 1979.

Kulik, Karol. *Alexander Korda: The Man Who Could Work Miracles.* New Rochelle, N.Y.: Arlington House, 1975.

Langer, William L., and S. Everett Gleason. *The Challenge to Isolation: The World Crises of 1937–1940 and American Foreign Policy.* 2 vols. New York: Harper Torchbooks, 1952.

Laqueur, Walter, ed. *The Second World War: Essays in Military and Political History.* London: Sage Publications, 1982.

Leigh, Michael. *Mobilizing Consent.* Westport, Conn.: Greenwood Press, 1976.

Lippmann, Walter. *U.S. Foreign Policy: Shield of the Republic.* Boston: Little, Brown, 1943.

Lovell, Mary S. *Cast No Shadow: The Life of Betty Pack, the American Spy Who Changed the Course of World War II.* New York: Pantheon, 1992.

McAleer, John. *Rex Stout: A Biography.* Boston: Little, Brown, 1977.

McCune, Wesley. *The Nine Young Men.* New York: Harper and Brothers, 1947.

Margolis, Michael, and Gary A. Mauser. *Manipulating Public Opinion.* Belmont, Calif.: Brooks/Cole, 1989.

Martin, Ralph G. *Henry and Clare: An Intimate Portrait of the Luces.* New York: G. P. Putnam's Sons, 1991.

Masterman, J. C. *The Double-Cross System in the War of 1939–1945.* New Haven, Conn.: Yale University Press, 1972.

Miller, Nathan. *Spying for America: The Hidden History of U.S. Intelligence.* New York: Paragon House, 1989.

Moore, David W. *The Superpollsters: How They Measure and Manipulate Public Opinion in America.* New York: Four Walls, Eight Windows, 1992.

Moscow, Warren. *Roosevelt and Willkie.* Englewood Cliffs, N.J.: Prentice-Hall, 1968.

Mosley, Leonard. *Dulles: A Biography of Eleanor, Allen, and John Foster Dulles and Their Family Network.* New York: Dial, 1978.

Murphy, Bruce Allen. *The Brandeis/Frankfurter Connection: The Secret Political Activities of Two Supreme Court Justices.* Garden City, N.Y.: Doubleday/Anchor, 1983.

Neal, Steve. *Dark Horse: A Biography of Wendell Willkie.* Garden City, N.Y.: Doubleday, 1984.

Ogden, Chris. *Life of the Party: The Biography of Pamela Digby Churchill Hayward Harriman.* Boston: Little, Brown, 1994.

O'Toole, G. J. A. *The Encyclopedia of American Intelligence and Espionage, from the Revolutionary War to the Present.* New York: Facts on File, 1988.

Parenti, Michael. *Inventing Reality.* New York: St. Martin's Press, 1986.

Parmet, Herbert S., and Marie B. Hecht. *Never Again: A President Runs for a Third Term*. New York: Macmillan, 1968.

Paterson, Thomas G., J. Garry Clifford, and Kenneth J. Hagan. *American Foreign Policy: A History Since 1900*. 2nd ed. Lexington, Mass.: D. C. Heath, 1983.

Pearson, John. *The Private Lives of Winston Churchill*. New York: Simon & Schuster, 1991.

Peterson, H. C. *Propaganda for War: The Campaign Against American Neutrality, 1914–1917*. Norman, Okla.: The University of Oklahoma Press, 1939.

Ponting, Clive. *1940: Myth and Reality*. Chicago: Ivan R. Dee, 1990.

Porter, David L. *The Seventy-sixth Congress and WWII, 1939–1940*. Columbia, Mo.: University of Missouri Press, 1979.

Pronay, Nicholas, and D. W. Spring. *Propaganda, Politics and Film, 1918–1945*. London: Macmillan, 1982.

Read, Anthony, and David Fischer. *Colonel Z: The Secret Life of a Master of Spies*. New York: Viking, 1985

Reynolds, David. *The Creation of the Anglo-American Alliance, 1937–1941: A Study in Competitive Cooperation*. Chapel Hill. N.C.: University of North Carolina Press, 1981.

Rose, Norman. *Vansittart: Study of a Diplomat*. New York: Holmes & Meier, 1978.

Roseboom, Eugene H. *A History of Presidential Elections*. New York: Macmillan, 1957.

Rout, Leslie B., and John N. Bratzel. *The Shadow War*. Hanover, N.H.: University Press of New England, 1986.

Russett, Bruce M. *No Clear and Present Danger: A Skeptical View of the United States Entry into World War II*. New York: Harper & Row, 1971.

Salisbury, Harrison Evans. *Without Fear or Favor*. New York: Times Books, 1980.

Sampson, Anthony. *The Seven Sisters: The Great Oil Companies and the World They Made*. New York: Viking Press, 1975.

Sanders, Marion K. *Dorothy Thompson: A Legend in Her Time*. Boston: Houghton Mifflin, 1973.

Schapsmeier, Edward L., and Frederick H. Schapsmeier. *Walter Lippmann: Philosopher-Journalist*. Washington, D.C.: Public Affairs Press, 1969.

Schneider, James C. *Should America Go to War? The Debate over Foreign Policy in Chicago, 1939–1941*. Chapel Hill, N.C.: University of North Carolina Press, 1989.

Schulzinger, Robert D. *The Wise Men of Foreign Affairs: The History of the Council on Foreign Relations*. New York: Columbia University Press, 1984.

Schwarz, Jordan A. *Liberal: Adolf A. Berle and the Vision of an American Era*. New York: Free Press, 1987.

Sherwood, Robert E. *Roosevelt and Hopkins, An Intimate History*. New York: Harper, 1948.

Shirer, William L. *Berlin Diary: The Journal of a Foreign Correspondent, 1934–1941*. New York: A. A. Knopf, 1941.

Shogan, Robert. *Hard Bargain: How FDR Twisted Churchill's Arm, Evaded the Law, and Changed the Role of the American Presidency*. New York: Scribner, 1995.

Short, K. R. M. *Film and Radio Propaganda in World War II*. Knoxville, Tenn.: University of Tennessee Press, 1983.

Shoup, Laurence H., and William Minter. *Imperial Brain Trust*. New York: Monthly Review Press, 1977.

Simpson, Christopher. *Blowback: America's Recruitment of Nazis and Its Effects on the Cold War*. New York: Weidenfeld and Nicolson, 1988.

Smith, Janet Adam. *John Buchan*. Boston: Little, Brown, 1965.

Smith, R. Harris. *OSS: The Secret History of America's First Central Intelligence Agency*. Berkeley, Calif.: University of California Press, 1972.

Soley, Lawrence C. *Radio Warfare: OSS and CIA Subversive Propaganda*. New York: Praeger, 1989.

Sparks, C. Nelson. *One Man—Wendell Willkie*. New York: Raynor, 1943.

Stafford, David. *Camp X*. New York: Dodd, Mead, 1987.

Steel, Ronald. *Walter Lippmann and the American Century*. Boston: Little, Brown, 1980.

Stevenson, William. *A Man Called Intrepid: The Secret War*. New York: Ballantine, 1976.

Stuart, Sir Campbell. *The Secrets of Crewe House: The Story of a Famous Campaign*. London: Hodder & Stoughton, 1920.

Swanberg, W. A. *Luce and His Empire*. New York: Charles Scribner's Sons, 1972.

Sweet-Escott. *Baker Street Irregular*. London: Methuen, 1965.

Tabori, Paul. *Alexander Korda*. New York: Living Books, 1966.

Talese, Gay. *The Kingdom and the Power*. Garden City, N.Y.: Anchor Books, 1978.

Tappert, Tara L. *The Emmets: A Generation of Gifted Women*. New York: Borghi, c. 1993.

Taylor, Philip. *The Projection of Britain*. Cambridge, England: Cambridge University Press, 1981.

Thompason, Robert Smith. *A Time for War: Franklin D. Roosevelt and the Path to Pearl Harbor*. New York: Prentice-Hall, 1991.

Thorne, Christopher. *Allies of a Kind: The United States, Britain and the War against Japan, 1941–1945*. New York: Oxford University Press, 1978.

Tifft, Susan E., and Alex S. Jones. *The Patriarch: The Rise and Fall of the Bingham Dynasty*. New York: Simon & Schuster, 1991.

Tompkins, C. David. *Senator Arthur H. Vandenberg: The Evolution of a Modern Republican, 1884–1945*. Lansing, Mich.: Michigan State University Press, 1970.

Troy, Tom. "George." In *In the Name of Intelligence: Essays in Honor of Walter Pforzheimer*, ed. Hayden Peake and Samuel Halpern, 479–98. Washington, D.C.: NIBC Press, 1994.

Ward, Irene. *F.A.N.Y. Invicta*. Foreword by HRH the Princess Alice. London: Hutchinson, n.d.

Wark, Wesley. *The Ultimate Enemy: British Intelligence and Nazi Germany, 1933–1939*. Ithaca, N.Y.: Cornell University Press, 1985.

Watt, Donald Cameron. *How War Came: The Immediate Origins of the Second World War, 1938–1939*. New York: Pantheon, 1989.

———. *Succeeding John Bull: America in Britain's Place, 1900–1975*. New York: Cambridge University Press, 1984.

Weidman, Jerome. *Praying for Rain*. New York: Hutchinson, 1955.

West, Nigel [Rupert Allison]. *MI-6: British Secret Intelligence Service Operations, 1909–45*. New York: Random House, 1983.

————. *The Circus: MI-5 Operations, 1945–1972*. New York: Stein & Day, 1984.

Whalen, Richard J. *The Founding Father: The Story of Joseph P. Kennedy*. New York: New American Library, 1964.

Wheeler, Burton K. *Yankee from the West*. Garden City, N.Y.: Doubleday, 1962.

Wheeler, Michael. *Lies, Damn Lies, and Statistics*. New York: Liveright, 1976.

White, Graham J. *FDR and the Press*. Chicago: University of Chicago Press, 1979.

Winterbotham, F. W. *Secret and Personal*. London: William Kimber, 1969.

Winkler, Allan M. *The Politics of Propaganda: The Office of War Information, 1942–1945*. New Haven, Conn.: Yale University Press, 1978.

Winks, Robin. *Cloak and Gown: Scholars in the Secret War, 1939–1961*. New York: William Morrow, 1987.

Dissertations

Brewer, Susan Ann. "Creating the 'Special Relationship': British Propaganda in the United States During the Second World War." Ph.D. diss., Cornell University, 1991.

Cull, Nicholas John. "The British Campaign Against American 'Neutrality,' Publicity and Propaganda." Ph.D. diss., University of Leeds, 1991.

Grabavoy, Leann. "Joseph Alsop and American Foreign Policy: The Journalist as Advocate." Ph.D. diss., University of Georgia, 1988.

Hanks, Richard Kay. "Hamilton Fish and American Isolationism, 1929–1944." Ph.D. diss., University of California Riverside, 1971.

Jaffe, Joseph, Jr. "Isolationism and Neutrality in Academe, 1938–1941." Ph.D. diss., Case Western Reserve University, 1979.

Schwar, Jane Harriet. "Interventionist Propaganda and Pressure Groups in the United States, 1937–1941." Ph.D. diss., Ohio State University, 1973.

Articles

Beale, Howard K. "The Professional Historian: His Theory and His Practice." *Pacific Historical Review* 22, no. 3 (August 1953): 248–55.

Bemis, Samuel Flagg. "First Gun of a Revisionist Historiography for the Second World War." *Journal of Modern History* 19 (March 1947): 55–60.

Bennett, Edward W. "Intelligence and History from the Other Side of the Hill." *Journal of Modern History* 60 (June 1988): 312–37.

Blum, Richard. "Espionage and the University." *Cambridge Review* 105 (July 1984): 143–48.

Bolles, Blair. "Bipartisanship in American Foreign Policy." *Foreign Policy Reports* 24 (January 1, 1949): 190–99.

Bratzel, John F., and Leslie Rout. "FDR and the Secret Map." *Wilson Quarterly* (January 1985): 167–73.

Cecil, Robert. "C's War." *Intelligence and National Security* 1 (May 1986): 170–88.

Clifford, J. Garry. "Grenville Clark and the Origins of Selective Service." *Review of Politics* 35 (January 1973): 17–40.

————. "Review Essay: Both Ends of the Telescope: New Perspectives on FDR and American Entry into World War II." *Diplomatic History* 13 (Spring 1989): 213–30.

Cook, Blanche Wiesen. "C.D. Jackson: Cold War Propagandist." *Covert Action* 35 (Fall 1990): 33–38.

Crockett, R. B. "The Foreign Office News Department and the Struggle Against Appeasement." *Historical Research* 63 (February 1990): 73–85.

Cull, Nicholas J. "Did the Mounties and the NFB Fake Nazi Atrocity Pictures?" *The Globe and Mail* (Birmingham, England), "FOCUS," Section D.

Davenport, W. "Hot Seats." *Colliers* (5 September 1942): 18–19.

Doenecke, Justice D. "Historiography: U.S. Policy and the European War, 1939–1941." *Diplomatic History* 19 (Fall 1995): 690.

Domhoff, G. William. "The Power Elite and Its Critics." In *C. Wright Mills and the Power Elite*, ed. G. William Domhoff and Hoyt B. Ballard, 251–78. Boston: Beacon Press, 1968.

Dorwart, Jeffery M. "The Roosevelt-Astor Espionage Ring." *New York History* 62 (July 1981): 307–22.

Elsey, George M. "Memoir: Some White House Recollections, 1942–53." *Diplomatic History* 12 (Summer 1988): 357–64.

Fishel, Edwin C. Review of *The Broken Seal* by Ladislas Farago. In *Studies in Intelligence* 59 (Winter 1968): 81.

Gaddis, John Lewis. "Intelligence, Espionage, and Cold War Origins." *Diplomatic History*.

Gregory, Ross. "Politics in an Age of Crises: America, and Indiana in the Election of 1940." *Indiana Magazine of History* 86 (September 1990): 247–80.

Hodgen, Godfrey. "The Establishment." *Foreign Policy* 10 (Spring 1973): 3–40.

Hulnick, Arthur S. "Learning about U.S. Intelligence: Difficult but Not Impossible." *International Journal of Intelligence and Counterintelligence* 5, no. 1: 89–103.

Ignatius, David. "Britain's War in America: How Churchill's Agents Secretly Manipulated the U.S. before Pearl Harbor." *Washington Post*, 17 September 1989, C-1, C-2.

Ikenberry, G. John. "Rethinking the Origins of American Hegemony." *Political Science Quarterly* 104 (Fall 1989): 375–400.

Jensen, Richard J. "The Causes and Cures of Unemployment in the Great Depression." *Journal of Interdisciplinary History* 19 (Spring 1989): 553–83.

Johnson, Thomas M. "They Told All." *American Legion Magazine* 26 (February 1939): 14–17, 38–39.

Jones, David Lloyd. "Marketing the Allies to America." *Midwest Quarterly* 29 (Spring 1988): 366–83.

Jordy, William, and Will Chasen. "Keep Them Out." *Nation* (24 October 1942): 415–17.

Keylor, William R. "How They Advertised France." *Diplomatic History* 17 (Summer 1993): 351–73.

Kirkpatrick, L. B. Review of *The Quiet Canadian* by H. Montgomery Hyde. In *Studies in Intelligence* 7 (Summer 1963): 122–25.

Kramer, Paul. "Nelson Rockefeller and British Security Coordination." *Journal of Contemporary History* 16 (January 1981): 73–88.

Langer, William L. "Scholarship and the Intelligence Problem." *Proceedings of the American Philosopical Society* 92 (March 8, 1948): 43–45.

Leutze, James. "The Secret of the Churchill-Roosevelt Correspondence: September 1939–May 1940." *Journal of Contemporary History* 10 (July 1975): 465–91.

Little, Douglas. "Crackpot Realists and Other Heroes: The Rise and Fall of the Postwar American Diplomatic Elite." *Diplomatic History* 13 (Winter 1989): 99–111.

Loory, Stuart H. "The CIA's Use of the Press: A 'Mighty Wurlitzer.' " *Columbia Journalism Review* 13, no. 3 (September/October 1974): 9–18.

MacDonnell, Francis. "The Search for a Second Zimmerman Telegram: FDR, BSC, and the Latin American Front." *International Journal of Intelligence and Counterintelligence* 4, no. 4: 487–505.

Matson, Robert W. "The British Naval Blockade and U.S. Trade, 1939–40." *Historian* 53 (Summer 1991): 743–63.

Naftali, Timothy J. "Intrepid's Last Deception: Documenting the Career of Sir William Stephenson." *Intelligence and National Security* 8, no. 3 (July 1993): 72–99.

Patterson, James T. "Eating Humble Pie: A Note on Roosevelt, Congress, and the Neutrality Revision." *Historian* 15 (May 1969): 407–14.

Porch, Douglas. "French Intelligence Culture: A Historical and Political Perspective." *Intelligence and National Security* 10 (July 1995): 486–511.

Reynolds, David. "Lord Lothian and Anglo-American Relations, 1939–1940." *Transactions of the American Philosophical Society* 73, part 2 (1983): 1–65.

———. "Rethinking Anglo-American Relations." *International Affairs* 65 (Winter 1988/89): 89–111.

Rhodes, Benjamin D. "The British Royal Visit of 1939 and the Psychological Approach to the United States." *Diplomatic History* 2 (Spring 1978): 197–211.

Roberts, Priscella. " 'All the Right People': The Historiography of the American Foreign Policy Establishment." *Journal of American Studies* 26 (1992): 409–34.

Rockefeller Foundation. *Annual Report, 1946.* Rockefeller Foundation, 49 West 49th St., New York, N.Y.

Ross, Hugh. "Was the Nomination of Wendell Willkie a Political Miracle?" *Indiana Magazine of History* 58 (June 1962): 79–100.

Rovere, Richard. "New Man in the Pantheon." *New Yorker*, March 24, 1962, 150–66.

Rubin, Louis D., Jr. "Did Churchill Ruin 'The Great Work of Time'? Thought on the New British Revisionism." *Virginia Quarterly Review* 70 (Winter 1994).

Ruetten, Richard. "Harry Elmer Barnes and the Historical Blackout." *Historian* 33 (February 1971): 202–13.

Stafford, David. "Britain Looks at Europe, 1940: Some Origins of S.O.E." *Canadian Journal of History* 10 (August 1975): 231–48.

———. " 'Intrepid': Myth and Reality." *Journal of Contemporary History* 22 (April 1987): 303–17.

Steele, Richard W. "Preparing the Public for War: Efforts to Establish a National Propaganda Agency, 1940–1941." 75: 1640–53.

———. "The Pulse of the People: Franklin D. Roosevelt and the Gauging of American Public Opinion." *Journal of Contemporary History* 9, no. 4 (October 1974): 195–216.

Stone, I. F. "Esso Family Reunion." *Nation* (12 July 1943), 826–27.

Sullivan, Brian R. " 'A Highly Commendable Action': William J. Donovan's Intelligence Mission for Musolini and Roosevelt, December 1935–February 1936." *Intelligence and National Security* 6 (April 1991): 334–66.

Theoharis, Athan G. "The 'Correct' Definition of Intelligence." *International Journal of Intelligence and Counterintelligence* 5, no. 4: 433–54.

———. "Researching the Intelligence Agencies: The Problem of Covert Activities." *Public Historian* 6 (Spring 1984):67–76.

Troy, Thomas F. "The Coordinator of Information and British Intelligence." *Studies in Intelligence* 18, no. 1-S (Spring 1974).

Tuttle, William M., Jr. "Aid-to-the-Allies Short-of-War versus American Intervention, 1940: A Reappraisal of William Allen White's Leadership." *Journal of American History* 56 (March 1970): 840–58.

Twohey, James S. "An Analysis of Newspaper Opinion on War Issues." *Public Opinion,* Fall 1941, 448–55.

Wark, Wesley K. "Introduction: The Study of Espionage: Past, Present, Future?" *Intelligence and National Security* 8 (July 1993): 1–13.

Warner, Geoffrey. "Britain's Special Relationship." Talk given at 1989 International Conference "NATO After 40 Years," Kent State University, 18 April 1989.

Watt, D. Cameron. "Intelligence and the Historian." *Diplomatic History* 14 (Spring 1990): 199–204.

———. "The Sender der deutschen Freiheitspartei: A First Step in the British Radio War Against Nazi Germany?" *Intelligence and National Security* 6 (July 1991): 621–26.

Williams, George. "Intelligence and Book Learning: A Comprehensive Survey of Public Sources on Secret Activities." *Choice,* November 1979, 1125–38.

Wyant, Rowena. "Voting via the Senate Mailbag." *Public Opinion Quarterly* 5 (Fall 1941), 359–82.

···

Index

•••

About
the Author

Tom Mahl teaches college history in Ohio. He holds a doctorate in diplomatic history from Kent State University.